# THE APPIAN WAY,
# A JOURNEY

THE

# APPIAN WAY, A JOURNEY

## DORA JANE HAMBLIN
## MARY JANE GRUNSFELD

 RANDOM HOUSE / NEW YORK

*Grateful acknowledgment is made to the following for permission to reprint previously published material:*

Dover Publications, Inc.: For excerpts from *Vitruvius: The Ten Books on Architecture,* translated by Morris Hicky Morgan, illustrations by Herbert Langford Warren.

Harvard University Press: For excerpts from the following books included in the Loeb Classical Library: *Livy* by Livy with English translations by B. O. Foster (Vols. 1–5), Frank Gardner Moore (Vols. 6–8), Evan T. Sage (Vols. 9–12), A. C. Schlesinger (Vols. 13–14), Loeb Classical Library 1919–1959. *Plutarch's Lives,* with an English translation by Bernadotte Perrin, Loeb Classical Library 1914–1926. *Procopius,* with an English translation by B. H. Dewing and G. Downey, Loeb Classical Library 1914–1940. *Seneca ad Lucilium, Epistulae Morales,* with an English translation by R. M. Gummere, Loeb Classical Library 1917–1925.

G. P. Putnam's Sons: For excerpts from *Memoirs of a Renaissance Pope: The Commentaries of Pius II,* abridged and translated by Florence A. Gragg and Leona C. Gabel. Copyright © 1959 by Florence A. Gragg and Leona C. Gabel.

The University of Chicago Press: For excerpts from *Satires and Epistles of Horace: A Modern English Verse Translation,* by Smith Palmer Bovie (1959).

*Library of Congress Cataloging in Publication Data*
*Hamblin, Dora Jane, 1920-*
*The Appian Way.*

1. *Appian Way.   I. Grunsfeld, Mary Jane Loeb, joint*
*author.   II.   Title.*
*DG29.A6H35   914.5   74-8722*
*ISBN O-394-47233-0*
*Designed by Antonina Krass*

*Manufactured in the United States of America*
9   8   7   6   5   4   3   2
*First Edition*

*For all the* nipotini:

GRUNSFELDS, HAMBLINS,
KLATZES, OVROMS

# *Preface*

It is necessary to explain some variety of usage — in distances, spellings of names, and dates — in the pages that follow.

Roman roads were calculated in Roman miles, which were slightly shorter than the modern English or American mile. But distances in Italy today are indicated in kilometers. For this reason we have referred to distances in miles when dealing with historical times, and in kilometers when this measurement could be useful to modern travelers wishing to find the precise location of monuments, remains or road traces.

Similarly, we have used the Latin names for Roman cities along the road when dealing with its history, but we have used modern names and references in chapters where this usage seemed sensible and logical. In cases in which there are different spellings for the ancient names — Erdoniae, Herdoniae and Herdonia for the same city, for example — we have in most instances accepted the spelling of the late Italian scholar Giuseppe Lugli. We have varied from Lugli's spelling only when some other version has become more common in books on the subject. The map of the route of the road includes a key which contains both ancient and modern names. The cities of Rome and Naples have been called by these modern English designations throughout the book, and we have also used the Anglicized versions of proper names, like Cicero, Livy, Caesar, Horace.

Because the history of the Via Appia spans centuries before and after the Common Era, we have used the traditional terms B.C. and A.D. when there was a possibility of confusion. When a date is clearly B.C. or A.D., it is given only in numbers.

All photographs in the book were taken by Dora Jane Hamblin, except those given individual credit.

Our debt to the ancient writers is inestimable, as is that to more modern students and scholars of the road. We owe particular thanks to Dr. J. B. Ward-Perkins of the British School at Rome and his library staff; to Mrs. Innes Longobardi of the library of the American Academy, to the German Archaeological Institute and to the Museo della Civilta Romana, all in Rome; to Lawrence Towner and James Wells and the staff of the Newberry Library in Chicago, and to Stanley Gwynn, University of Chicago Libraries; to R. A. G. Carson of the British Museum's Department of Coins and Medals; and to the Istituto Geografico Militare in Florence.

Among the many individuals who took time and trouble to help us on our way we remember particularly Professor Dinu Adamesteanu, superintendent of antiquity for the province of Basilicata; Dr. Giovanna Alvisi of Aerofototeca in Rome; Dr. Daniele Sterpos of Autostrade S.p.A. in Florence; Professor Baldo Conticello, director of the Archaeological Museum of Sperlonga; Professor S. P. Vinson, Classics Department, University of Arizona at Tucson; and Mrs. Dorothy Patton and Mrs. Marcia Preble Stolz of Chicago, who translated documents which defeated us.

Paul R. Reynolds of New York City, gentleman and literary agent, planted the seed of idea for this book several years ago and waited a long time for it. We thank him, Mrs. Elsie Stern, Barbara Willson, and the book's editor, Robert D. Loomis, for their patience and aid.

Finally, the authors wish to salute three friends and colleagues in Rome whose help and enthusiasm never wavered: Ann Pearce Natanson, Fiammetta Bises Brumetti and Simonetta Toraldo-Serra.

All of these persons and institutions are innocent of any error of fact or judgment which may appear in the following pages. The responsibility for accuracy rests upon us.

Dora Jane Hamblin
Mary Jane Grunsfeld

# Contents

# Contents

# THE APPIAN WAY, A JOURNEY

# I
# THE APPIAN WAY, QUEEN OF ROADS

The most famous of all the world's roads was built by convicts, slaves and soldiers. It was named Queen by a poet.

Publius Papinius Statius in the first century A.D. called it *lungarum regina viarum*—Queen of Long-Distance Roads. Strange, in the muscular military world of first-century Rome, that Statius should call this flinty triumph of engineers and impressed laborers a queen and not a king. Yet Statius was right.

The Appia doesn't stamp and march its way from Rome to the Adriatic Sea. It seems almost to slide, sinuous and feminine. It flows softly between rows of cypresses and umbrella pines south of Rome, glides across the Pontine Marshes, slithers up the rocky slopes of the spine of the Apennine Mountains and down their valleys. It arches over rivers, rides viaducts up hills, goes on and on, quiet and enigmatic as a force of nature.

Then it ends below a tall column at Brindisi, facing Greece across the sea, and in the pungent portside air, lovers of the road hear a sigh mixed with the slap and slosh of water. It was here the queen was coming, all that way. All that hot, hard, often bloody way.

There are older roads than the Appia. There are longer roads. There are topographically more dramatic roads. But no other highway on earth has seen so much of the traffic, the turbulence, the trade and triumph and bloodshed and glory which form the tapestry of Western civilization. No other road ever had so many poets.

The Appia was the first of the great Roman roads which within five hundred years laced together the whole civilized world. Born when Rome was young and eager, the Appia was the brainchild of an arrogant man who ignored wise counsel and aimed it, in 312 B.C., straight into the heart of Rome's biggest and most dangerous neighbor, the Samnite League. It was almost entirely an inland road; yet when it reached Brindisi it had touched all the seas which encircle the Italian peninsula: the broad white beaches of Terracina and Formia and Mondragone south of Rome on the Tyrrhenian Sea, where the surf breaks like rows of flounces on a lacy skirt; the rocky coast of Taranto facing Africa across the Ionian Sea; the broad sweep and shallow harbors of the Adriatic. It was toward the east that Rome yearned, across the Adriatic to Greece and the lands of the Bible, the Turkish peninsula and the site of Troy, to the exotic riches of Asia Minor.

Dusty Roman legionnaires, headed wearily home from incessant wars against Carthaginians, Samnites, Greeks, must have set their sandals on the smooth gray stones with an agony of anticipation, straining their eyes into the reddish glow which still suffuses the Via Appia at sunset, looking for a first glimpse of the walls and towers of Rome.

Mark Antony went off to court Cleopatra down this road, and Julius Caesar was once its *curator*, its overseer. Hannibal seized a section of it and almost brought down Rome. The followers of the rebellious slave Spartacus were crucified along the road and left there as a lesson to other slaves.

Jews from Jerusalem traveled on the Appia in the second century B.C. to appear before the Senate and obtain the friendship and protection of Rome. They came again, a century later, as prisoners of Pompey, the conqueror of Palestine, and still later as prisoners of Titus.

The apostle Paul, who said in his Biblical letter to the Romans that he had long wished to visit "God's beloved in Rome," finally got his wish in about A.D. 60, but then he, too, was a prisoner attended by a Roman centurion named Julius. Paul trudged along the Via Appia to Rome to plead his case with the emperor. Peter, having escaped from a Roman jail, was walking on the Appia the day he had a vision of Jesus, and shamed by his own intended flight, turned around and went back to Rome and martyrdom.

Perhaps the best-known journey of all was made by the poet Horace in 38 B.C. Horace traveled "From Rome to Brindisi, with Stops." Lovers of Latin and of Horace can recite the short work from memory, including his bawdy complaints about a "nocturnal omission" when a lady failed to keep an appointment with him in the town of Trevicum. This reference is omitted, replaced by several lines of asterisks, in a paperback edition of Horace printed in Rome in 1935 and still for sale in some outpost cities of the Appia.

On the same historic trip, Horace set up a topographical controversy by deviating from the Appia's established route and wandering off on muleback to visit friends and stop at way stations he failed to identify specifically. So important is the road, and so important is Horace, that two thousand years after him his precise route is the subject of scholarly analysis and dissertation.

Such famous figures were not the road's chief users, however. Soldiers, colonists, merchants, geographers, tourists, messengers, slaves, postmen trod the road or jolted their spines along it in rude carriages unblessed by rubber tires. Gladiators and wild animals and bands of roving athletes wandered up and down to provide entertainment in the amphitheaters and markets and sprawling private villas which lined the road.

Anyone who was anyone expected to be buried along the Via Appia, and to leave a monument to dazzle future generations.

There was even the grandfather of all road shows, "The Great Sacred Antonine Travelling Company of Artists of the Whole Empire," which performed theatrical works along the road in the second century A.D.

These events took place in the first four hundred years of the life of the Queen of Roads. Its engineers were charged to make a road which would last "forever," and their product survived far longer even than the Roman Empire. The Via Appia was in regular use, for most of its distance, for one thousand years.

· · ·

Starting from a gate in the first masonry wall of Rome, the road struck straight south following an existing track which passed the Temple of Mars and the town of Bovillae, and proceeded toward the Alban Hills, to which the popes today still flee during summer heat, to the heights and waters of extinct volcanoes and volcanic lakes. The same volcanos whose eruption millennia ago created the lakes spewed out basalt, the dense dark igneous rock from which the familiar stones of the Via Appia are carved.

From the Alban Hills the road ran gently downward toward Tres Tabernae, where Christian pilgrims hiked out to meet Paul, across the Pontine Marshes to a fortress called Anxur, high above the sea and the site of Roman Tarracina. There the road bent inland to avoid a lake, returned to the sea near Formiae, where Cicero had a summer villa, and shortly after that made its decisive turn inland to cross the peninsula. It leaped the mighty Volturno River at Casilinum, and a few miles later arrived at Capua, a former Samnite stronghold. It was 132 miles from Rome to Capua; the road reached the city at the end of 312 or early in 311 B.C.

Within a decade it was extended eastward toward Beneventum. En route it passed the grim site of the Romans' humiliating defeat at the Caudine Forks, the narrow, still-wild confines of river valleys between mountains. From Beneventum the road crossed a high Apennine plateau, passed Aeclanum, and by 291 B.C. it had arrived at Venusium, where Horace was born. Then it coasted down the eastern slope of the Apennines to Tarentum on the Ionian Sea, and shot across the narrow heel of the boot to Brundisium. By 244 B.C., less than a century after it began, the Appia was completed — 360 miles of road.

It wasn't all made of the familiar great gray basalt blocks like those on the edge of Rome. Some of it was simply gravel, some just rocky outcrop scraped clear of vegetation and marked with milestones. Yet it was a permanent, all-weather road.

After four hundred years the Emperor Trajan decreed an alternate route for more than half the length of the road. Beginning at Beneventum in A.D. 114, the highway known as the Via Appia Traiana set out to cross the spiny ridge and reach the town of Aecae, modern Troia. There it turned southeast to pass through Herdoniae and Canusium — near the site of another disastrous Roman defeat at the Battle of Cannae — and to reach the sea at Barium. From Barium the route

*The Via Appia on the outskirts of Rome, as it looks today.*

was straight and easy down the coastal plain to Brundisium. Though longer in miles, the Appia Traiana was so smooth a route that it was shorter than the original Via Appia.

Wherever they ran, the Appia and the Appia Traiana were engraved into the landscape of Italy by the thin smooth grooves of thousands of iron-rimmed chariot and carriage wheels, millions of tiny marks left by the hoofs of horses and mules.

As the swirling, untidy centuries passed, the heroes and villains of history left their marks and memories on the road. Goths, Vandals, Longobards, Saracens, warring Italian noblemen and contending dynasties of Germany, Spain, France and Austria fought on it and over it. Only England seems not to have coveted the route and the lands of the Queen of Roads, but her blockade of the Italian seas during the struggle with Napoleon forced all Paris–Naples cargo to go by road and subjected the poor old Queen to such a crunch of heavy traffic that even its sturdy old stones were turned to gravel on some sections of the route south of Rome.

Charlemagne marched up the road from Capua in the eighth century to liberate Rome from the Longobards. Thomas Aquinas died on the Appia in the thirteenth century, en route to the council of Lyon. The poet Torquato Tasso was almost captured by highwaymen in 1588 on the Appia near Formia. In the Roman Catholic jubilee year of 1600, more than 1,200,000 religious pilgrims trekked to Rome, thousands of them on the ancient road.

Then came the romantic travelers of the eighteenth and nineteenth centuries, men and women searching for the wheel tracks and the memories, the crumbled walls and arches of Roman amphitheaters along the way. They sought gateways, arches, aqueducts, tombs, graceful stone bridges some of which still arch over rivers the Romans knew.

George Gordon, Lord Byron brooded over the ruins and wrote of "the stern round tower of other days," the Tomb of Cecilia Metella on the Appia just south of Rome. Johann Wolfgang von Goethe in 1787 traveled along the road and kept a meticulous journal.

No doubt the Brownings tarried there on soft summer evenings during their Roman sojourn, sighing or holding hands or mulling over bits of verse as they achieved the proper melancholy attitude for surveying the traces of long-lost men and dreams and loves.

*The great column facing the sea at Brindisi, where the Via Appia ended.*

Henry Wadsworth Longfellow spent a month in Ariccia in 1826 and wrote of "The Appian Way [which] leads you from the gate of Rome to the gate of La Riccia." Beneath the heights of the city the landscape, he wrote, was "blotted with ruined tombs, and marked with broken but magnificent aqueducts that point the way to Rome."

Nathaniel Hawthorne first found the ruins disturbing and not very aesthetic. But then, after some indoctrination from a lame old lady named Mrs. Jameson who took him out to see the Appia and its monuments in "a little one-horse carriage," he confessed that "now that I have known it once, Rome certainly does draw into itself my heart."

Herman Melville, consummate man of the sea, toured the world under sail, but alighted from his ship to make the trip from Naples to Rome on the Via Appia.

Mark Twain teased both tradition and his guides, and was so annoyed by the claims of miracles put forth for holy relics along the road that he invented a very Mark Twainish joke: "After they had exhausted their enthusiasm pointing out to us and praising the beauties of some ancient bronze image or broken-legged statue, we look at it stupidly and in silence for five, ten, fifteen minutes—as long as we can hold out, in fact—and then ask, 'Is—is he dead?'"

"He," whoever he was, surely was dead. The Appia was not. It echoed to the tramp of soldiers just over a century ago, when Garibaldi led his brave "one thousand" up the Appian Way to capture Rome and to create modern Italy.

Today it lives as SS 7, *strada statale* 7 of the Italian highway network, a smooth asphalt secondary road by-passed by the six-lane *autostrade,* or superhighways, of the past twenty years. Much of it follows the track of the original Appia, from the foot of the Alban Hills through Terracina and Capua and Benevento to Taranto and Brindisi.

The first few miles, from inside Rome until a connection with modern state road 7, remain marked "Via Appia Antica." They are navigable for automobiles with sturdy shock absorbers and patient drivers, though they are seen far better on foot.

Gina Lollobrigida and Marcello Mastroianni now own homes on the Appia Antica, side by side with rich foreigners and religious institutions and ruined walls. Italian peasants too poor to rent apartments put up corrugated iron shacks in the ruins; some raise

chickens in the vaulted tomb which the Emperor Maxenti
A.D. 309 for his fallen son Romulus.

Roman car thieves have taken to hiding their four-wl
dence in abandoned catacombs along the road, and mu……,……
thorities in 1972 found it expedient to remove from their niches the few
remaining examples of marble funerary busts and tablets on the
Appia, to frustrate antiquities collectors.

Travelers still turn up. Millions every year go out reverently
through the towering Porta San Sebastiano, once the Porta Appia, to
gaze at the worn stones. There are bespectacled Japanese who fret
because Roman sightseeing buses are seldom on time, and sturdy
hiking Germans who scorn buses, and French visitors who flatten
themselves against medieval walls trying to photograph the narrow
street without being run over, and excited Americans who on hot
days do not deign to alight from air-conditioned transport to see the
stones up close.

Among the pilgrims are archaeologists and historians, and all the
world's Latin teachers, nice old parties in tennis shoes whose eyes
mist at the sight of the road and whose souls are transported back to
a better and braver world despite the all-too-visible remains of other
people's picnics and the bumps and giggles emerging from parked
Fiat cars in which athletic young Romans attempt to make cramped
love in defiance of gears, brake levers and door handles.

If roads had hearts and memories—and how tempting it is to
ascribe them, absurdly, to a road so amenable to imagination as the
Queen—then the Appia would be content. Battered and burdened,
neglected, mindlessly ravaged still, it is used. The babble of languages of all the centuries continues. The incessant coming and
going. Fires. First the signal fires of the legions; always shepherds
trying to keep warm; now wieners over twigs. Use.

Used things eventually wear out, but they don't just die. As
Hawthorne wrote:

> It is a very wonderful arrangement of Providence that these things
> should have been preserved for a long series of coming generations by
> that accumulation of dust and soil and grass and trees and houses over
> them, which will keep them safe, and cause their reappearance above the
> ground to be gradual, so that the rest of the world's lifetime may have
> for one of its enjoyments the uncovering. . . .

# II
# APPIUS CLAUDIUS, HIS WATER AND HIS ROAD

The man who started the Appia was a fifth- or sixth-generation Roman citizen of Sabine descent. For most of his life he held both public office and public attention; he was a man so willful, so stubborn, so talented that thunder and lightning accumulated around his head.

When he was old he was called Appius Claudius Caecus—"the Blind." This final name was appended without explanation; hence nobody knows today whether he suffered from some debility of old age, whether the nickname was symbolic or whether, as his enemies insisted, he was struck blind by the gods for his sins of pride and arrogance.

Appius Claudius was born a patrician, prosperous, well connected, privileged, in a Rome which was still a truculent settlement of small tribes and clans, farmers, herdsmen, huddled along the Tiber River and up the slopes of the seven little hills. The Romans were defended by a primitive earthen agger and by a later stone wall built in the fifth and fourth centuries B.C. against marauders from the north,

*13*

Etruscans and Gauls. They had come to terms with the Sabine people to the northeast, and had subdued the tribes of Latini, Volsci and the Oscan-speaking peoples in the immediate south. But they were still battling with the Samnites, a complex of tribes which formed the largest political unit in Italy and controlled thousands of miles of territory south of Rome from one sea to the other, thus blocking their passage to the Adriatic and the glittering cultures of Greece, Egypt and the Middle East.

In 312 B.C., Appius Claudius was elected a censor of Rome, together with a man named Gaius Plautius. In the Roman Republic the two censors, chosen by an assembly of citizens, ranked just below the consuls in power and prestige. Their title meant roughly "evaluator," and their tasks were to guard public morals—the honor of women, treatment of slaves, education of children—and to authorize and supervise public works.

Rome in that year was about four hundred years old, and it was threatening to burst the seams of its walls or to drown in its own refuse. It was still using, for roads, the trampled paths of shepherds and their flocks, pathways traveled since prehistoric times by men and beasts who came from the surrounding hills and plains to the Tiber for water. It was still relying on that same river, and on some adjacent springs, for drinking water and bath water, for cooking and cleaning.

The new censors immediately turned their attention to public works. Appius Claudius chose to provide a viable, all-weather road southward where he felt Rome's interests lay, and Gaius Plautius set himself to finding a new water source which could be piped to the city. Both men had prompt success. Plautius located some springs ten miles east of Rome whose water could be conducted to the city easily, most of the way underground. Claudius knew there was a wide track leading southward out of the Porta Capena, a gate in Rome's first masonry defense wall, toward the Temple of Mars on the outskirts of town, and from there to the village of Bovillae twelve miles outside the gate. From Bovillae the path led into the Alban Hills, and it was well worn. The Romans and the Albani, the residents of the hills, had had frequent dealings with one another, some of them belligerent. Thirty years before Appius Claudius assumed the censorship, there had been heavy traffic on this old track when some mutinous soldiers marched on Rome and made camp "under the ridge of Alba Longa," and moved to within eight miles of the Roman wall. Livy reported upon the event, and noted that the soldiers "marched . . . on what is now the Appian way."

Appius Claudius had only to hire engineers, foremen, laborers, and order them to refine the track. He decreed that it should be leveled, confined within retaining curbs, graveled against rain and mud, lifted on stone supports across valleys, "floated" on piles in marshes. To direct the work he hired the best engineers he could find. For the heavy labor he used thousands of convicted criminals, a cheap force he could command as one of his censor's prerogatives.

It is impossible to assess just how much he involved himself in the specific, day-to-day details of construction. Certainly he decided the route and the surface, and he ordered that the road should run to Capua. The combative Samnites had temporarily been battered into alliance with Rome, and Rome had poured out both money and citizens to establish colonies as buffer strongholds between the two centers of power.

This particular route was a triumph for the "southern lobby" of senators of Appius Claudius' era. Invaders from all sides had been repulsed for the moment, but the Senate was split on whether to expand to the north into Etruscan territory or to the southeast into the lands of the splintered and myriad tribes which lived there. Moving south, they thought, would involve dangerous dispersal of Roman strength, because the enemy was elusive. The Samnites, furthermore, were still dangerous. In 321 they had humbled the Roman legions at the Caudine Forks. Which way to go? Appius Claudius came down firmly on the side of the southern lobby: the road went south.

The decision was a bold and canny one. Appius understood before most Romans did that a road link was a vital artery, that it would bind forever to Rome not only the new colonies but also the cities of restless, newly conquered peoples along its route. The experience of later centuries proved that he was correct, but he made the decision without this experience, and he made it in lofty grandeur. His was the first of the roads which all the world was to admire.

Shortly after it reached Capua, however—sometime in 310—he was embroiled in one of the first and loudest of the public controversies which were to dog both the man and his policies for the rest of his life. The point at issue this time was that he refused to give up his job as censor. When the post was created, a censorship lasted for five years, but a series of bad experiences with despots and crooks and self-seekers had impelled a ruler called Aemilius to enact, shortly before 400 B.C., the *Lex Aemilia,* which limited the censors' terms to eighteen months. Gaius Plautius dutifully resigned, in mid-310, but Appius Claudius refused.

This blithe arrogance, according to a detailed report by Livy, so outraged a tribune named Publius Sempronius that he called Appius Claudius to public trial before the elected magistrates of Rome. Passionately Sempronius invoked the *Lex Aemilia,* and righteously he named the censors who had obeyed it. In his defense Appius Claudius remarked that he had not been alive when the *Lex Aemilia* was passed. Anyone elected at that time, he said, might indeed have been constrained to obey it. But since he *was* not, he *would* not. He was arrested for his defiance, but on appeal he persuaded three tribunes to vote for him. In an early equivalent of a hung jury, he got off free and went right on being a censor. He was, furthermore, the sole censor for the next eighteen months because his flouting of the law caused such disorder that no other man was elected to serve with him.

Now, it does not happen to every nation, nor even to every century in the same nation, to see the likes of a Charles de Gaulle or a Franklin Delano Roosevelt or an Appius Claudius Caecus. When these men happen, they rise above their time, attracting the lightning, and remain forever historical enigmas. Opinions and judgments of them vary so widely within their own eras that later students, attempting to separate fact from partisanship, are defeated as much by the anguished wails of their enemies as by the overblown praise of their sycophants. The cacophony, perhaps regrettably, seldom stays the fingers of writers. But it does boggle their minds.

Appius Claudius, like others of his type, got mixed reviews. Cicero and Plutarch tended to admire him. Livy usually deplored him, but sometimes grudgingly paid some respects. "Behold," he wrote, "the descendant of that Appius who, having been elected decemvir for one year, himself declared his own election for a second year, and the third . . . retained the fasces and authority, and relinquished not his hold on the magistracy until he was overwhelmed by his ill-gotten, ill-administered, and ill-continued powers."

Livy was so angry that one can imagine him now, spluttering in his studio, fracturing pen after pen and hurling the shattered instruments against the wall as he poured out his righteous rage. Although he wrote three hundred years after the acts of Appius Claudius which so offended him, he was a good reporter and set down as accurately as he could the oratory which had flown in clouds around the person of Appius: "'Will this be your contention, Appius, that the people is not bound by the Aemilian law? Or that the people is bound and you alone are exempt?'" Or, a bit later: "'Is it enough to add a day, or a month to his censorship? "Three years," quoth [Appius], "and six months beyond the time permitted by the Aemilian law will I administer the censorship, and administer it alone." Surely this begins to look like monarchy!'"

Appius Claudius went serenely on. References to his ancestry bothered him not a whit. All Rome knew about the family, anyway. Its founder was a Sabine named Attius Clausus who in 505 B.C. had decided that further combat with the feisty Romans was useless. He thus argued with his own people against continuing the wars, and then he picked up himself, his family and several thousand followers and moved to Rome. He was received with honor, awarded instant citizenship, and in 495 was chosen one of the two consuls of the city. By then he had Romanized his name to Appius Claudius.

After him came a long line of Appius Claudiuses, in such bewildering profusion that they can be separated from one another only by noting carefully the years of their power. Right after the first one came a holy terror called Appius Claudius Crassus who was beastly to the plebeians, the rising class of artisans and tradesmen, and who violated so many land laws that even the patricians felt he had gone too far. There was a Gaius Claudius who so lusted after a free-born girl that he tried to arrange to have her sold as a slave so he could seduce her. The girl's father averted this fate by murdering her with his own hands, but Claudius was in disgrace forever after. There was another Appius Claudius who tried to make himself dictator of all Rome. And there was the Emperor Claudius, of whom Robert Graves wrote.

Within the framework of the family, and its penchant for sticking like glue to any public office against which it rubbed, Appius Claudius of the road appears almost dangerously liberal. He ap-

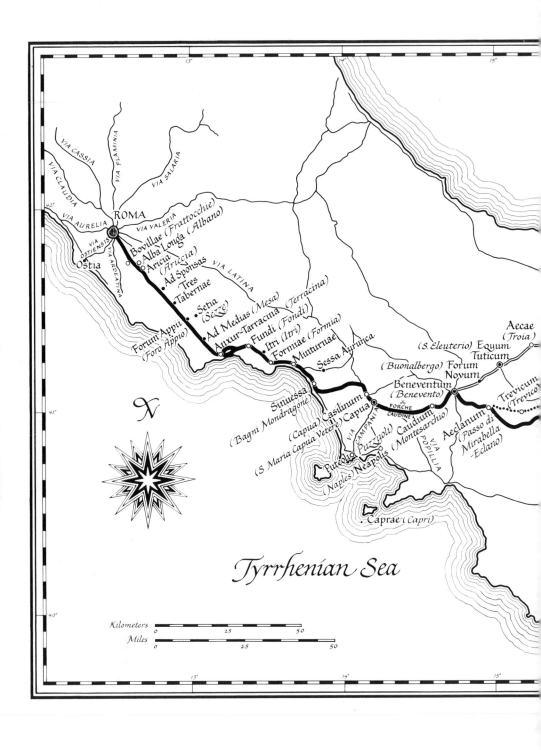

VIA CASSIA
VIA CLAUDIA
VIA FLAMINIA
VIA AURELIA
VIA SALARIA
ROMA
VIA VALERIA
VIA OSTIENSIS
Ostia
Bovillae (Frattocchie)
VIA ARDEATINA
Alba Longa (Albano)
Ariccia (Ariccia)
Ad Sponsas
Tres Tabernae
VIA LATINA
Setia (Sezze)
Ad Medias (Mesa)
Forum Appii (Foro Appio)
Anxur-Tarracina (Terracina)
Fundi (Fondi)
Itri (Itri)
Formiae (Formia)
Minturnae
Sessa Aurunca
Sinuessa (Bagni Mondragone)
Casilunum
Capua
(Capua)
(S. Maria Capua Vetere)
VIA CAMPANA
Puteoli (Pozzuoli)
Naples Neapolis (Naples)
Caprae (Capri)

(S. Eleuterio) Equum Tuticum
(Buonalbergo) Forum Novum
Beneventum (Benevento)
FORCHE CAUDINE
Caudium (Montesarchio)
VIA POPILLIA
Aeclanum (Passo di Mirabella Eclano)
Aecae (Troia)
Trevicum (Trevico)

N

Tyrrhenian Sea

Kilometers
0        25       50
Miles
0        25       50

# THE APPIAN WAY

Adriatic Sea

Via Appia
Via Appia-Traiana
Horace's route
Other roads

Modern names in italics

Herdoniae
(Ordona)
Cannae
VIA APPIA-TRAIANA
Asculum
(Ascoli
Satriano)
Canusium
(Canosa)
(Bari)
Barium
Rubi
(Venosa)
(Ruvo di Puglia)
Butuntum
(Bitonto)
Venusium
quilonia
acedonia)
(Gravina di Puglia)
Ad Pinum
Silvium
Egnatia
(Murgia Catena)
Blera
VIA APPIA
Speluncae
(Torre S. Sabina)
Brundisium
(Brindisi)
(Mesagne) Scamnum

ITALY

Valentium
(Valesio)
Tarentum
(Taranto)
Lupiae
(Lecce)

Hydruntum
(Otranto)

16°    17°    18°
42°
41°
40°

pointed the sons of freedmen to the Senate, filling posts which had formerly gone only to landowners or wealthy citizens. His fellow aristocrats accused him of "debasing" the Senate, and some tried to frustrate him after his censorship by calling the roll and seating the senators as they had been before Appius Claudius tampered with the list.

He also assigned poor men and landless residents into the administrative units of large *gens,* or clans, further outraging the patricians, but the final insult came when he took away from the Potitian *gens* the hereditary right of ritual sacrifice to Hercules at the god's main altar in the city. Appius Claudius turned the ritual duties over to public slaves and had them instructed in the rites. Just what his motives were is not clear, but Livy in one of his blasts says that within one year the "twelve families of the Potitii, and grown men to the number of 30," had perished and the name died out. It was for this offense, says Livy, that Appius was stricken blind "by the unforgetting ire of the gods."

Among the charges brought by the tribune Sempronius against Appius Claudius when he refused to cede the censorship was that he had apparently never read the Law of Twelve Tables, a body of traditional civil law which had been applied for centuries. Had he ever studied this law, Sempronius indicated, Appius Claudius would know that he was bound to follow the later Aemilian Law and resign. Livy adds that Appius' escape from punishment for all this was "greatly to the indignation of all classes."

Neither Sempronius' charge nor Livy's judgment seems, upon examination, logical. A man who had opened the Senate to plebeians, found clan homes for freedmen and the poor, would certainly have remained popular with those classes. As for knowing the Law, there is considerable evidence that Appius Claudius actually made copies of it available to his secretary, one Gnaeus Flavius, a plebeian and the son of a freedman, so that it could be published for the edification of the populace. This was a step of overwhelming importance, for the Twelve Tables had been held in the secret archives of the patrician rulers, and interpreted to common people, the plebeians, by a select group of jurists who, milords, embodied the law.

Flavius, with the connivance of Appius Claudius, broke this monopoly: he first had copies made, for which the grateful Romans elected him tribune. Later, while serving as curule aedile, he put up notice boards in the Forum and mounted upon them legal calendars so that ordinary citizens could know on which days their grievances against either the state or the neighbors might be heard. By one simple gesture the power of the interpreters of the law was fractured because it was no longer a total mystery.

After all this, Appius Claudius fought successfully against the election of plebeians to the consulship. His critics could never be consistent about him because the man was not consistent himself—or at least his public stance was not consistent. He curried favor with the plebs when their favor would serve him; he behaved as an arrogant patrician when he thought he dared or had the strength to behave thus. His only real consistency was toward his own interests. He was a consummate politician.

He believed more in the mystique of the law than in its specific application. Having connived in the commendable opening of the Twelve Tables to public knowledge, he then openly flouted several of them. While he was still censor he campaigned illegally for the office of consul. That time he didn't succeed, but later he was elected consul for two separate terms. His powers were not increased much because he had already managed to make a censor as powerful as a consul, but he enjoyed the grander title. He also became praetor, and a general of troops.

No matter where or how he served, Appius Claudius caused trouble and shattered tradition. In addition to tampering with the performance of the rites of Hercules he also invaded religious affairs in a tawdry fight with the *tibicines,* the sacred flute players. First he forbade them to conduct their annual feast at public expense. When the flute players protested, he threatened to cancel their license altogether. Thereupon the flute players went on strike. Their piped ministrations were expected, respected and traditional at all grand public affairs, and the silence caused consternation in Rome. The tone of both religious and funerary events was lowered severely until the Thunderer and the Flautists worked out a compromise.

Between controversies, Appius Claudius translated Greek into Roman, wrote dissertations, won from later scholars the accolade of "the first prose writer in Latin." He probably regarded as his finest hour the day in 280 when, old and blind and infirm, he single-handedly altered the direction of Roman history one more time by talking the Senate into fighting King Pyrrhus of Epirus.

This was another of the threatened moments of Rome, a crucial hour in which the Senate wavered. The legions had driven invading Gauls back north across the Po Valley, and had subdued the Samnites in the south. Rome was master of the entire peninsula from the Po to the thin arc of Greek colonies planted along the instep of the Italian boot.

To these Greeks, Rome had offered an alliance and protection against the obstreperous "barbarians," the Italianate tribes that lived precariously between the Greek area of control and the Roman. Not only did Tarentum refuse alliance, it also sent for Pyrrhus and offered all its warriors to his banners. This combination of Eastern force and local colonists had already defeated the Roman legions once, and the Senate was disposed to sue for peace.

Appius Claudius, the unregenerate curmudgeon, objected. It had been thirty years since his road drove south, and he had seen it used as a highway by the triumphant troops of his beloved city. He had even marched down it himself, leading the legions to fight the Samnites. He knew that it worked, that it was an instrument of power. He knew that it was in this moment stretching toward Tarentum on the sea, toward communication with the East. It could never reach there, never link with the seas and across them to Greece and Egypt if Tarentum, with Pyrrhus' aid, should prevail.

For this, as well as the simpler reason of patriotism, Appius Claudius could not tolerate the Senate's equivocation. He dressed up in his finest toga, summoned his slaves to carry him by litter to the Forum, and there ordered his sons and sons-in-law to lift him and carry him inside. Witnesses wrote that the senators were awed by his blind and white-haired presence, as silent as he until he chose to speak. Plutarch recorded his words:

> "Up to this time, O Romans, I have regarded the misfortune to my eyes as an affliction. But it now distresses me that I am not deaf as well as blind, that I might not hear the shameful resolutions and decrees of yours which bring low the glory of Rome. . . . Do not suppose that ye will rid yourselves of this fellow [Pyrrhus] by making him your friend; nay, ye will bring against you others, and they will despise you as men whom anybody can easily subdue, if Pyrrhus goes away unpunished for his insults. . . ."

*One of the Samnite warriors whom Appius Claudius defeated. This fragment is now in the Benevento archaeological museum.*

When the old man ceased to speak, says Plutarch, "his hearers were seized with eagerness to prosecute the war."

Pyrrhus won two battles but failed to gain his objective. His chagrin gave to all the languages of modern Europe, and to the English-speaking world, its most bitter adjective for the price of victory. In 275 Pyrrhus finally was defeated by the Romans and sent packing.

Once again, after his oratory, Appius Claudius basked in public admiration. Cicero praised him in words which are not entirely sympathetic: "his slaves feared him, his children revered him, all loved him." But Cicero added a moral. In old age, he said Appius Claudius "did not languidly succumb, but kept his mind ever taut like a well-strung bow." Old age, Cicero concluded, is honored "only on condition that it defends itself, maintains its rights, is subservient to no one, and to the last breath rules over its own domain. . . ."

This was a grand-exit performance, but the Roman world was treated to a series of Claudian curtain calls for several more generations. The family reputation for courage and military acumen— though not, in truth, for outrageousness—was tarnished badly a few years later by Appius' son Publius Claudius Pulcher, who suffered a humiliating defeat as commander of a Roman fleet against the Carthaginians in southern waters. The disaster was attributed at the time to Publius' cavalier treatment of a batch of sacred chickens.

The comportment of chickens, like the flights of birds, the movements of fish, and the color of animal entrails, were in those days used as omens, read and interpreted by priestly augurs, and were entitled to respectful treatment. But at one point Publius Claudius' chickens refused to eat. So he, in an impatient action characteristic of both his *gens* and his genes, ordered them thrown in the sea. "If they won't eat," he decreed, "then let them drink."

Thus passed also the family's hard-won reputation for sophisticated oratory. Even before "Chicken Claudius" had smirched the escutcheon, one of the most liberal of "Road Claudius'" reforms had been brought to naught. Two less courageous censors than he had yielded to the pressure of the patricians and culled from each and every *gens* of Rome the poor whom Appius Claudius had enrolled there. These censors separated what they considered the plebeian riffraff, organized the whole unruly mob into four new and distinct groups and gave them the name *Urban*. In the view of those who hated him, "that man" Appius Claudius may thus have contributed even to the urban crisis of his own and later days.

It is one of the supreme ironies of Appius Claudius' turbulent life that he risked his first public censure and defied the sacred laws of Rome not to ensure the completion of his road—which was finished to Capua by the time his censorship expired—but instead to take credit for having brought water to the city.

Gaius Plautius, who found the springs, had not had time in his eighteen-month term to complete Rome's first aqueduct, partly because engineers had not yet mastered the high arch which carried later water supplies vaulting over the countryside. Plautius' water started in a sewerlike pipe fifty feet below the surface and ran almost all the way to Rome underground, where it poured out near the banks of the Tiber.

All this excavation, this pipe laying, could not be completed as rapidly as could a graveled road. Poor Plautius, who had every right to expect that his water would be called Aqua Plautia, had to be content with the appended nickname Venox, "the Hunter," because he had discovered the spring.

Devious devil that he was, though, Appius Claudius had a shrewd sense of what was important to his time and to his city: roads and water. All the legends of military glory and conquest, all the triumphs of poetry and oratory, all the sonorous laws and their contention pale before the twin Roman achievements of roads and water. These were simple, sensible amenities of such immense importance that the Romans carried them to all corners of their world, to the great benefit of all who lived there.

One of the favorite conceits of scholars from Appius Claudius' time to our own has been a comparison of the life styles, the aims and dreams of Greece and of Rome. Often these debates are conducted to the detriment of Rome. They differ very little, actually, from lesser arguments about the relative merits of Paris, London, New York or San Francisco, except that the Greece-Rome battle is couched in lofty terms and is amenable to manipulation by quotations of ancient writers. A great deal of the argument boils down to things like water and roads, as symbols even if not as entities. They are used to epitomize the practical, pragmatic character of Rome as distinct from such soarings of the Greek spirit as the creative urge or grace of living.

One of the first participants in the great debate was the Greek geographer Strabo, who went on record that the Greeks aimed "most happily in the founding of cities, in that they aimed at beauty, strength of position, harbors, and productive soil." The Romans, Strabo was bound to admit, "had the best foresight . . . in construction of roads and aqueducts, and of sewers that could wash out the filth of the city. . . ."

Pliny considered the aqueducts Rome's greatest achievement. He asserted that "the whole globe offers nothing more marvelous." Even more effusive was an engineer named Sextus Julius Frontinus who was chief of the Rome water department at the end of the first century A.D. "Who will venture to compare with these mighty conduits the idle Pyramids, or the famous but useless works of the Greeks?" he asked.

In this passage Frontinus sounds like all the soulless, utilitarian Romans to whom the Hellenophile always points, but Frontinus knew a lot about water. He had personally checked and controlled Rome's sources, had caught everybody from noblemen to courtesans illegally tapping the aqueducts in defiance of both public cleanliness and public health. And he knew what happened to a city when its water taps went dry.

Until Plautius and Appius Claudius brought the first of eleven aqueducts into Rome, the patricians thought themselves lucky to be able to bathe once a week. The plebeians queued up for water at springs and public fountains.

It was water, after all, in the Tiber, which had brought the first settlers to the site of Rome. Water remained for centuries a near-sacred thing. One of the most revered springs in the old city filled a fountain near the site of the Porta Capena in the first masonry city wall. This was the holy water of the Camenae, four water nymphs who had bestowed their liquid blessing as a way of befriending the fledgling city. Their water was used first by the vestal virgins from temples nearby. The vestals were forbidden to use water which had either passed through pipes or touched the earth, so they trooped off to the spring every morning carrying special water pots with rounded bottoms. If the virgins put the pots down for any reason, they would promptly tip over and spill.

The same spring, and fountain, and grove of trees, were considered also sacred to the god Mercury. Best known as the messenger of the mighty, Mercury was also the god of commerce, thievery, eloquence and science. In his honor many merchants trekked to the fountain on the Ides of May (the fifteenth day was called "Ides" in each month of the Roman calendar). Here they filled vessels with water, dipped laurel branches into it, and sprinkled both their pious heads and their merchandise. The poet Ovid, who seems to have harbored a low opinion of merchants, wrote that once they had performed this damp rite they uttered a special prayer: "Wash away the perjuries of past time . . . let the swift south winds carry away the wicked words, and may tomorrow open the door for me to fresh perjuries, and may the gods above not care if I shall utter any! Only grant me profits,

*The remains of an aqueduct on the outskirts of Rome, best visible from SS 7 as it goes out to Ciampino Airport and Cinecittà. A branch of the Aqua Claudia, this was built by the Emperor Commodus in the second century* A.D.

grant me the joy of profit made, and see to it that I enjoy cheating the buyer!" And, concludes Ovid, "At such prayers Mercury laughs from on high, remembering that he himself stole the Ortygian kine."

With all these merchants, vestal virgins, overseeing nymphs, thirsty neighbors, the holy grove and the holy water pots, the area around the Porta Capena must have been a traffic jam when Appius Claudius chose to begin his road right there. It was an auspicious place for the beginning of a road.

The Aqua Appia went nowhere near it and was, by comparison with later aqueducts, a very short-lived wonder. Even by the time of Frontinus, four hundred years later, the Aqua Appia was considered the work of "the ancients." It was still in use, but it had been far surpassed by other, more productive and far more dramatic-looking aqueducts.

By the third century A.D., Rome had eleven of them. Never did a city have such rushings, gushings, splashing of water. At that time the population was about one million, and the network of aqueducts provided to it 250 million gallons of water a day, a proportionate figure probably never achieved again. New York City, when it had three times the population, could produce less than twice the volume. New York probably made more conservative use of its water, however, because it could be controlled by taps. In Rome the water just ran, day and night. Aqueducts were not designed to be turned on and off, and by A.D. 410 they poured their sparkling, leaping bounty into 1,212 public fountains, 11 majestic imperial baths, 926 more modest baths, and Frontinus–knows how many private homes.

There is an endearing Roman story about Queen Christina of Sweden, who visited the Vatican in the seventeenth century and assumed that the two exuberant fountains within the embrace of the Bernini Colonnade had been turned on especially in her honor. Having marveled at the gay spurt of their white water into the blue sky, she graciously gave permission to have them turned off. She was appalled to learn that they never stopped. There is another story, which says that the same eccentric sovereign playfully shot off three cannonballs from the top of the nearby tomb of Hadrian toward the French Academy a mile away on the Pincian Hill, just to warn a friend that she would be late for lunch. So it may be that both tales have been embroidered.

Nowadays the Vatican fountains can be stopped, as they are occasionally to extricate an eel which has made its precarious way for twenty-five miles through the pipes from the Lake of Bracciano to an unscheduled audience with the pope. Others are stopped for repairs, at intervals, but it is a fact that most of the aqueduct-fed street fountains and spigots of Rome run steadily today, as they did in ancient times, even when supplies of water are cut off to hotels and restaurants.

Many of the aqueducts were cut in the sixth century A.D. by bar-

*This eulogy to Appius Claudius was found during excavations of the Forum in Rome. The original marble is in the Florence archaeological museum.*

barian invaders, and Appius Claudius' aqueduct had vanished even before this interruption. Remains of it exist deep under the city, however, and in times of heavy rain their crumbling pipes still contribute to the central sewer of the city, the *cloaca maxima,* a construction so mighty that it could have been the nave of a medieval cathedral had it been built a millennium later and above the ground. Water in Rome still sweeps through homes, baths, fountains, over the cobblestones and then at last into the old drain which was there before Appius Claudius, before Frontinus, performing its final service to a water-worshiping people by helping to flush out the trash from the streets into the old passage toward the sea.

Appius Claudius died before "his" aqueduct had been either destroyed or superseded. Perhaps he was happy that it bore his name, for on it he pinned his main hope for immortality. Yet no sentimental traveler for centuries has ever seen one of its few arches inside the city.

In the late nineteenth century diggers found a carved stone *elogio* to Appius Claudius' memory, in the ruins of the Forum. In 1932 archaeologists commissioned by Mussolini unearthed the final portions of a rectangular Roman portico attached to a temple. The portico had curving sides almost like the Bernini Colonnade, and into their walls at two levels the builders had set niches for half-sized statues and for inscriptions which listed the *cursus honorum,* or public career, of their heroes. Into one of these niches the *elogio* to Appius Claudius fit perfectly. It reads:

> HE CONQUERED MANY SAMNITE CITIES. HE DESTROYED THE
> SABINE AND ETRUSCAN ARMIES. HE REFUSED TO MAKE
> PEACE WITH PYRRHUS. DURING HIS CENSORSHIP HE CON-
> STRUCTED THE VIA APPIA AND BROUGHT WATER TO THE
> CITY. HE MADE THE TEMPLE OF BELLONA.

Long before the world knew it, and after Appius Claudius himself ceased to care, his peers had listed the most important contribution of his life, the road, before the water.

# III
# SKELETONS IN
# THE OUTSKIRTS

Nowhere are the remains of the road so brushed still by spirits, so haunted by eloquent voices and turbulent events as in the few miles of roadbed which reach through the southern outskirts of modern Rome. Nowhere else, either, are the worn stones so accessible to those who yearn to put their feet, just once, where some personal hero trod. By the simple act of walking here, a person who wishes it can be projected far back, into an earlier column of the long procession of mankind, and he can march along with that column thinking his own thoughts.

The track of the Appia begins in a patch of grass under a semicircle of tall evergreens, beside a stubby pile of brick and mortar just a few hundred yards from the Roman Forum, the Colosseum, the Arch of Constantine. Children kick soccer balls beside the worn masonry core, and workmen in their undershirts nap in the grass. Traffic surges past on a six-lane inner-city highway; few drivers have time to glance at the little ruin.

On its side is a neat marble plaque which says: "Beginning

of the Via Appia." Tradition identifies it as the last pitiful remnant of the Porta Capena. The wide square which faces it repeats the name: Piazza di Porta Capena. Across the piazza stands the cement-and-glass structure of the Food and Agriculture Organization of the United Nations, housed in a building which Mussolini had planned as his Ministry of African Affairs before World War II demolished his African affairs.

Between the FAO building and the Porta Capena is an eighty-foot obelisk from the holy city of Axum in Ethiopia. Carved in the fourth century A.D., it is a trophy brought back to Rome in 1937 by Italian soldiers who had just subdued the barefoot troops of Haile Selassie. Important visitors to Rome usually are escorted from the airport through this piazza, to see the starting point of the Appia, the column of Axum, and from there around the Colosseum, past the Forum, and to the Quirinale, the White House of Italy. In 1970, when the then seventy-eight-year-old Emperor of Ethiopia came to call, the cortege made a tactful detour so that Haile Selassie's eyes would not fall on that pilfered pillar from Axum, a reminder of Roman perfidy.

*Remains of the Porta Capena, where the road began, inside Rome, with modern traffic passing it.*

Dwarfed now both by the pillar and the FAO building, the Porta Capena is serene in its park. No traces of the old paving stones are left anywhere near it, however, so a visitor longing for a first glimpse of the road would do well to commence inside the Roman Forum. Here the paving of the sacred road, the Via Sacra, is intact for long distances. It is almost identical in width and composition to the paving of the Appia, and it led from the Forum out to the Porta Capena and the beginning of the road.

Once the Porta Capena was not only gate but also underpinning for a water reservoir. The latter leaked. Early users of the Appia called it the "dripping arch," because every time they entered or left the city by this road they received instant baptism en route.

From the Capena, the road went southeast toward the flat fields and intervening undulations of the Roman Campagna, the beloved countryside described by ancient writers. All traces of the original road have been obliterated, but the track is followed by the Via delle Terme di Caracalla, a wide avenue which passes the towering ruins of public baths begun in A.D. 206 and finished eleven years later.

Though not the largest baths in Rome, the ones called Caracalla could accommodate sixteen hundred persons at a time in a labyrinth of sweat rooms, warm rooms, cold rooms, gymnasiums, libraries and art galleries. No wonder that Roman homes had no bathtubs.

The vaulting arches of Caracalla's circular *caldarium,* or hot room, form the backdrop today for outdoor summer opera. Measurements of size rendered into square feet or cubic yards are incomprehensible to anyone who isn't an architect, so suffice it to note that the stage of this theater in the mighty ruins can accommodate three hundred extras for the triumphal march of *Aïda,* the star singers, the chorus, a couple of camels, an elephant or two, and a four-horse chariot which clatters onstage, to the visible apprehension of the ladies of the chorus, bearing inside it the tenor Radames, who is expected to sing at full voice while clutching for dear life to the sides of the chariot. On one occasion in the 1950s the directors of the Caracalla opera borrowed some spirited horses from the *Ben Hur* movie set, and watched with horror as the horses galloped across the stage, down the exit ramp, out the gate and off in the general direction of the Colosseum. The Italian audience rose as one and proclaimed "*Bis!*" — "Encore!"

The Baths of Caracalla had not been built when the Appia first passed this way. But thousands of Roman citizens walked the route, going to their baths, two millennia before *Aïda* was written.

Between the Porta Capena and the baths, hidden in the trees, is a church named for two early Christian martyrs, Nereus and Achilleus. Its origin predates them; originally the church was *titulus fasciolae,* sacred to the memory of the apostle Peter. Peter, who had been locked up in Rome's Mamertine Prison during a persecution of Christians, managed to escape and fled the city along the Via Appia. At this point in the road, tradition says, he lost one of the bandages which he had wrapped around his chain-chafed legs. No one knows exactly when the first church was erected on the site, but inscriptions from A.D. 377 mention it. It was one of the oldest titular churches of Rome, named for the bandage, *fasciola.*

From the church of the bandage and the baths of Caracalla, the Appia went straight and level into a saucer in the landscape. Now it is a big piazza called Numa Pompilius, after a Sabine king of Rome in the seventh century B.C. From here three roads branch off into the

Campagna. One, to the right, is the Cristoforo Colombo leading to Ostia, the modern sea resort near the site of Rome's ancient seaport. One is the Via Latina, older even than the Appia, which heads obliquely toward the Alban Hills. The third, between the other two, is the Appia, with a signboard indication: "To the Appia Antica."

The road rises perceptibly between encasing villa and garden walls. Behind the walls lie treasures: the tomb of the aristocratic Scipio family; a *columbarium,* which originally meant "dovecote" but which was the name applied metaphorically to subterranean vaults with rows of small niches for the ashes of the dead; a church which Italians call matter-of-factly San Giovanni in Olio—St. John in Oil, on the spot where the apostle John was alleged to have been boiled in oil but emerged "as from a refreshing bath."

Here the road is like a tunnel. Two small Italian cars can pass on it; three, more often than not, attempt the feat. Tourists awaiting a city bus are constrained to flatten themselves against the restricting walls, or cower in the set-back entrances of private villas, to avoid being squashed when the bus comes.

A mile from the Porta Capena the tunnel-like road arrives at the Porta San Sebastiano, an imposing opening in the defense wall built by the Emperor Aurelian in the third century A.D. Originally it was called the Porta Appia and it was a much lower, more modest gate. In the Middle Ages the tall flanking towers were built and the name was changed.

Just inside the arched Porta San Sebastiano is a picturesque ruin called the Arch of Drusus. Maybe it was a triumphal arch erected to the honor of the Roman general Drusus in the first century B.C. More likely, it was part of an aqueduct which carried water to the Baths of Caracalla. The aqueduct theory is supported by the presence of a tall brick archway standing just to the side of the Arch of Drusus. Whether it was arch or aqueduct, the charming little ruin was there in the early years of the Appia. Traffic passed under and through it, as it still does.

In 1970 the city of Rome created a "wall walk" along the ramparts of the Aurelian Wall beside the Porta San Sebastiano, and opened it to visitors with energy and curiosity enough to wish to walk where Roman archers stood. Walltop affords an exciting view of the Arch of Drusus, the red brick ruin of Caracalla, the route of the Appia both

back toward the Porta Capena and out toward the tombs. It also affords a brief history of the vicissitudes of both city and road: embedded in the walls of the often-restored Aurelian rampart are inscribed stones bearing the names and crests of popes and emperors who restored them, scratched signatures of workmen, the sealed-in clay pots and broken fragments placed by contractors who saved both money and weight by using debris instead of brick. There is even a primitive fresco of the Madonna, done in the late sixteenth century by a nameless hermit who lived in an abandoned tower and left his painting as thanks. By the late 1500s, much-sacked Rome had shrunk to 20,000 souls huddled around fortress Vatican, and the Aurelian Wall was way out in the country, a suitably remote place for a hermit.

Somewhere near the wall, a few yards inside or outside the gate, was the first mile of the Appia, and the first milestone. The road here curves gently downward and slightly to the right. It is bordered by restaurants, factories, filling stations, advertising billboards, discarded plastic bags and more walls. Just outside the gate, on the left going south, is a fountain whose basin is a marble sarcophagus, and whose decorations, some funerary figures. Nothing marks it or identifies it. Few visitors see it, though both dogs and pedestrians stop to drink from it, and Italian drivers trapped in traffic jams sometimes use it for a quick car wash.

About half a mile farther on, or seven tenths of a kilometer,* is the first of the striking monuments on the road outside the walls. This is a tall brown stone ruin, roughly pyramidal, with on top of it a neat little house and two windows facing the road. The eroded stone core is believed to be the remains of the Tomb of Geta, son of the Emperor Septimius Severus. Geta was murdered by his brother Caracalla, he of the baths, in a fraternal dispute over succession.

A few yards beyond it, lying on the right behind a wall and almost covered by later construction, is the ivy-covered top of a rounded tower. This is the Tomb of Priscilla, wife of a friend of the Emperor Domitian. The poet Statius, who named the Queen of Roads, wrote a

---

* All measurements to follow in this chapter will be indicated in kilometers, using Porta San Sebastiano as zero. This is convenient, as measurements of distance both on the road itself and on the gauges of European automobiles are in kilometers. 1 km. = 0.6 mile.

*The Porta San Sebastiano, once the Porta Appia, which led the road out of the city. This view is from outside the wall.*

letter of condolence to the bereaved husband in which he said: "To love a wife while she lives is a pleasure, to go on loving her when she is dead is a cult." He also predicted that "Centuries will have no power to destroy this splendid marble edifice." In this case he was wrong. No marble remains at all, and even the tower is difficult to see.

At 0.9 kilometer outside the wall, where the Via Appia veers to the left, is the church of Domine Quo Vadis? It is a very small building with a stark and dirty façade, but inside it is clean, well lighted and appealing. It takes its name from the legend that Peter, having lost his bandage but still fleeing, met a vision of Christ at this spot. Startled, Peter asked, *"Domine, quo vadis?"*—"Lord, where are you going?"—and Christ replied, "I go to Rome to be crucified a second time." Chastened, Peter turned around and walked back along the Appia to his own martyrdom at the hands of Nero.

The church is almost always open, though unattended. Two steps inside the door are several rows of big neat paving blocks, quite possibly the stones of the first Appian pavement, and fixed firmly with steel rods to the floor is a piece of marble showing two human footprints. To the pious and credulous of the Middle Ages these were the miraculous prints of Jesus himself—or maybe of Peter, versions vary—on the site of the dramatic encounter between master and disciple. In 1620 the original marble was removed and taken to a museum in the Church of San Sebastiano. The one now visible in Domine Quo Vadis? is a copy.

For centuries the tradition of the meeting, the presence of the footprints has attracted pilgrims to the church. Many of them have been skeptical. Mark Twain had a look, got from his guide the impression that the footprints were Peter's rather than Jesus' and with a fine eye for discrepancies in doubtful stories he noted that the prints were so long—almost eleven inches—and so wide that in his opinion they could have belonged only to a man ten or twelve feet tall. Further, as Twain commented in *The Innocents Abroad*, "It was not stated how it was ever discovered whose footprints they were, seeing the interview occurred secretly and at night."

Footprints in stone, often with one print going forward and the other backward, were common in pagan religious sanctuaries, perhaps as an indication of the devotion of the worshiper in making his way to the sanctuary and then trudging the long way back home again.

*Footprints in marble in the church of Domine Quo Vadis?*

The most logical explanation for the miraculous footprints of Domine Quo Vadis? is that some early Christian, having made his way to the site of Peter's meeting with his Lord, decided to leave a symbol of his piety and a deathless memorial to his belief. He may have dug up the footprint stone somewhere else along the Appia, from a pagan shrine, and lugged it along with him. He couldn't have known that it would be accepted centuries later as a miracle, one of the relics so prized by the churches of Rome.

At 2 kilometers south of the gate a later road, the Via Appia Pignatelli, forks off to the left. Just a few yards before, it is the entrance to the Catacombs of St. Callistus, geographically the first of a series of underground burial chambers which line the road and which have become its best-known monuments.

There still persists the romantic notion that catacombs were created for the courageous, secret worship of early Christians who burrowed under the earth to escape pagan Roman persecution. This is not true. Small bands of worshipers may have gathered there from time to time to honor or to inter their relatives, but the catacombs were burial places, period.

Roman respect for the dead extended to the precincts in which their remains were committed to the afterlife; these precincts were sacred. Before the Christian Era, the prevailing Roman practice was to cremate the body and then erect a monument which enclosed the ashes. When the Appia was built, most funerals were conducted at night so that other citizens should not be saddened by the rites and so that the sacrifices offered to the gods would not be interrupted or cheapened by the stares of the curious.

Toward the end of the Republic and during the Empire, this custom changed. Members of wealthy and influential families wished their funeral processions to be seen by the public. Funerals were held by day, and they became as elaborate as weddings and triumphs, as carefully choreographed as theatrical performances. When an important man died he was laid on a bier spread with purple and gold-embroidered coverings; the body was dressed in the full regalia of the highest office the man had occupied in his career. All of his relatives accompanied him in a procession from the family home to the Forum and thence to his final resting place. All wore black; sons wore black veils.

At the head of the procession was a party of hired female mourners, selected for the volume and poignancy of their wails. At some time in history these mourners must also have pulled out their hair, because later Romans passed a law specifically forbidding this excess of professional grief.

Behind the wailing women came the flute players, dancers and a party of actors. One actor impersonated the dead person, others wore marks or carried wax images of the deceased's most distinguished ancestors. One kinsman pronounced a eulogy in the Forum. The salient points of this speech were repeated in incised marble on the monument which was his tomb. Further public honor and acclaim were assured by burial along one of the great roads, so that all who passed would be reminded of the fame of the family, the worthy deeds and characters of the men and women whose ashes lay here.

So strong was the Roman attachment to funeral rites that even birds, if they were favorites of important persons, were accorded ceremony. Pliny tells of a raven, a bird which the Greeks had revered because of its "understanding of auspices," which was given a splendid funeral on the Via Appia. Pliny's raven was hatched in a brood on top of the Temple of Castor and Pollux and then flew down to take up residence in a cobbler's shop in the vicinity. Soon it "picked up the habit of talking," and flew off every morning to a platform facing the Forum, where it called out cheery greetings to the Emperor Tiberius, generals and senators, and even to ordinary citizens whom it recognized and liked.

This amazing bird, having performed its daily salutations, then returned to the cobbler's shop. There one sad day it fell afoul of a jealous cobbler nearby who accused it of having dirtied his stock with its droppings. Filled with rage, he killed it. Everybody from the emperor to the generals to the local beggars was outraged. The murderous cobbler was driven from the district, and the raven had a fine funeral.

"The bird's funeral was celebrated with a vast crowd . . . flowers . . . the draped bier being carried on the shoulders of two Ethiopians and in front of it going in procession a flute player and all kinds of wreaths," Pliny said.

Then, having provided all this, the raven's devoted admirers burned up its *corpus,* somewhere near the field of the god Rediculus. (The name comes not from "ridiculous," which it suggests, but from *redire,* to return.) The exact location of the raven's funeral pyre has been lost, but the remains of a temple to Deus Rediculus, the god of the return journey, lie to the left of the Appia in the valley of the Caffarella. Roman legend holds that on this spot the invader Hannibal was suddenly persuaded to abandon his siege of Rome and to return home. A more likely explanation is that the Romans, having elevated the road to such an important, quasi-deified entity, also appointed a god and built a temple to supervise the safe return of wayfarers from the long journeys they undertook.

Pliny's raven perished early in the first century A.D. The oldest documented human funerary inscription on the Appia dates from a hundred years before. Its carved and weathered words are dedicated to the memory of one Marcus Caecilius, whose choice of sentiment marks him as a man of noble nature and beguiling friendliness. "Stranger," says his memorial, "I thank you for having stopped by my resting place; may thy business prosper, keep well, sleep peacefully."

Almost as old is another, which exhorts: "Stop, stranger, and turn towards . . . this sepulcher, which contains the ashes of a good and kind man, a friend of the poor."

These requests for the attention of the passer-by were, like the grand funeral processions of later years, pathetic implorations for immortality. The Roman concept of hell was less a place of punishment than a vast emptiness in which drifted formless shades, indistinguishable one from the other. To be indistinguishable, anonymous, unidentified, was hell. To be identified forever, in stone, to have one's name proudly displayed where men would walk for generations, was to be immortal.

Burial became more complicated after the birth of Christianity. The Christianized Romans, like the Jews before them, inhumed their dead instead of cremating them. This created a need for space in which to lay out intact bodies. The dovecote *columbaria*, accommodating dozens or even hundreds of urns of ashes, would not do. Since both Christians and Jews were, after all, also Romans, they wanted to put the remains of those they loved into honored positions along the great roads. That was the custom, a tradition which rose above religious belief. Neither group was rich enough, in money or influence, to obtain enormous tracts of such valuable land. Both suffered from intermittent persecution, which made them nervous of flaunting in the face of their death-respecting fellow citizens a burial practice which might seem dangerously foreign.

Their solution was to go underground. Romans who already owned land along the Appia, and who then were converted to Christianity, offered space. It was simple for them to tunnel both deeper and wider into the softish native stone of the Roman Campagna and transform a small family plot into a labyrinth hundreds of meters long and three or four stories deep. Six miles of subterranean galleries have been explored and measured in the catacombs of Callistus, eight miles in those of Domitilla.

Christians and Jews also profited from a Roman custom of forming "burial clubs." When they began, the clubs were groups of humble citizens who pooled their resources to buy a bit of precious land along the Appia for the interment of their ashes and those of their relatives. Many a burial club no doubt masked the nucleus of political organization and land acquisition for the minority groups.

There are at least seven catacombs on the Appia, including the Jewish one now called Vigna Randanini. *Vigna* means "vineyard," and on top of all the invisible galleries and chambers, the corridors and the memorials, flourish vineyards and villas, used-car lots and *trattorie*.

Most of the present catacomb entrances are of medieval construction. Down below, despite the grisly appearance of entire skeletons laid out on musty, cobwebby shelves, the explicit sense of silence and finality, the catacombs are not dreary places. Pleasant multilingual priests with soft voices dispense candles and information as they lead groups of tourists through, translating the enigmatic scratched symbols of Christians and Jews incised into the brown rock.

Catacombs can be delicious cool relief from the Roman sun, and a boon to hay-fever sufferers. Pollen doesn't penetrate easily into these damp homes of the dead. Children try to scare one another and themselves down in the tombs, but their hearts aren't really in it. They look as if they would like to come back on Halloween, to have a party here.

The Catacombs of St. Callistus, whose entrance comes first along the road, were named for a man as rambunctious as Appius Claudius himself, and even more controversial—if such a thing is possible. Callistus was a third-century pope whose enemies swore that he was born a slave. He grew up to become an embezzling banker, once started a riot in a synagogue, was sent into exile, and finally was commissioned by a near-illiterate predecessor to supervise the papal cemetery in Rome. Whether all these charges are true or not, the fact remains that Callistus succeeded to the throne of Peter. One of his first acts was to decree that the bones of previous popes be dug up from wherever they were buried and transferred to the catacombs upon which he bestowed his name.

Callistus did not bestow the generic name "catacombs" upon the subterranean burial places, however. That nomenclature comes from the Catacombs of San Sebastiano, half a mile farther out on the

Appia. Though the date of their origin is not clear, they were the only burial chambers on the road which were never forgotten during the long night of the Dark Ages. Pilgrims believed that the bodies of both Peter and Paul were hidden here during the persecutions of the third century. The holy site was called *catacumbas.* Some scholars trace the derivation to the Greek *kata,* meaning "near" or "beside," and *cumbas* from either the Greek *kumbos,* meaning "valley," or the Latin *recumbere,* to "lie" or "recline." Quick judgment would assume the correctness of *recumbere,* but Jesuit scholars have judged that the name came instead from the Latin *coemeterium ad catacumbas,* a combination of "cemetery" and the Greek words for "sunken valley."

Because the specific site of the Catacombs of San Sebastiano was so well known, the name *catacumbas* passed from it eventually to all other subterranean burial places. Graffiti on the walls there attest to the belief of pilgrims who for centuries felt that they had been in the presence of the holy remains of the apostles. The graffiti have in this century received some support from science. Vatican archaeologists in the late 1940s dug up, from a crypt deep under the central church of Catholicism, St. Peter's in Rome, bones believed to be those of Peter. After the terror of the third-century persecutions, the remains must have been carried reverently back to Rome and reburied.

Through all the centuries since Jesus and his disciples, the worship of and traffic in religious relics has been a source of both strength and embarrassment to the Roman Church. An early-seventeenth-century list of relics published with Vatican approval and compiled by a canon named Ottavio Panciroli included the following: pieces of Jesus' natal crib in three Roman churches; most of his cradle at Santa Maria Maggiore, but bits and pieces elsewhere; swaddling clothes at three sites. The umbilical cord alleged to be in the church of Salvatore delle Scale Sante. The holy foreskin was also there for a while,

*The figures of Peter and Paul, a graffito made by a pious pilgrim sometime after 313 A.D. The original is in Rome's Lateran Museum.*

but unfortunately it disappeared. There were stones upon which Jesus had either slept or stood to speak, remnants of the loaves with which he fed the five thousand, locks of his hair in four churches, and pieces of his shirt in two others. There were enough bits of the "true cross" to make a giant redwood. One church even had the very sponge which cynical soldiers had soaked in vinegar and raised up to Jesus' lips.

Tourists still go, with varying degrees of faith or curiosity, to see the relics. Organized tours of the Via Appia pause first at the church of Santa Maria Maggiore inside Rome, where Americans gape at the gold on the ceiling. This is alleged to be the first gold extracted from North America, given by Christopher Columbus to Queen Isabella of Spain, and presented by her religious majesty to the Pope in Rome, who installed it on the ceiling. German tourists, who are more assiduous readers of detailed guidebooks than are Americans, ignore the ceiling and kneel near a sunken crypt to sing Christmas carols over the little casket which purports to contain remnants of Jesus' cradle.

The *Catholic Encyclopedia*, published by the Vatican, cautions the faithful to maintain discreet reservation about the relics, and it is at pains to relate the story of a ninth-century deacon of the church of St. Peter in Chains, "the most unfortunately notorious counterfeiter of relics." This infamous canon even stooped so low as to send emissaries to Germany to steal bodies from cemeteries and bring them to Rome as the remains of holy Christian martyrs. Nowadays people go to his church mainly to see the great statue of Moses, made by Michelangelo.

Beyond the Catacombs of St. Callistus, beyond those of St. Sebastian, at about 2.6 kilometers, are the remains of the best-preserved Roman circus in the world. It was built by the Emperor Maxentius early in the fourth century A.D. as a monument to his son Romulus and as a gift to the Roman people. The Circus of Maxentius was the spiritual ancestor of Indianapolis and Churchill Downs, one of the grandest race tracks ever conceived. Along a graceful loop five hundred yards long and eighty yards wide the charioteers, standing upright, whipped their horses to run seven times around the *spina,* the "spine" or dividing wall, and the *metae,* sturdy masonry turning posts set into either end of the track. If the chariots got too close to the *metae,* their inner wooden wheels hit the post and flew into bits. If they went too wide, they lost time and were passed on the inside.

The circus held eighteen thousand spectators, all of them brought to a frenzy by music, a procession of dignitaries, the paraded effigies of the gods. Betting was encouraged and frantic. There was the alluring possibility of death and destruction on the curves. When a chariot splintered against a barrier, the followers had to veer sharply left or right and even they might brash. When the dust settled, slaves sprinted to haul away wreckage of chariots, horses, charioteers. The Romans loved it.

Maxentius' circus may be glimpsed, but poorly, from the Appia. There is a better view from the Appia Pignatelli, though it too is narrow and has no convenient parking place for sightseers. Two friendly prostitutes are accustomed to sit along the Appia Pignatelli, near the western end of the circus, within sight of the arch which marked this end of the race track. One of them has become an expert on photography. "Not from here, dearie," she counsels helpfully. "The light is against you. Go back down there, about twenty-five meters. Everybody takes pictures from there."

Beyond the circus, the Appia begins another incline, up to a ridge on which stands the road's best-known single remnant, the circular tower of the Tomb of Cecilia Metella, 3 kilometers outside the wall. Just who Cecilia Metella was is a mystery. Probably she was the daughter-in-law of M. Licinius Crassus, a wealthy supporter of Julius Caesar. Whoever she was, she was accorded one of the grandest tombs on all the road, and also the tribute of George Gordon, Lord Byron, who wrote in *Childe Harolde* of "the stern round tower of other days."

Cecilia's tower stands on a square concrete base, dominating the landscape, almost innocent of the marble covering which once gleamed in the Roman sun. Along its top were once the sculptured heads of bulls, which led Italians of later epochs to refer to it as the farm or the tower of *Capo di Bove* — Bull's Head.

Survival of this magnificent monument rests upon the cupidity of a thirteenth-century pope who gave the whole thing to his relatives, the Caetani family. The noble Caetani transformed the tomb and tower into a fortress which blocked the Appia, and they extracted tolls from anyone who wished to pass this way. Tourists and mer-

*The Tomb of Cecilia Metella, as it looks today.*

chants quite sensibly objected, and they began to turn off to the left
from the Appia and use alternate tracks to avoid the block. Thus this
reach of road fell into disuse, disrepair and even dis-remember. Its
tombs and monuments, its paving and sidewalks were lashed by rain
and wind, flooded and saved. Weeds grew over the marbles, silt rose
in layers on the stones. Shepherds blackened the walls of chamber
tombs by making brush fires in inclement weather. Sheep munched
their way where chariot wheels had passed. Several kilometers of the
Via Appia vanished, not to be seen again until nineteenth-century
popes ordered excavation and restoration.

An architect and archaeologist, Luigi Canina, followed the papal
excavations and studied the foundations which the spades uncovered. His meticulous drawings are fascinating. If his reconstruction of the original appearance of the road is correct, then the
Appia once was a horror of a long thin Forest Lawn, a gallery of bad
taste created in the name of respect. Much as one may regret the
destruction of their elaborate exteriors, it is perhaps merciful that
these pretentious monuments, shouldering one another for attention,
have been plundered. In its heyday, the Appia must have been more
of an assault on the eye than on the emotions, for anyone not personally involved.

Now emotion has a fighting chance. Past the Tomb of Cecilia Metella, the road proceeds serenely across a high flatland, between rows
of fifty-foot umbrella pines and tall, dark, thin cypresses. The most
beautiful stretch begins a kilometer after Cecilia Metella and runs
for three kilometers. It's a nice place to walk. Most of the roadbed
is covered with asphalt to accommodate automobiles, but every
few hundred yards a bit of old stone is exposed. There are traces
of curbing, and of *crepidines,* the sidewalks which used to edge the
highway.

Here trees are green even in a Roman August, casting a greenish
shade across the headless marble statues, the austere bas-reliefs of in-
terred noblemen, the thin brick and solid stone which is all that
remains of some lesser monuments to the dead. Though the cypress
grows wild and beautiful across Tuscany, Umbria, Sicily and the
Veneto, it remains associated in the Italian minds with cemeteries.
Superstitious workmen near Rome ask foreigners to please not plant
cypresses in their gardens—at least not until construction is finished

*The bend in the road at the Tomb of the Horatii and Curiatii.*

and they are safely away from the area and immune to the aura of death which the cypress carries.

Though the Appia meanders a little outside the Aurelian Wall and the church of Domine Quo Vadis?, the first sharp deviation from dead straight comes at 6 kilometers. Here the road takes an abrupt turn to the left, traverses several hundred meters, and then lurches back to the right. The detour is short, specific and obvious. It was made by Appius Claudius' engineers out of respect for the dead. They were intent on building the shortest possible route from Rome to the Alban Hills, and they had the skill to do so. Here they sacrificed skill to convention: they altered the route of the road to avoid desecration of the legendary tombs of the Horatii and Curiatii, the protagonists of a war between Romans and residents of the Alban Hills in the fourth or fifth century B.C. According to the legend, Roman and Alban armies met on the plain five miles south of the city, determined to settle once and for all which group should dominate the area.

The armies were of near-equal strength and armor. In a triumph of common sense, the leaders decided not to engage all their troops but instead to pit three warriors from one side against three from the other, in hand-to-hand battle. There were, by a stroke of coincidence worthy of the plot of a Gilbert and Sullivan opera, three brothers Horatii on the Roman side and three brothers Curiatii on the Alban side. Eureka, it was done: the Horatii and the Curiatii fought it out.

The Roman historian Livy recorded the outcome: the brothers rushed at one another. At the first clash of weapons, two of the Horatii fell dead. Before they died they wounded all three of the Curiatii. The third Horatius pretended panic and fled. He was, the legend says, unhurt, but he wanted to lure the wounded Curiatii to chase him for the kill. The farther they ran, the weaker the Curiatii became. Horatius was able to stop, turn, and kill, three times, eliminating all of the opposing brothers in sequence. This Horatius probably was the same one made immortal to generations of schoolchildren in the *Lays* of Thomas Babington Macaulay as Horatius at the Bridge. That was another day and another battle, however. To return to the battle of the brothers, Livy wrote that after Horatius' victory, both sides "set to bury their dead in a very different frame of mind, the victors proud of their increased dominion, the conquered mourning their lost freedom."

Livy also said that he had seen five tombs, two Roman ones in the south toward the Alban Hills, three Curiatii ones along the Appia near Rome. Today there are three tumuli on the Appia, low and grass-grown, one of them with a medieval tower on top. Because the whole war was occasioned by competition between Albans and Romans, it is appropriate that 14.5 kilometers south of the tumuli on the Appia, on the outskirts of the town of Albano, there is another large monument bearing the identification "Tomb of the Horatii and the Curiatii." This is a far more impressive ruin than any of the tumuli, but archaeologists date it to a much later period than the six-man war.

Modern Romans, who enjoy a joke and enjoy most of all a cynical joke, love to total the tombs and point out that six warriors who may never have existed are honored by two notable, and quite far-apart, burial places.

Just beyond the tumuli on the Via Appia lie the sprawling, scattered remains of one of the grandest villas on the road, that of the brothers Quintili. Unlike the Horatii and the Curiatii, the Quintili were not legendary at all. They were very real, but their end was just as bloody.

Condianus and Maximus Quintilius were descendants of one of the oldest families of Rome, the Quinctii, a *gens* older than the city. They were wealthy, educated, brave, devoted to each other. Together they wrote a book on agriculture which was a classic of its time. They served as governors of provinces in Asia Minor, where they fought repeatedly and gallantly against barbarian intruders. Then they built their villa, whose gardens, fountains, cisterns, statue-lined walks and outbuildings stretched for almost one kilometer between the Via Appia and the present Appia Nuova, on family-owned lands. The gardens must have been particularly magnificent, created on the fertile silt lands of the Campagna, watered by the cisterns, tended by slaves and supervised with the special expertise of the agriculturally knowledgeable brothers.

All was taken over by the villainous Emperor Commodus in the second century A.D. Commodus so coveted the layout that he had the brothers Quintili first proscribed, then murdered. Ancient writers said that this fate had been foreseen by an oracle in the East where the brothers had served. The oracle predicted that Condianus and Maximus would die and that Sextus, son of one of them, would wander the world lonely and wretched.

Unhappily, it all came true. Sextus Quintilius was in Syria when he heard of Commodus' vile act, and the deaths of his father and uncle. He knew that he, too, was doomed. One story says that he drank the blood of a hare, climbed on his horse, galloped away and then purposefully fell from his horse and vomited up the hare's blood as if it had been his own. He was carried into a house where he and the residents conspired to feign his death. A coffin was carried from the house and burned, but it contained the body of a ram instead of that of Sextus.

What happened next is the stuff of legend. In an echo of the slaughter of the innocents which attended Jesus' birth, Commodus' troops ranged over the Roman provinces to seek out and murder young men of Sextus' age and physiognomy. Some historians believe that Sextus himself perished in this pogrom. Others say that he survived to wander the world, changing his lodging and his costume frequently to avoid capture.

Even this bloodbath failed to satiate Commodus. When simple

murder palled, he aspired to become a gladiator. He was in a gladiators' school on the last day of December, A.D. 192, when his enemies caught him and did him in.

After he was gone, a young man who claimed to be the long-lost Sextus Quintilius appeared in Rome. He demanded from Commodus' successor, the Emperor Pertinax, the restitution of the lands and fortune of his family. Though he carried documentary evidence to support his claim, he was undone by Pertinax when the emperor addressed him in Greek. This was a language Sextus should have known well, but the man who called himself the heir did not and could not reply.

From the Appia it is difficult to see the great villa of the unfortunate Quintili. At 6.6 kilometers from the Porta San Sebastiano is a ruin of the nymphaeum, a complex of fountains and gardens and columns. Probably this was built by Commodus. In front of it is a ten-meter stretch of exposed Appian paving stones, but the land on which the villa stands is in private hands. There is no public entrance.

The other remains, of cisterns and walls, porticos and foundations, are best seen from the Appia Nuova, state road 7, which runs out of Rome past Ciampino Airport and Cinecittà, Rome's postwar "Hollywood on the Tiber." The same road provides the best perspective of a dozen arches of a branch aqueduct which Commodus had built to carry the Aqua Claudia to the Villa Quintili after he occupied it. He moved his entire personal household and the imperial hangers-on to the site, and all those people required more water than had the Quintili. The Aqua Claudia gushed from a spring near the site of Ciampino Airport, and it issued from the ground so hot that even in winter it was 63 degrees Fahrenheit. When it reached Rome it was mixed with the Aqua Julia to reduce it to a bearable drinking temperature.

From the Villa Quintili to the south, the Appia now is devoid of trees and tombs until it arrives at the largest circular monument of the entire route. Casal Rotondo it is called today, the "round castle." Its sides have been totally stripped of their marble, and somebody has built a house on top. In front of it is another reach of Roman paving stones, here sharply grooved by chariot wheels and worn by weather. Beside it is a brick wall into which fragments of marbles and inscriptions are cemented. Many of the lower, accessible bits have been stolen. Above theft level is a block which carries the single name "Cotta."

This one name, found by the archaeologist Canina, convinced him that the Casal Rotondo was built by Marcus Valerius Messalinus Cotta, a lawyer and art lover who was a friend of Julius Caesar's, to the memory of his father Messala. Just past it is a crossroad, but the Appia plunges straight on toward the blunt peak of Monte Cavo. There is little to see on this piece of road except the dramatic ruin, 8.2 kilometers south of the city gate, of a four-sided tall tower with a white stripe in its middle. This is the Torre Selce, built in the twelfth century as a fortress. The white stripe was designed to make it visible for miles across the Campagna. The foot of the tower is planted on much older Roman remains, probably the core of a tomb. The top has been struck repeatedly by lightning and is falling apart.

Near here was found the marble inscription of the man who described himself as "good and kind" and "a friend of the poor." He added that he was called Caius Attilius Evhodus, freedman of Serranus, jeweler of the Via Sacra. He asked modestly that the passer-by "do no harm to this sepulcher," but his request was ignored. Person or persons unknown have destroyed every trace of whatever structure once was here.

The aspect of the Appia at this point is as dreary as the fate of the jeweler Evhodus' tomb. Nothing is left except, at 9.6 kilometers, the ruin of a semicircular *exedra*, a resting place for Roman travelers. A little farther on, on the right, is a disintegrating tall quadrangular monument of uncertain origin. Just before these two ruins, the Appia crosses the modern Grande Raccordo Anulare, the "ring road" which circles Rome and permits cars to transfer from one main artery to another without crossing the city. The intersection is a death trap, with neither visibility nor traffic lights, and four lanes of thundering trucks and darting Fiats. Beyond it the Appia goes on past small funeral mounds crested with tufts of ruin weed, wild fennel, aromatic mint. To the right of the road, 10.6 kilometers from the city wall, lie the remains of a Temple of Hercules, a pattern of short dark columns in two rows, and between them the tumbled pieces of their upper sections.

Half a kilometer beyond these, on the left, is a little round brick tower which Italians call *la berretta da prete*, "the priest's cap," because of the odd peaked shape of its top. And just beyond this, at 11.4 kilometers, the carriage road ends at a crossroad called Via di Fioranello.

Cars proceed from here at their peril, but the track of the road stretches straight on for another three or four kilometers, to the site of the Roman city of Bovillae and to a junction with the modern Appia Nuova. The roadbed is visible, running down into a valley, up the other side, and ending on the horizon in a squarish monument whose tower is medieval but whose base is massively Roman.

Only the hardy and the determined explore this last reach of road near Rome. The beginning of it, as it crosses the Via di Fioranello, is less than inviting. Here neighbors dump their trash. Rain turns it into a bog. It smells. Prostitutes sit on upended oil drums or while away unemployed hours by ragpicking in the refuse. They are amiable, however, and they have accurate information on the depth of the stagnant water in the rutted roadway. Most of their clients are truck-drivers or lusty youths in beaten-up old cars, so the ladies of the road know far more about local road conditions than does the Automobile Club.

Once past these hazards, the seeker of the Appia embarks upon its most achingly lovely stretch. Traffic roars to the left, enormous silver airplanes drift downward toward Ciampino. It is they, however, which are unreal. Reality is the stone, solid underfoot, visible in snatches. Reality is the thrust of a curbstone through the encroaching fennel, the rocky remains of a sidewalk, the flash of white as the sun catches a marble fragment.

An old man gathers snails from humid bushes, and cautions his small dog not to attack the *stranieri*. He assumes that only foreigners take the trouble to walk here. Sheep graze quietly over a tomb mound. Gray basalt Roman paving stones appear across a trickling stream, their covering of silt and weeds, accumulated for centuries, washed away by the runoff of a sudden storm.

On the track goes. After half a kilometer the walker ceases to hear the traffic or see the planes. There is a scurry of lizards in the underbrush, the squish of one's own shoes in the damp. A vague wish for rubber boots, an apprehension about snakes. Above all the desire that this road should never end.

From feet to heart to brain, a walker here feels the Appian Way.

# IV
# HOSPICES AND
# HAZARDS

Once out of "lofty Rome" and headed southward on the Appia, past
tombs and monuments, the traveler encountered practical problems.
Where could he eat, change horses, spend the night?

Goods and services were provided, with less than uniform efficiency, along the entire length of the road. The best-known of them,
*mutationes* and *mansiones,* were established during the Empire to provide facilities for imperial envoys and messengers, and persons either
of importance or on state business. *Mutationes* were changing stations which offered fresh horses or mules, cartwrights, smithies,
wheelwrights, every six to nine miles. *Mansiones,* with rooms and
meals, were located from every eighteen to about thirty miles, depending on the terrain.

If these official government facilities were not fully occupied, they
could be used by ordinary travelers. If they were, the common citizen
had to make do with inns and taverns, called *cauponae* or *tabernae.*
These accommodations left something to be desired. A hapless "traveiler" ran the risk of being robbed, mugged, poisoned and over-
charged. Quite a number of notable citizens were even murdered.

Virtually nothing remains of these two-thousand-year-old equivalents of the filling station and the highway motel, but the existence of hospices and the prevalence of hazards is eloquently attested to by everyone from Horace to the adventurers of the sixteenth to nineteenth centuries. Most ancient of all sources are poetic accounts of trips along the Appia made by the Roman satirists Gaius Lucilius about 150 B.C. and by Horace.

Supplementing them are several "itineraries," listing distances, names and locations of towns, rivers, obstacles and stopping places along the route in the third and fourth centuries A.D. One of the most precise and detailed of the itineraries was made by a religious pilgrim from Bordeaux, France, who trekked to Jerusalem in about A.D. 333. The document is known alternatively as the Bordeaux Itinerary or the Jerusalem Itinerary, a slight confusion complicated by the fact that "Jerusalem," in the Latin text of the original, is rendered as Hierosolymitanum and is often cited this way in references.

The Bordeaux–Jerusalem/Hierosolymitanum pilgrim made his way for four thousand painful miles across what are now France, North Italy and Yugoslavia, through old Constantinople and across Asia Minor, then back by sea to Hydruntum on the Italian peninsula, up to Brundisium and, via the Appia Traiana, to Rome, and home. He intended his work to be an aid to other devout travelers wishing to go from Western Europe to the Holy Land, but it is of most interest today because of the meticulous listing of "changing stations" and "overnight halts."

On this itinerary, as on almost all others, including Horace's, the first overnight stop on the Appia south of Rome is Aricia, 16 miles from the walls of the city. There is still a town, spelled Ariccia, on or near this site, perched on a hillside between two valleys. Also there, today, a secondary highway lies on top of one of the most mighty masonry works of all the Appia, a viaduct built in the second century B.C. to carry the roadbed up from the valley floor and through the little city.

Covered with modern pavement, its sides overgrown with weeds, the viaduct is difficult to identify, but it is there. It is made of *opus quadratum*, large blocks set in alternate rows lengthwise and end-on, more than 800 feet long, 18 feet wide at its widest point, and once almost 45 feet high. Erosion and repair have lowered it now to about

*The viaduct at Aricia, the first stop out of Rome. This is an engraving by Carlo Labruzzi (published 1854). Courtesy German Archaeological Institute, Rome.*

36 feet. Still visible in winter, when ground vegetation dies back, are two arches set into the bottom by its builders to permit the passage of winter rain and flood without damage to the viaduct. Perhaps the most telling tribute to the quality of their work is the fact that within the past decade another viaduct, built in the mid-nineteenth century at a higher point in the valley, broke down in a storm. For several months, twentieth-century traffic was detoured to pass again across the old squared stones of its predecessor.

Romans called the viaduct the Pons Aricinus, and if they admired its construction, they didn't say so. To them it was infamous as a haunt of beggars and robbers. Around A.D. 120 the poet Juvenal heaped scorn on a man by describing him as "a blind flatterer, a dire courtier from a beggar's stand, well fitted to beg at the wheels of chariots and blow soft kisses to them as they rolled down the Arician hill." Rolling down was one thing; rolling up, slowly against the incline, made the traveler far more vulnerable to the incantations of beggars, the hit-and-run tactics of purse snatchers.

*Arrival at a* mansione, *or inn. The vehicle is a* carpentum; *a coachman sits in front of the two passengers, a runner out in front of the horses. Man looking out of window may be the innkeeper.*

Of the inn in Aricia we know almost nothing except that Horace said it was quiet. This must have been the equivalent of four stars on a tourist itinerary of the day, because inns then were raucous, roistering places of almost universal ill repute. They were both run and patronized by individuals whose business it was to prey upon the unwary, including pious pilgrims, honest merchants and wandering poets.

Innkeepers themselves had such a bad reputation that they were not admitted to military service, nor permitted to form a guild. On the list of suspect citizens kept by soldiers and by police, they were lumped together with thieves, gamblers and panders. It is likely that many innkeepers were accomplished practitioners of all three professions. Their female staff members often doubled as prostitutes, and both they and the publicans were suspected of spying for pay. Certainly they were in a good position to overhear information about movements of men and troops up and down the road, shipments of precious goods, and details of plot and counterplot among the warring nobles.

Even innkeepers' wives were tarred with the brush which marked their husbands. One scholar has reported that these women were so ill regarded that they were exempt from the Roman laws covering adultery and other sexual triangulations and misdemeanors. The implication is that the very law itself would have been offended had it been obeyed by the likes of these ladies, and that it was thus more honored in the breach.

The physical arrangement of these nefarious institutions may be reconstructed most logically from the ruins of Pompeii. Pompeii was not on the Appia, but its streets, shops, taverns must have been nearly identical with others of the first century A.D. One Pompeian establishment, called the Inn of Hermes, had a rather wide entrance from the street, with wine rooms on either side. There were three bedrooms on the ground floor, and two or three more reached by a flight of steps to an upper story. Also on the ground floor were a stable, a shelter for vehicles, a watering trough and a toilet.

Another inn there had a large public room, perhaps for dining, just inside the entrance, a hearth with a water heater beside it, a wine room, kitchen and six bedrooms. In the walls of both hostelries, guests had scratched rude remarks about the service or the accommodation, or earthy comments on just how, and with whom, they had passed the night. As in Pompeii, inns located in towns were used not only by legitimate travelers but also by local roisterers and gamblers who could enter the premises discreetly through narrow side entrances opening from alleyways.

Even when they weren't being actively aggressed upon, inn clients were tormented. Again and again, ancient accounts tell of pillows stuffed with reeds instead of feathers, of filthy sleeping pallets crawling with fleas and bedbugs. Lizards and spiders dropped from the rafters onto the guests. Bad smells swirled from both kitchen and toilet; gusts of smoke smarted the eyes. In case of temporary overloads, two or three clients were piled into the same bed, and latecomers had to camp out with the beasts on piles of hay in the stables.

Always there was a din. Guests quarreled with one another or the landlord; late arrivals shouted for attention and noisily unhitched their beasts. Some travelers constantly "chanted," perhaps having taken counsel from Plutarch, who recommended loud uninterrupted conversation as an aid to the health while on a trip. This cryptic advice may have been designed to drown out the other loud noises or even, perhaps, to impel the speaker to breathe the foul air through his nose and expel it with some force through the mouth.

Not even bad weather and miserable traveling conditions were enough to make men greet an inn with gratitude. In an Epistle to a friend, Horace wrote:

> But surely, friend, the man who gains an inn
> Besplashed with mud, and soaking to the skin,
> When on his way from Capua to Rome
> Will not desire to make that inn his home.

Fire, too, was a terrible hazard, though its occurrence was noted only once in the best-known of the extant travel diaries. This again is Horace, and his account of near-disaster is so graphic and so good-natured that it is hilarious.

> Here our painstaking host set his house afire while basting
> Some skinny little thrushes. The fire slipped out of the grate,
> Took a nonchalant stroll around the old kitchen, then rushed
> Toward the roof, soaring upward and beginning to lick at the
>     beams.
> You should have seen the starved guests and the quavering
>     slaves
> Grab their food, and all trying to put out the fire at once.

Though the thrushes were skinny, they seem to have been otherwise edible, a situation which did not always obtain on the road. The Greek physician Galen warned travelers of A.D. 200 to beware of meat which looked like pork but might turn out to be human flesh. Galen reported that he knew someone who had been fed human flesh at a wayside tavern and who perceived the truth when he found a finger bone in the pot.

St. Augustine in the fourth century A.D. had even more ominous news: some innkeepers' wives were really witches, he said, who put strange Circean drugs into their cheeses. The hapless man who ate them would turn into a mule, though retaining his human faculties. Only by the demonic performance of immoral acts could the victim regain his human configuration.

Water and wine, whether separate or combined, caused strife

between host and client. Horace noted that the water was so bad at Forum Appii, the traditional second step on the Appia, that "I made war on my stomach and waited fuming while friends finished their dinner." At an unnamed stop, probably Asculum, just before Canusium over toward the Adriatic, he was outraged because the natives sold their water. As compensation, the bread in this place was "so good that the smart tourist loads up his slaves." In Canusium itself the bread was "made of gravel," and the water scarce. How strange it must have been for any Roman, accustomed to the flood of water rushing from that city's fountains, to arrive at places within their own hegemony in which the locals dared sell water, or to permit it to be in short supply.

How even stranger it is, though, to find Horace's complaints repeated by an English writer, Crauford Tait Ramage, in 1868. Ramage had read Horace, and he reported that Canusium—which by his day was called Canosa—still had bread "full of sand." Ramage attributed the defect to the soft local rock used for millstones. His landlord, he said, told him that sometimes the residents couldn't even eat the local spaghetti because of the same problem. Ramage found a Roman aqueduct still standing, though partly ruined, and he complained that Canosa suffered from the same water shortage which Horace had noted.

In 1973 the bread in Canosa was fine. There may perhaps still have been a water shortage, but the authors were not aware of it, having been so well satisfied by the delicious dry white wine of the region.

Wine was seldom in short supply in ancient times, even in the inns. Its quality in public places was, however, often suspect. All men except drunkards added water to their wine, but innkeepers were alleged to exaggerate the practice. One Roman writer chided a friend for complaining about unseasonably heavy rains: "how many amphorae of wine our friends the publicans have filled," he said. The epigrammatist Martial jotted a jingle on the same subject:

> The rains this year left sopping wet
> The grapes on every vine.
> So, barkeep, don't you try to say
> There's no water in your wine.
> The other day down Ravenna way,

A barkeep did me wrong.
I ordered up a glass of weak,
And he makes me pay for strong.

Inn fare in Roman times, as even today in Italy, was based primarily upon seasonal fruit and vegetable crops. "In season" on the peninsula tends to mean "available," and "out of season" is translatable not as "more expensive" but as "we don't have it." There were, and are, always such staples as fish and figs, bread and spaghetti. Even these, however, could be in short supply from Horace's time until the seventeenth century.

In 1625 an erudite and poetic Jesuit priest of Siena, Alessandro Donati, set forth along the Appia to see the sights, and buried in ten quite sentimental and beautiful *Elegies* is a horrendous account of an inn he found along the road. He found the hostelry with the aid of a tree branch tied to a post, a sign which had been used for centuries to mark the roadside tavern. The host rushed out to invite him in, assuring him that here was truly his home away from home. He could offer the priest a bedchamber with frescoes which even the kings of France and Spain would envy. As for the cuisine—well, if such a thing as songbird's milk existed, it would be found in his establishment.

Somewhat doubtful but surrounded by "swarms of inn workers, travelling parties, horses, and mules," the Jesuit agreed to stop for the night. Once inside, he discovered that the only painting the walls had ever seen had been applied by the greasy smoke of cooking fires. The entrance door was so low that he had to stoop; the central beam was propped up with a post. The bed was a sack of river rushes with a cover which did not fit.

"To table, with trepidation," wrote the priest with commendable good humor. "One chair leg was too short, and the table danced on its unequal legs. The bread seemed made of hay or oats . . . the eggs were tiny and black . . . salad with two drops of oil."

Choked with almost equal parts of rage and laughter, Donati announced that he had eaten enough. But the host would not let him go. There was another plate, produced with a flourish, which turned out to be boiled cabbage. Then the *pièce de résistance*, touted falsely by the innkeeper as "a plump little dove just snatched from under its mother's wings." At last the priest lost his temper. "But here doves perhaps hatch crows?" he shouted. "No, this is a country of monsters."

For all this dubious food and service, inn guests felt themselves unjustly charged. "How glad we are at the sight of shelter in the desert, a roof in a storm, a bath or a fire in the cold, and how dear they cost in inns," wrote Seneca.

Luke noted that lodging and dinner for two en route to Rome cost as much as a day's pay for a praetorian guard, infinitely more than a day's pay for an ordinary soldier.

Against this testimony are some early-twentieth-century studies which translated food costs in Roman times into 1920 U.S. monetary rates: about four cents for a pound of beef or mutton, six cents for lamb and pork, two cents for twenty turnips or ten cucumbers or for forty apples. These are practically useless figures, however, because of the impossibility of equating monetary values from one era to another with all the variables involved. Probably the clearest sense one can get is the scale of relative charges. Records from the second century B.C., when the Via Appia and its inns were in full and heavy usage, report that a portion of meat cost twice as much as a combined portion of bread and a pint of wine. Mule feed cost as much as one portion of meat. A girl cost four times as much as either meat or mule feed. Presumably the last charge was for overnight rental, not outright purchase.

There were alternatives to the inns and public eating places along the way. There were tents, for instance, which could be both carried and clean. There were farmhouses, and there were hospices erected by wealthy landowners who staffed them with personal slaves to provide service. Horace mentions having stopped at three farmhouses on his way to Brundisium; one of them he complimented for its well-stocked larder. Of another he said that the *padrone*, the owner, was required by law to supply the traveler with fresh food and fodder for the animals. This smacks of privilege, or of official business. Horace was traveling with a coterie of important people, including his patron the patrician Maecenas, close friend of the young Octavian, who had been adopted by Julius Caesar as son and heir. This group surely was given some assurance of accommodation on the road, some access to government facilities.

There was also, for the rich or influential, hospitality. The tradition of hospitality, which existed from prehistoric times among the tribes of the Near East, was elevated to a positive virtue in the Hebrew and early Christian religions. Careful reading reveals an astonishing emphasis on this quality. In his Epistle to the Romans, Paul says that every good Christian should distribute to the necessity of the saints, and should be "given to hospitality." He repeats the admonition in his First Epistle to Timothy, by describing a bishop as a man who should be "blameless, the husband of one wife, vigilant, sober, of good behaviour, given to hospitality. . . ."

Peter echoed the phrase in his First Epistle General: "Use hospitality one to another without grudging." The instruction was even clearer in the Epistle to the Hebrews: "Be not forgetful to entertain strangers. . . ."

Such specific instructions, hammered home repeatedly, could have been inspired only by the woeful condition of public, commercial "hospitality" on the roads of the Christian and Roman worlds. By inciting the early Christians to hospitality the apostles were only broadening, democratizing, a usage common among the pagan Romans: the extension of shelter and safety to one's friends and kinsmen.

Most well-connected Romans had mutual agreements with friends. Cicero had a friend in Greece, Lyso, with whom he stayed when he went there. In return Lyso stayed with him when he was in Italy. Once, to Cicero's despair, Lyso spent almost a year with him. Other Romans concluded alliances of mutual defense against bedbugs, watered wine, pimps and pickpockets by making formal agreements of hospitality and by having cut a small die called a *tessera hospitalis.* This *tessera* they solemnly broke into two pieces, each partner retaining his half. When the owner, or one of his descendants or trusted friends, turned up on the Appia in need of food and lodging, he had only to present his half, match it to the portion held by his prospective host, and clean beds and well-stocked kitchens were his. When parties to the *tessera hospitalis* fell out, or changed their minds, both pieces of the die were smashed to bits. The ritual must have been much more impressive than the revocation of a credit card.

Some habitual travelers, like Cato the Younger in the first century B.C., sent ahead of them servants charged with locating a suitable place to stop. Cato usually sent two, one of whom seems to have been his private baker. These worthies entered the town discreetly and inquired as to whether or not their master had kin or close friends about. If there were none, they applied to city officials for lodging, and they accepted what was offered. Because Cato was the great-grandson of a Roman consul, and because he was himself soldier, statesman and philosopher, it is unlikely that municipal authorities would ever offer him less than the best that they had.

Other men, who were either reluctant or unable to command official and personal hospitality in the days when the Appia was young, bought and built villas and small stopping places along the road. Cicero had either eight or seventeen of them, depending on which impeccable source one consults. They weren't all on the Appia, but at least four of them were.

Seneca, on the other hand, rather fancied traveling light and without provision for the night. Once he wrote a friend that "I was shipwrecked before I got aboard," meaning that he traveled with as few possessions as a shipwrecked man. He went out "with very few slaves—one carriage load—and no paraphernalia. . . . The mattress lies upon the ground, and I upon the mattress." He did take along several writing tablets and some dried figs. "If I have bread, I use figs as a relish; if not, I regard figs as substitute for bread."

Part of Seneca's motivation for voyaging on land like a shipwrecked sailor was a simple objection to being robbed. He took along little that anybody would want to steal. Highwaymen and bands of recalcitrant slaves preyed on travelers not only on the viaduct of Aricia but also wherever the road was narrow, steep or lightly defended. Most often they conducted their forays toward the frontiers of the advancing roads, but sometimes they operated right on the outskirts of Rome and other major cities of the peninsula.

During civil disturbances, when plebeians and patricians lined up in bloody war against each other, the bandits were so fierce that Augustus, the first emperor, erected forts for troops at key points along the Appia. Later, Tiberius expanded them. When imperial troops captured highway predators, they executed them summarily and often exposed their bodies by the roadside as warnings to any other inhabitants who might be tempted to lives of crime. Now and again this barbaric treatment was instructive to scientists: the physician Galen happened upon the corpse of an executed thief and found it so picked of carrion that he stopped in his tracks and had a good study of this conveniently revealed structure of the human skeleton.

Matters got worse when the Emperor Septimius Severus decided that Roman stalwarts were too corruptible and excitable to serve as praetorian guards. He recruited his protectors from young men of the conquered provinces and nations, and the more combative of the native Romans joined the alternate ranks of gladiators and highwaymen.

One of these, Felix Bulla, became a bandit in the tradition of Robin Hood or of that Sicilian Giuliano who in the early 1950s captured the Italian imagination by defying authority. Felix Bulla, at the head of six hundred disaffected citizens, terrorized travelers on the Appia for more than two years. His informers always knew which rich Roman had landed at Brundisium, coming home from Greece or the Roman colonies in Asia Minor. They also knew which well-endowed gentlemen had left Rome going east. Bulla stopped them all. If they were simple tradesmen he sometimes exacted only a small ransom. If he liked them, he was capable of giving them money to continue their journey. Once he captured a centurion sent to trap him, and was content to shave the man's head and send him home with a message: "If masters treated their slaves better, there would be no robbers."

This attitude, plus some acts of derring-do in defense of his troops (once he masqueraded as the Roman district officer in charge of hiring gladiators and bought back two of his own captured thieves) made Felix Bulla a hero to many. When he was caught at last, betrayed by a mistress and asleep in a cave, he was taken to trial in Rome. A jurist asked him why he was a bandit, and Bulla retorted, "Why are you a prefect?"

In the end Bulla was sentenced to be torn apart by beasts in a public spectacle. He and his kind became central figures in popular literature so familiar that Lucius Apuleius in about A.D. 125 could write to an appreciative audience about the "brave, steadfast, faithful robber of the better sort."

Despite the hazards, the Appia and the other Roman roads were much safer in ancient times than most public highways ever were again for centuries. By the Middle Ages, when the power of Rome and its emperors was only a fading memory, the Appia was still in use but its perils had sharply increased. Opportunities for variegated vice in the stopping places had become more ample even than fifteen hundred years before. So much so that the sturdy Jerome Turler of the warnings about "naughty conscience and empty purse" found it necessary in 1575 to admonish his countrymen about their behavior abroad. The Italians had a popular expression, he wrote, which held that *"Thedesco Italianato, Diabolo incarnato,"* that is, a German "become in manners lyke an Italian putteth on the nature of the Deuill, and is apt unto all kinde of wickednesse."

A little later in the same century an intrepid Englishman, Fynes Moryson, made a tour of Europe on a fellowship from Peterhouse College. He read everything he could find on the perils of travel, including the book Turler had written, and he added some advice of his own: "In all Innes . . . let him bolt or locke the doore of his chamber: let him take heed of his chamber fellowes, and always have his Sword by his side . . . ; let him lay his purse under his pillow, but always foulded with his garters, or some thing hee first useth in the morning, lest hee forget to put it up before hee goe out of his chamber."

Having almost miraculously achieved Rome without incident, Moryson decided to set forth toward Naples, and he made a deal with a travel agent to provide a horse, meals and lodging along the way. This was necessary, he noted, because "The Italian Hosts are notable in fawning and crouching for gaine . . . they extort so unreasonably, as nothing can bee added to their perfidiousness and covetousnesse."

Moryson prudently attached himself, further, to a caravan of merchants and tourists which had formed around the august nucleus of the papal mail carrier. The mailman had with him a retinue of heavily laden mules and an escort of armed horsemen to defend him against *banditi.*

Thus surrounded and protected, he managed to traverse Rome-to-Aricia without mishap even though, as he noted, the woody mountains around Aricia were "infamous for the robberies by banished men."

Moryson's nervousness was caused partly by a whole new threat, the international warfare between Catholics and Protestants. Having forgotten the apostles' admonitions about Christian hospitality, both wings of the church were being beastly one to another. Moryson left Elizabethan England full of misgivings about how he would be treated in Catholic countries, and he advised all Englishmen who might follow him to Italy to avoid conversation with strangers upon the road. Such solitary, isolated travel could be lonely, so he advised tourists to take along some good books. These volumes should, he admonished, "treat not of the Common-wealth, the Religion thereof, or any Subject that may be dangerous. . . ."

Once he had seen Naples, Moryson returned to Rome and then left just before Easter because he was sure that Catholic priests were making a census of strangers in the lodging places. Taking extraordinary evasive action, he departed for Siena, darted to Florence, dodged to Pisa, and wrote later with satisfaction that "by often changing places I avoyded the Priests inquiring after mee, which is most dangerous about Easter time, when all men receive the Sacrament."

Papal convoys similar to the one which Moryson joined were common in the sixteenth century, but even they were not always safe. In August 1590, brigands hijacked the papal convoy from Rome to Naples, on the Via Appia, and then perhaps just to show their strength also captured the one going the other way up the road on the same day. Travel had become so dangerous that gentlemen in Italy and abroad made book on their chance of survival. Ben Jonson, in *Every Man out of his Humour,* has a character wager "some five thousand pound, to be paid me five for one, upon return of myself, my wife and my dog" from a voyage via Italy to Constantinople.

The same year that Jerome Turler toured on the Appia, a young German prince made a similar trip. Because of his exalted position, he was met at Terracina by an escort of cavalry sent by the Spanish governor of the province (Southern Italy had been under Spanish rule since 1442) to protect him from the dangers of the road.

As late as 1820 an English lady wrote that "Our manner of travelling between Mola [today's Formia] and Terracina was as follows: the military posts situated at each mile sent out a patrol as soon as they heard our carriages. Then we had a choice, either the guards came in our carriages with us, or we had to proceed slowly enough so that they could accompany us." The entire area from Terracina to Fondi, to Itri, to Mola was traditionally infested by "some of the most notorious highwaymen of modern times," she added. A French traveler of the same period described this stretch of the Appia as "one long army camp."

It had been even worse two centuries earlier. In 1592 the most noted poet of his time, Torquato Tasso, was held up for days on the Appia at Mola by a bandit named Marco di Sciarra and his troop of highwaymen. Tasso had been in Naples as the guest of a powerful friend, the Prince of Conca, and he had timed his departure carefully to accompany an official convoy headed for Rome. Despite the precaution, the whole party was blocked by bandits at a narrow stretch of the road between the sea and a tall circular medieval defense tower which stands still at the site of today's Formia.

From his near-captivity, Tasso sent a stream of letters back to friends in Naples. In the first he sounded merely excited: "Yesterday [Marco] killed many men of this zone, and took others prisoner. Therefore one must make provision, as if in the war with Spartacus." In the next letter he still seemed to be savoring the situation: "Every day there is a skirmish, with the killing of some of our men. The other night the area resounded with the cries and screams of women . . . I wanted to rush out and bloody the sword given to me by Your Lordship."

Before long, Tasso tired of the drama, however, and began to blame his discomfort on his friend the prince. In a fretful letter he demanded that somebody dispatch another convoy immediately to rescue him and help him get on back to Rome. The Prince of Conca could, he wrote pettishly, "have let me go sooner, in more notable company, and with more security."

Finally, ten days after he had left Naples, Tasso arrived in Rome looking pale and thin, but otherwise undamaged. It is not clear just how he and his companions finally got through. Tasso's first biographer stated that the bandit Marco, when he was informed of the identity of his near-captive, was so impressed that he withdrew his forces and let the convoy pass. This sounds like biographical flattery; it is more likely that troops of the Prince of Conca combined with papal soldiery and drove Marco di Sciarra and his men from the pass, at least long enough to let Tasso's party proceed to Rome.

Apart from bandits and bad inns and broken axles, there were still other hazards on the road, the most notable of them illness. What would happen if the traveler got sick en route, was bitten by a viper or contracted a raging infection in a public house? Some inns in-

MOLA

CASTEL NOVO.

VIA Appia

cluded "medical attention" in their price list, but it must have been rudimentary at best and downright dangerous at worst.

Prudent travelers did two things. First, they consulted the augurs, official soothsayers trained to observe and interpret omens, good and bad. Second, they armed themselves with a supply of reliable home remedies for common ailments.

Augury could involve everything from sacred chickens, the vessels which Appius Claudius' son treated so cavalierly, to sacrifice, to sudden flashes of light or even rainstorms. The ancients believed in all of them, but they progressed from one system to another and regarded earlier generations' signs and precautions as either stupid or primitive. Thus Cicero could write that "Just as nowadays we seek omens by the inspection of entrails . . . so in former times the flight of birds was studied when weighty decisions had to be made. Wherefore, by reason of our failure to be on the watch for sinister portents, we fall into calamities unspeakable."

Cicero seems to have been of two minds about the whole question. He recounts in one place the experience of an illustrious visitor, King Deiotarus of Galatia, who was warned of trouble by the flight of an eagle and turned right around and went home, canceling a long-planned journey. "The very next night," Cicero recounts with awe, "the chamber in which he would have slept, had he continued his trip, crashed in ruin." He did not say where this fragile sleeping chamber was located.

On the other hand, Cicero points out that the also illustrious Marcus Marcellus, five times consul of Republican Rome, disdained "divination by flashes and spear points, employed only in war." Marcellus so thoroughly disliked receiving any augural signs when he was in the midst of vital maneuvers that he "had his litter closed, on the march, in order not to be impeded by omens."

Simple travelers seldom had the means or connections to consult the augurs before a journey, so they tried to attach themselves to the trains of the mighty or to tag along in the wake of official convoys. They had their own small superstitions: it was, for example, the custom to salute anyone who sneezed; the sneezer was immediately

*The locale of the famous episode when Torquato Tasso was held up en route from Naples to Rome by outlaws for more than a week. In this engraving by Braun in Florence, the Rome-Capua road is rendered with loving care; note road sign "Via Appia" in left foreground. Courtesy Autostrade S.p.A.*

71

wished "*Salubritas*" — health. The Emperor Tiberius was particularly insistent upon this custom. Everyone riding in a vehicle with him was constrained to utter the incantation instantly, and to repeat it as often as the emperor sneezed.

Some citizens carried face masks to prevent sunburn as they walked or jogged along, and almost all had some standard medicines in their saddlebags or traveling valises. One of the staples was olive oil, believed to be efficacious for cooling fevers. Wayfarers believed that old oil was much better than new, for it had acquired more odor and more strength.

Salt water, accepted then as now to alleviate local infections, was not always available on inland portions of the Appia, so well-prepared tourists carried little packets of marine salt which could be mixed with any water available. The best medical wool, all agreed, was obtained newly shorn from the neck of a lamb, and honey, an important ingredient in many medicines, was best if it contained dead bees.

Other potions involved the ashes of birds or other small creatures, ashes best obtained by cremating the animal in a new pot, covered with a lid, smeared over with potter's earth, then fired in a furnace.

Many of these cures had been set down in the third century A.D. by a horticulturist named Quintus Gargilius Martialis. He based his medical handbook for travelers on recipes for homemade potions included in the *Natural History* of Pliny two centuries earlier. Gargilius included not only exotica like cremated birds but also most of the common garden herbs, plus thistles, garlic, truffles, fruits, acorns and mushrooms. From the length of the list it is clear that a sick man taking his medicine would have such a nutritionally rich diet that he would get well on vitamins alone.

Pliny's and Gargilius' work was used again fifteen hundred years later in an aid to travelers edited and amplified by a German, Valentin Rose, in Berlin in 1874. Rose noted in a foreword that both he and several of his friends had been victims of quacks and frauds while abroad, and that he had therefore gathered together prescriptions for good health and put them into "one little book" as a service to those setting out on a journey. With an earnestness and sense of order worthy of the Romans themselves, he announced that "We shall begin at the head . . ." and listed such complaints as pains, dandruff, gray hair, bloodshot eyes and dripping nose. He then proceeded downward.

Rose may have been a hypochondriac, but he was thorough in his approach. The wonder is that in all the centuries between Pliny and Rose the common cures had changed so little. They were at least more specific than they had been in Horace's time. He, having spent a horrid night along the Appia in the Pontine Marshes, complained of being kept awake by carousing sailors and fellow passengers, quarreling porters and "resonant swamp frogs." He got up the next day with painfully inflamed eyes and treated them with something he describes vaguely as "black salve."

Even the early equivalents of aspirin and seasick remedies and Band-Aids ceased to suffice for travelers of the plague-ridden Middle Ages. Mass death swept Europe in waves, and anyone brave enough to make a trip found himself not only in personal peril but also regarded with suspicion at every port of call.

That same English Fynes Moryson who had played hide-and-seek with the priests in Italy included in his travel notes the extraordinary protective measures enforced in the late sixteenth century:

> Whosoever comes into Italy, and from whence soever; but more especially if hee come from suspected places, as Constantinople, never free from the plague; hee must bring to the Confines [of Italy] a certificate of his health, and in time of any plague, hee must bring the like to any City within land, where he is to passe, which certificates brought from place to place, and necessary to be carried, they curiously observe and read. This paper is vulgarly [i.e., in the local Italian, not in Latin] called *Bolletino della sanità;* and if any man want it, hee is shut up in the Lazareto or Pest-house forty dayes, till it appeare hee is healthfull.

Moryson himself was never locked up in the pesthouse, but in explaining how the lockup functioned he unwittingly revealed the origins of a key word used today in the languages of Europe and the United States in connection with contagious diseases. Being held inside for the prescribed period, he said, was called "doing the forty" by the natives — *far' la quarantana.*

# V
# MILESTONES, MAPS
# AND GUIDEBOOKS

Second stop south of Rome on the Via Appia was Forum Appii, a
settlement which probably owed its existence to the road and thus
was named for its builder. All traces of it have vanished, except a
small sign, which says "Foro Appii," attached to a red farmhouse in
the minuscule village of Faiti, which now stands on or near the site
of the ancient town.

Yet Forum Appii sounds elusively familiar to the modern ear because of the Biblical account of the journey of Paul to Rome.
". . . and so we went toward Rome," Luke wrote in the Acts. "And
from thence, when the brethren heard of us, they came to meet us as
far as Appii forum and The three taverns . . ." Forum Appii was 43
miles from Rome, and the spot called Tres Tabernae was 33 miles, a
long way for Christians in the year 60 or so to trudge to greet the
bearer of the message of faith. No wonder that Paul, who had been
escorted out of Jerusalem by Roman soldiers, shipwrecked on Malta,
urged along for miles on the Appia, at Forum Appii "thanked God,
and took courage," at the sight of the faithful who had come to meet
him.

He must also, like Quintilian, have taken heart from the measurement of the weary way he had come. No one knows for sure when the first milestones were erected on Roman roads, but along the reaches of the Appia which Paul trod there was at least one, and he must have seen it. This one, the oldest ever discovered in Italy, turned up during excavations more than two hundred years ago near a place now called Mesa, in the middle of the Pontine Marshes. Unlike most later road markers, it carried an inscription on the top instead of on the rounded side, and it indicated only that it had been erected by the aediles P. Claudius and C. Furius. There were only the names, and the Roman numerals X and LIII.

It is known that these two men were aediles from 251 to 249 B.C., and that in this era the work of aediles included both the preservation of public order and the maintenance of public property. The number X, because of the location in which the column was found, must have indicated that it was another 10 miles to Forum Appii, and the number LIII that it was 53 miles to Rome.

Many have believed that the Romans invented the milestone, and also the road map, but this is not true. Both had existed before. Babylon had maps, Persia had roads and maps, way stations and markers. Egyptians, Persians, Greeks had devised simple and ingenious methods for marking routes with heaps of stones or pebbles which carried clues to direction and distance. It fell to the Romans, however, with their passion for organization and standardization, to develop both milestones and maps into reliable and easily comprehensible aids to travelers.

When Appius Claudius built the first of the great Roman roads, he did not use milestones. Perhaps those aediles of sixty-odd years later were the pioneers of signposting. Their work was expanded by the famous Gracchi brothers of the second century B.C., Tiberius and Gaius. The Gracchi, born into impeccable nobility and notable wealth, were political realists and honorable citizens who devoted their brief lives to the good of Rome—a good which in their minds involved a great deal of reform. Dutifully they fought Rome's wars, loyally they accepted the political positions incumbent upon the well-born and wealthy, and valiantly they fought for things like land distribution, a limitation of military demands on the poor and defenseless, the granting of Roman citizenship to worthy men of all provinces and all professions.

Tiberius, the elder brother, was murdered for his political stance, and his brother Gaius determined to further Tiberius' works. To Gaius Gracchus is usually credited the idea that the employment of the otherwise unoccupied would be an honorable way to perform necessary public works. Thus in a two-thousand-year-old forerunner of the New Deal, the unemployed were set to work in the construction and labeling of milestones. One of the sources for ascribing milestones to Gracchus is a notation of Plutarch, who states specifically that Gaius Gracchus, who was tribune in 123 B.C., "caused the roads to be all divided into miles . . . and erected pillars of stone to signify the distance from one place to another."

The markers were instantly of inestimable value. Travelers knew where they were, and how much farther they had to go. Outlanders, whether from the Italian provinces or from abroad, could ask of more experienced travelers just how far it was from one place to another, and receive reasonably accurate information. "Two days' walking" or "two days by mule" could at last be separated from the surely variable capacities of two different walkers or two different mules, and put into a linear category. Areas of danger, or in need of repair, could at last be established by some measurement more accurate than "after the grove of trees, beside the sacred spring, before the place of the flight of birds."

The Rome milestones most familiar to our eyes, about six feet high, cylindrical, often set on a square base, were not universal when the roads were made. In the early periods some were shaped like pyramids, some were set horizontally, some were painted at the top. They varied in height from four feet to twelve, and the material from which they were carved depended upon which kind of rock was most easily available near the road.

Almost all carried at least one Roman numeral indicating distance, but few explained from where to where. Presumably, they were understood to mean to or from Rome or the nearest important city in the provinces. Some of the *miliaria,* as milestones are called in modern Italian, are found to have no numbers at all. One explanation for this could be that they were mass-produced in a central place with a good supply of usable rock, and then shipped out to be set in place with the appropriate mileage mark added later in paint.

At first, milestone texts were simple. They indicated a distance, and the name of the responsible public official in charge of the work.

Later inscriptions became more complex, to include the exact year, and whether the road had at this point been constructed, repaired or rebuilt. When a man paid for the work from his own pocket, the responsible consul or aedile or emperor said so by instructing the stone chiselers to inscribe the words *Sua pecunia stravit*—"He had it done at his own expense"—into the columns.

Sometimes emperors noted that they had shared the expenses with someone else. A fine example of this type was found between the cities of Beneventum and Aeclanum in which Hadrian, emperor between A.D. 117 and 138, confesses in stone that he paid for only part of the road and that the adjacent landowners paid the rest.

As the Empire grew, and as ambitious heads of state tried to exaggerate their own importance or commemorate themselves by inscriptions in stone, the milestones became very wordy. Even short-lived emperors appended lists of laudatory titles to their own names, and commanded the sculptors to carve them into the milestones. Perhaps the prime example of this genre was a column erected by Caracalla on the Via Appia in A.D. 216 at Mile 71 near today's Fondi. It says the following:

> THE EMPEROR, CAESAR M. AURELIUS ANTONIUS, INVICTUS, PIUS, FELIX, AUGUSTUS, PARTICUS MAXIMUS, BRITTANICUS MAXIMUS, GERMANICUS MAXIMUS, PONTIFEX MAXIMUS, DURING HIS 19TH YEAR OF TRIBUNE'S POWER, ACCLAIMED EMPEROR FOR THE THIRD TIME, CONSUL FOR THE THIRD TIME, PROCONSUL: REBUILT THIS ROAD, WHICH WAS WORN OUT AFTER HAVING AT FIRST BEEN USELESSLY PAVED WITH CALCAREOUS STONE, USING NEW FLINT, SO THAT IT WAS MORE SOLID FOR TRAVELLERS, AND HE DID SO AT HIS OWN EXPENSE, FOR A DISTANCE OF 21 MILES.

Literate and accustomed to sententious pronouncements as the Romans were, they must have found this a bit much.

Today the verbiage is lost upon anyone who cannot decipher the eroded, blurred, abbreviated Latin letters and numbers. From a car, however slowly it passes, little is legible except the incised numeral which appears above or below the text.

More than four thousand of these milestones still exist, and they

*This milestone, on the Appia Traiana, is set up on a streetcorner in the town of Cerignola, near the Adriatic.*

turn up in strange places. Many have been built into the walls of churches, either inside as décor or outside as corner posts. Others are upside down or sideways, used as building blocks in peasant houses and medieval walls, road foundations and bridge supports.

Some have been re-erected on or near the road. There are two clearly visible, flanking the entrance of a minor administrative head-quarters and apartment house on the present route of the Appia at Mesa, just a few kilometers north of Terracina. There are two more between Fondi and Formia near the sea and five stand like sentinels in a tiny park just outside the Castello in Benevento, near the main square, and the only hotel, of the city.

Most of the finest examples, outside of museums, remain on the route of the Appia Traiana, the road which Trajan made from Bene-ventum to Brundisium to shorten the old Appia across the Apennine ridge. One of these Traiana milestones stands in the middle of an arc of Roman columns on the esplanade at Bari; there are eight in a delightful public park in Trani just a few miles up the coast from Bari on the Adriatic. Near Canosa, on a hill created by centuries of destruction left by man and nature, are at least five of them, turned every which way in the jumble of stone on the site of what was, most likely, Cannae, where Hannibal and his Carthaginians adminis-tered a disastrous defeat to the Roman legions in 216 B.C. In the village of Cerignola nearby there is one on a streetcorner, and there are two in the shadowy arcade of the city hall.

Among the most evocative are two in the otherwise uninteresting village of Ascoli Satriano. Both are set in the tiny main square, one almost hidden under the leaves of a scrubby tree beside a bar, the other almost obliterated by the red paint of some local partisan with a political message to impart to the populace.

No matter where they are, or how much they have been defaced, damaged, reused, the milestones manage to tug at the heart. Mute, blurred, stonily serene and vaguely phallic, they still exude a sense of identification, of kinship, with all nameless, faceless fellow humans who must once have scanned them with such eager eyes. Were those others breathless with anticipation at reunion with some beloved? Were they apprehensive, as Paul must have been as he neared Rome and his audience with the emperor? Were some of them as ignorant as we, unable to decipher Latin? Were they lost? Were they even perhaps on the wrong road?

No people from their time to our own traveled so much, or traveled so far. Perhaps this is the link which binds us to those worn stones, which loads them with such a freight of emotion. No artifacts along the road, not even the tumbled stones of the roadbed itself, nor the soaring arches, nor the bridges, nor the cavernous amphitheaters, go more straight to the heart than do those symbols saying that "it is 40 miles to. . . ." They speak so clearly of the coming and going, of the farewells and reunions, of those ancient people we almost know, so nearly can remember.

Even with the wealth of milestones still around, it is ironic that no scholar knows precisely what distance they measured. It is agreed that the Roman mile was based on 5,000 Roman feet, or more specifically, on 1,000 paces. This is the *milia passuum,* or M.P., of the ancient itineraries and of the milestones. Yet 1,000 steps surely couldn't have been exactly the same for each Roman soldier, or each Roman surveyor.

It is possible that even the Romans didn't know, to a foot or an inch, and that they simply accepted as *milia passuum* each mark made by the man who paced it off. Certainly they accepted the measurement as standard, and erected their milestones accordingly. The problem today is that not one of the four thousand markers stands at the site upon which it was first erected. Every single one has been moved, at one time or another, and no two adjacent ones were ever left *in situ* long enough, or measured carefully enough, to establish the distance between them.

As a rule of thumb, the Roman mile is defined as 1,480 meters, slightly shorter than the standard English/American mile of 1,760 yards. Conversion from meters to yards is simple arithmetic, but boring: a meter is 3.37 inches longer than a yard.

When these calculations are projected upon the traces of the Via Appia, however, they become more complex because the Roman world, having invented the mile and bequeathed it forever to the English-speaking world, no longer uses it. Modern Italy quite sensibly abandoned the mile several decades ago for the metric kilometer, five eighths of a mile, and all distances within the nation today are measured thus. So are the calibrations of "mileage" in cars. Trying to measure a mileage reference along the old road, using an automobile which indicates kilometers, can be frustrating.

Many opportunities to make an accurate measurement of the

Roman mile have been lost. One of the first chances came in 1574 when a cylindrical column marked I, and bearing the name of the Emperor Vespasian, was dug up somewhere outside the Porta San Sebastiano, once the Porta Appia, on the edge of Rome. About twenty-five years later a similar column, marked VII, came to light.

The Italian architect and archaeologist Luigi Canina reported that column I was found 114 "spans," or about 115 meters, outside the city gate and that it must have marked the first Roman mile on the Appia from the Porta Capena. Later scholars have criticized Canina for accepting vague geographical reports of where it was found, but he could do little else, since he had not been present when rescuers found it. Some even have said that this could not have been the first milestone, or else that it already had been moved, because the first Roman mile would have fallen just inside the gate at the Porta San Sebastiano.

Column VII, like I, was carried away before its exact location had been marked and recorded. Both may be seen today, tall and graceful, flanking the extreme right and left of the balustrade of the Piazza del Campidoglio in Rome, site of the city hall and the Capitoline museums.

However one may deplore the casual disregard for their provenance, this present placement is fitting. For what modern Romans call the Campidoglio was the site of the ancient Roman capitol, on top of one of the seven hills which have become so obscured by building and topographical change that they are hardly recognizable any more as hills at all. A twelfth-century book of *Mirabilia Romae* described the Capitoline Hill as "the head of the world, where the consuls and senators abode to govern the earth. . . ."

It was to the Capitoline Hill that Petrarch went in 1341 to receive the laurel crown of a poet, and it was here in 1764 that Gibbon was so moved by the remains and their memories that he decided to write the *History of the Decline and Fall of the Roman Empire*. It was also here, in the late 1950s, that the representatives of Great Britain, France, the Netherlands, Belgium and Luxembourg came to sign with Italy the pact which created the European Common Market. It was a fitting symbolic choice, for never since the *Pax Romana* and the fall of the Roman Empire had Western Europe been united.

*The milestone marked I, which was moved to the Campidoglio and set on a new base, marked S.P.Q.R., as decoration for the balustrade.*

For centuries in between great events, the Capitoline was abandoned, looted, left to fall to pieces. There were many years in which only goats grazed there, chewing at the tough weeds and grasses which could find nourishment between the broken stones. How much it must have meant, in the sixteenth century, when Michelangelo turned his talents to redesigning the hilltop, reconstructing its buildings. The survivors of the Middle Ages crawled out of the caves, physical and mental, of the long darkness to blink in the sunlight of the Renaissance. No wonder that with sweat and muscle they dragged up to Michelangelo's piazza the two great columns, physical remnants of their glorious past, and erected them proudly on rectangular bases. Into the bases they carved the ancient initials which still are inscribed on mailboxes, manhole covers, lampposts, and sometimes sidewalks: "S.P.Q.R.," symbols for that stirring, sonorous phrase, *Senatus Populusque Romanus* — "the Senate and the People of Rome."

Other remnants of the road, other milestones, were treated far more carelessly years later. In 1637, for example, there were seven of them on the Appia, still standing in their proper places, half in and half out of the water which had flooded the road in the Pontine Marshes. Manuscripts in the Vatican Library in Rome identify them specifically as milestones 40 to 46. This was a period in which many popes allotted both money and time to try to drain the marshes and reopen the Appia, and the records of their various engineers and contractors have been kept almost intact in the bulging Vatican archives.

Study of these records has become a near-hobby of modern road scholars, including one road detective named Daniele Sterpos, an official of Autostrade S.p.A., the Italian corporation which has constructed the huge, often beautiful network of superhighways up and down Italy since the end of World War II. The Autostrade's directors commissioned, as a public service, a study of the Roman roads, and under Dr. Sterpos' supervision have published a five-volume work in Italian on *Road Communications Through the Years.*

Sterpos' meticulous scholarship turned up both documents and drawings of those seven milestones, and revealed another lost opportunity for study: in 1777 Pope Pius VI commissioned work on the Appia in the Pontine Marshes, and appointed an antiquities-loving cardinal, Guglielmo Pallotta, to supervise the work. Roadmen found two milestones still standing—numbers 46 and 42—but they didn't measure the distance between them either accurately or carefully. They made a rough measure of about 1,471.23 meters per Roman mile, eighteen or nineteen feet short of the accepted length of 1,480 meters. Then they permitted workmen to drag away the milestones to get them out of the way of the new road building.

It seems to have mattered not at all, in 1777–1779, that stones which had stood for almost two millennia should be displaced so abruptly. Their fate may still have been better than other remains of the road, which were either stolen, broken up and used as fill, or pulverized to make cement. Workmen knocked down everything in their path, including ancient brickwork, though one of the foremen reported weekly, routinely and impassively, upon the "bits of columns and inscriptions" which he asked dredgers to turn over to the papal authorities. If it was convenient to do so, some of the diggers did. If it was difficult, or they were behind in their work schedule, they simply didn't waste time on such things.

Cardinal Pallotta, who often visited the scene of works, was horrified by the destruction in 1779. He issued an edict which bristles with invective and which may still be read in Vatican archives. He threatened punishment of any person who took away from the site "medals, metals, marbles, inscriptions, bas-reliefs, statues, intaglios . . . in whole or in part."

It was a noble effort, but too late. By 1779 most of the submerged stretches of the road, with its adjoining tombs and monuments, had emerged from the water, had been cleared and remade. Any remains which had once been there had already vanished.

In the middle of the reclaimed marshes, near where the old Roman stopping place Ad Medias once had stood, Pope Pius VI erected a new postal station called Mesa, and two of the milestones were set into its portico. These are the two visible today in this stretch of the road. One is marked with a V at the top of the column, and XLVIII at the bottom; the other has VI at the top, XLVIIII at the bottom. The distances marked were, like the archaic milestone Paul had seen years earlier along the road, to Forum Appii and to Rome itself.

This stretch of road, built right on top of the original Appia and renovated endless times, still carries the modern Appia straight through the marshes. To the right of the road, going south, is a canal which follows the track of the canal which flanked the road in Roman times. Horace took a night boat along this stretch, with mules plodding along the road to pull the boat. No traffic goes by canal nowadays, but the water is there at almost road level. Occasionally it carries the rowboats or fishing dinghies of neighbors, and always it reflects the willows and rushes along its side, the oleanders which modern Italy plants along the fringes of southern highways. Under the canal's glittering surface, one knows, lie still some of the stones and broken columns of Appius Claudius' road.

It is this particular reach, from about the town of Cisterna to near Terracina, which gave the Appia its somewhat overrated reputation of having gone always straight, direct, unswerving, toward its destination. It did go dead straight whenever possible, leaving aside deviations made for religious reasons like avoiding the Tomb of the Horatii and Curiatii just outside Rome, but its objective was normally of short duration and then it could bend or turn and drive straight toward the next one. Across the marshes there was no need to deviate, and there was every reason to cross the area as quickly as possible. Here the original Appia shot straight across the worst hazard known to the roadbuilder: mud and muck. Water can be bridged, stone can be cut, but ooze is a trial and a terror. Insects thrived in it, and the air was heavy and unpleasant with the miasma which rose from it. The word "malaria" comes from the Roman description of the *mal aria*, the bad air, which hung over the marsh.

Supported by piles driven deep into the mud, paved heavily on top, the straight stretch first became known as *la fettuccia,* then as *il diciannovenne.* Both words exist in modern Italian, the first meaning "broad flat ribbon"—or broad flat pasta, as in *fettucine*—the other in daily usage meaning either "the nineteen-year-old" or the nineteen Roman miles of the road itself.

The most famous milestone of all the Roman era has not survived, but was never really a milestone in the first place. It was called the *miliarium aureum,* the Golden Milestone. It wasn't really gold, either. It was a big column of gilded bronze, erected in the Roman Forum in about 20 B.C. by the first emperor, Augustus. On it were the names of the major cities of the Italian peninsula and their distances from

Rome. Tradition had it, erroneously, that the distances were calculated from the Golden Milestone itself. They were calculated instead from the Servian Wall, which in the case of the Via Appia meant the Porta Capena in that wall.

Some fragments of the *miliarium aureum* were excavated in the nineteenth century inside the Forum, near the Temple of Saturn, in a hemicycle which Constantine the Great called the *umbilicus urbis Romae*, the navel of Rome, and thus of the Roman Empire. The imagery was exquisite: by calling it the navel instead of the heart, Constantine acknowledged and made specific the vital function of the roads themselves, the umbilical cords by which the growing Roman hegemony was nourished.

Perhaps the Romans of Augustus' day reckoned that the roads began with the Golden Milestone, and that the "first mile" on the Appia, way out to the first milestone, seemed inordinately long because they were so reluctant to leave, or so eager to get home. In any case, the Golden Milestone's significance superseded simple mileage because it also marked and commemorated the first comprehensive mapping of the Roman world, the first accurate calculation, reduced to a map, of just how far the distances truly were.

Julius Caesar had launched the project of mapping the world, and he had even hired some Greek geographers to work on it. But his murder in 44 B.C. halted the plan. It was completed under his successor, Octavian, who later became known as Augustus, by one of the most fascinating men of that whole astonishing era. This man was Marcus Vipsanius Agrippa, soldier, writer, aqueduct builder, visionary, map maker. Agrippa was born in 63 B.C. of such humble parentage that nothing is known of his father except that he was called Gaius. When Agrippa was eighteen, he was serving in the army. Caesar decided to launch an expedition against the Parthians in the Middle East, and he wanted to send the young Octavian, whom he had adopted as son and heir, to fight with the expeditionary force and gain military experience. He instructed Octavian to choose two young men of his own age, but of humble origin, to go along as his companions. Agrippa was one of the two whom the young Octavian selected.

History might have been quite different had they actually gone together to the wars. Octavian, by all accounts, was a quite indifferent soldier, Agrippa a very good one. Before they could start for the Parthian campaigns, Caesar was dead, Octavian took over in Rome, and Agrippa went to do the fighting. For the rest of their lives the two friends worked together, Octavian running the state and Agrippa winning its battles on land and, extraordinarily, even on sea. It was Agrippa who defeated Sextus Pompeius at Naulochus in 36 B.C., and it was he who completely reorganized and rebuilt the Roman fleet and vanquished Antony and Cleopatra at the battle of Actium in 31 B.C., driving the pair eventually to suicide.

All this would have won him fame and fortune in Rome, but he didn't stop there. He served as governor in Gaul; he pacified the Germanic tribes; he dealt with Roman interests in what are now Greece and Israel; was a friend of the Jews. Even when his friend Octavian was acclaimed Emperor Augustus, in 27 B.C., Agrippa demonstrated no jealousy of the great honors which he had done so much to procure. Augustus made him proconsul, aedile, almost co-regent, and brought him back to Rome where Agrippa created his lasting monuments: roads, fountains throughout the city, the Pantheon, and the great survey of Roman roads.

To make his map, Agrippa called in Caesar's Greek geographers and consulted all the work they had done. He collected the measurements of army veterans who had tramped the roads, of sailors who had cruised the coasts and made charts of their own landmarks, harbors, shoals. He drew on his own certain knowledge of the routes in provinces of today's France, Germany and parts of the Near East. Some of the roads he studied had been built under his supervision; some he had ordered built. He relied somewhat, as did his sources, on the milestones erected beside the roads across the known world.

When the massive work was finished, he made his map. There was at first probably only one copy, presented to his friend, emperor and father-in-law, Augustus. The first copy was on painted marble; no remnants of it exist. After Agrippa's death in 12 B.C., Augustus ordered two copies of the map. One, in marble, was set up for public use in or near the Forum. The second, a small reproduction in gold, with the chief cities of the Empire marked in precious jewels, was for Augustus' own use. This latter extravagance probably impressed the nobles, but the marble map set up in public was a more effective landmark. It was the first known municipal aid to travel and geography, available to all who wanted to consult it.

It was also, as the canny Augustus must have known, a powerful propaganda weapon, a tribute to the glory and grandeur of his fledgling empire. This map has vanished, but a modern equivalent of it may be seen today in Rome, near the site of the first one, affixed to retaining walls beside the Via dei Fori Imperiali, which reaches from the foot of the Campidoglio to the Colosseum. Mussolini razed slums to have a road driven through, in 1933, to open a broad and dignified vista to the ruins of the Roman Forum and the Colosseum itself, and he had four huge stone maps put up on the walls. They show the gradual growth of Rome, from a white dot on the Tiber to an empire which stretched from England to Palestine, from North Germany to the Sahara Desert. Mussolini's motives were dual: mainly he wanted to indicate, to Italians and to the world, that he intended to re-establish that empire's might and prestige. He also harbored a respect which verged on awe for the accomplishments of Romans two thousand years his seniors, and he hoped to inspire the same respect and pride in the citizens.

Almost a hundred years after Agrippa's death another copy of his map, in marble, was ordered by the Emperor Vespasian and set up for public use near the Pantheon, which Agrippa had built. It is intriguing to think that travelers preparing to set forth on a journey probably made special trips to the Forum, or to the Pantheon, to consult the maps. Perhaps some took along a stool, a pen and a handful of papyrus sheets to make notes. Some probably just committed the major details to memory. If the maps were low enough to touch, the very outlines of the roads themselves must have blurred in time under the fingers of those who traced them and studied them.

Agrippa's great work has been criticized by some scholars, in another skirmish in the old battle over the relative merits of the life styles and systems of the Greeks and the Romans. The Greek Eratosthenes, these critics point out, managed to read the size of the earth by measuring the stars, while the Roman Agrippa had to calculate the length and breadth of provinces by grubbily counting milestones.

There is no reason to labor the argument here. Undoubtedly there were maps before Agrippa's. Babylonian records indicate that they had maps by 600 B.C., and the historian Herodotus wrote in the fourth century B.C. of a tyrant of Miletus, one Aristagoras, who wanted to enlist the help of Cleomenes of Sparta in a projected war

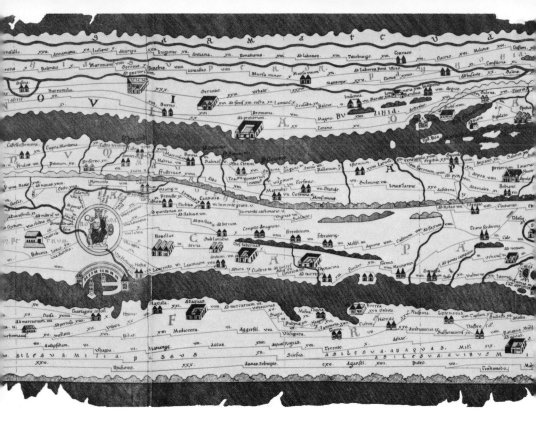

against Persia. To tempt Cleomenes to join him in the attack, he described the wealth of the lands they might conquer together, and produced "a brazen tablet, on which was engraved the circumference of the whole earth, and the whole sea, and all rivers."

It is possible that Agrippa saw this map, if it truly ever existed, during his sojourns in the Eastern provinces. It is almost certain that a man of learning and experience would have read Herodotus. Even if he plagiarized the idea, and even if his methods of measurement were prosaic, Agrippa did produce a map which was seen by many more people than two kings plotting together somewhere in a palace. It was Agrippa's effort which was enlarged, adapted and refined through the centuries and which became the first workable compendium from which road maps, guidebooks, itineraries and travelers' aids are descended.

Early maps were called *itineraria picta,* as distinct from *itineraria adnotata.* The first gave a general plan of the route of the road, with

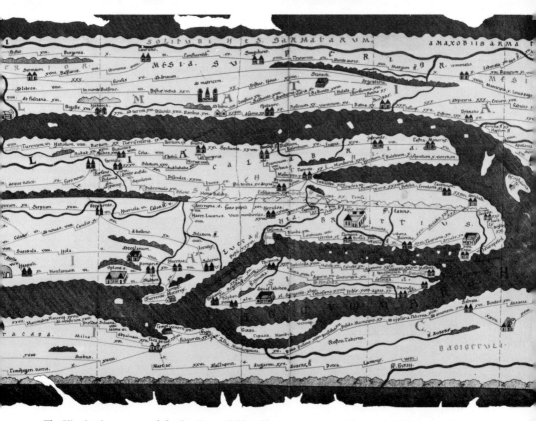

*The Via Appia segment of the Peutinger Table, oldest extant map of the road. Although made in the thirteenth century, it was based on very early, perhaps third century A.D., Roman maps of the world. Courtesy The Nationalbibliothek, Vienna.*

pictorial symbols for cities, rivers, mountains, way stations, and the like. The second were unillustrated lists of roads with their principal cities, indications of mileage, and information about taverns, inns, stations for changing horses.

Several of the *itineraria adnotata* have survived the centuries, among them the *Itinerarium Provinciarum Antonini Augusti*, which seems to have been a collation of the records of several travelers. Some Roman emperor in the third or fourth century A.D. ordered its compilation. It, like the *Itinerarium Hierosolytanum,* the journey of the religious pilgrim from Bordeaux to Jerusalem, includes each stop from Rome south and east on the Via Appia. The important points and mileages on these two itineraries agree with one another and with Horace, though there are small discrepancies.

The only *itinerarium picta* which still exists is a grotesquely distorted and utterly fascinating specimen called the Peutinger Table, now in the possession of the Nationalbibliothek in Vienna. The

*Tabula Peuteringiana* comprises eleven pieces of parchment, painted in five colors, originally pieced together and rolled up as one long scroll. It is almost twenty-three feet long and just a bit more than a foot wide.

This *Tabula* was probably done by a monk in Colmar, France, in 1265. Making a heroic effort to trace the lines of main roads throughout the then-known world, with distances marked and major cities and topographical details illustrated, the monk was forced into fantastic distortions of continents and countries. It is not easy to reduce the world to narrow rollable strips.

He painted the map in color to indicate seas, roads, rivers. There are symbols for large and small towns. Watering places are shown by little sketches of bathhouses with a tank in the center. Small towns are marked with one small house. Large towns have a circuit of pictured walls and towers. Three grand cities—Rome, Constantinople and Antioch—are indicated by a seated throned figure inside a circle. Rome and Antioch's seated figures wear crowns; Constantinople's has a plumed helmet.

The symbolism of the three seated figures is obscure. It may be that they had been added to the standard map of the Roman Empire after the death of Constantine in the fourth century, when the Empire was divided into three parts ruled by the late emperor's three sons. The pious monk himself added some special touches to the map which Agrippa and Augustus would never have dreamed of. He made the Mount of Olives prominent, for example, and he carefully noted the Vosges Forest and the Black Forest, topographical features which few ancient Romans could ever have seen. From the windows of a monastery in Colmar in 1265 both forests were visible, and the monk's careful rendition of them is an appealing demonstration of the human urge to "improve" any document or manuscript which comes to hand.

Just where the Peutinger Table resided, from its creation in 1265 until its discovery in a German library in the sixteenth century, is a mystery. So is the source from which the monk of Colmar made it. Interior evidence indicates that the monk had one, or possibly more, parchment maps from Roman sources. Some scholars believe he may have had a parchment version of Agrippa's map as model, but a German, Konrad Miller, advanced the theory that the basic source was a Roman geographer called Castorius. Miller based his case on the published work of an unnamed "Ravenna geographer" of about 670, an era in which Ravenna was the seat of a German Holy Roman emperor. The Ravenna geographer, Miller said, referred to at least thirty-seven specific places which turned up five centuries later, in the same form, on the Peutinger Table—and the Ravenna geographer named Castorius as his source.

Whether scholar Miller's theories as to the source of the table are correct or not, he deserves credit for tracing the history of the only extant version of the handmade map. This was no easy task because, unwieldly as the thing is, it kept getting lost. A man named Konrad Celtes found it in 1507 in what he called simply and vaguely "a library" and gave it to his friend Konrad Peutinger, from whom it takes its present designation. Celtes made it a specific condition of his gift that the manuscript should be published. For patriotic reasons Peutinger turned down a French offer to publish. Then he lent the document to a friend in Ravensburg, Germany, who died before the type was set. After this the whole thing was lost again, for fifty years. It turned up in the estate of a later Peutinger, in 1714, and then was bought by the Prince of Savoy "for 100 ducats." The prince willed it to Vienna's Nationalbibliothek in 1737.

No such monetary value was placed on Agrippa's map, but copies of it were produced for military commanders who needed to know the territory through which they were to march, and for civil governors who required them for the efficient management of their territories. These copies, meticulously transferred by hand to strips of parchment, must have been costly and highly perishable. Yet there is written evidence that not only generals and governors possessed them, but also private citizens. Under the Emperor Domitian in the first century A.D. a man named Mettius Pompusianus got into trouble for having a map of the world on the walls of his house, and for carrying a smaller copy of it around with him. The suspicious Domitian probably suspected him of some obscure plot.

A writer in the third century pleaded on patriotic grounds that the schools of Autun, in a northern Gallic province, should be provided with maps "for the teaching of geography."

Even earlier, in the first century B.C., the Roman poet Propertius makes one of his heroines study "a map of the eastern front" while her lover is off at the wars. Propertius may have been exercising poetic license as he wrote, because he suffered from the occasionally unrequited love of a Roman lady named Hostia, and he had studied in Athens. He was thus familiar with the "eastern front," and he may have had wistful dreams of a lady who would even study a map to remain close to her beloved. Perhaps he invented the notion of map study, but he did know about maps.

Gradually through the years, the straightforward itineraries and military charts which gave rudimentary information and mileage were embellished with more symbols and travelers' aids. As religious shrines and famous places of pilgrimage were marked, the documents changed subtly from maps to guidebooks. Traffic in them must have been intense. In 1852 diggers found in some curative baths at Vicarello, just north of Rome, four silver vessels shaped like milestones which listed the full road itinerary from Gades (Cadiz, in Spain) to Rome. The vessels bear different dates, but they are all from early

*One of the four "Vicarello vases," probably used as combination road maps and votive offerings. The place names are clearly visible, as is the mileage in Roman numerals.*

first century A.D. Why the vessels were abandoned in the baths can only be guessed; perhaps they were pious offerings for a magical religious cure. The fact that silversmiths found it profitable to turn out these expensive cups indicates that there was a flourishing market.

The first commercial, mass-produced maps and guidebooks had to wait for centuries. During the Dark Ages, little "scribbling" was done except in the monasteries. Not until the year in which Christopher Columbus set sail from Spain to find a route to China did a real, commercial map for road travelers make its appearance. This was Erhardt Etzlaub's *Way to Rome,* published in 1492 for the aid of religious pilgrims wishing to find and explore Rome, and was the first *printed* map to show roads. Illustrated with wood-block prints, it went through several editions in twenty years. It was printed with movable type, had color illustrations rendered by hand, and was oriented in a way that we consider upside down, with north at the bottom.

This map was inspired, as had been the silver cups of Vicarello, by the urge to pilgrimage to Rome. So was the first real guidebook, published by a Mr. Schott of Antwerp, on the occasion of the jubilee year of 1600. Schott's book, written in Latin and compressed into 450 pages of very fine print, was advertised "for anyone who visits Rome in the Holy Year of the Jubilee." At least 1,200,000 persons did.

This guide, full of descriptions of cities and sites and cemeteries in Rome, was so popular that it was translated into Italian the next year, and went through innumerable editions until 1670. Perhaps the estimable Mr. Schott got rich, but it is doubtful that he ever saw the roads and sites he described. His text bears a telltale resemblance to the journal kept by a scholar named Stefan Pighius, who twenty-five years earlier had accompanied to Italy the Crown Prince of Germany, Karl Frederick. Jubilees are held by the Church in Rome every twenty-five years, and in 1575 Pope Gregory XIII had rolled out every red carpet in the Vatican to welcome the young German prince and his scholarly companion Pighius. These were the years of the Protestant revolution, and the Pope needed a faithful prince in the land of Luther. Young Prince Karl Frederick and Pighius were received with honors in Rome, then sent out on the Via Appia to visit Ariccia in the Alban Hills, Minturno, Terracina and Naples. They were provided with horses and carriages for the Appian trip, because the young prince wanted to keep his own steeds and vehicles at top form for the trip back north across the Alps.

Pighius kept voluminous notes, and he wrote movingly of "the vast but watery Pontine fields where once passed the superb straight line of the Via Appia, of which now one sees only the miserable ruins under the water, while on both sides appear mausoleums, tombs, buildings, villas and palaces which once ornamented it."

Schott's guide to Rome and the roads pirated most of Pighius' words, leaving out only the lavish descriptions of honors accorded to the young prince.

Within two years Schott was challenged by another book, the title of which is so outrageously long that it merits repetition: *Itinerarium Italiae totius, in quo situs, origines, imperia civitatum ed oppidorum, mores populorum, item montes, lacus, flumina, fontes, aquae calidae, metalla, cunctaque miracula, monumenta, incredibilesque antiquitates mira arte experientiaque descripta leguntur.*

To wit, all about Italy, its location, its origins, its cities, its manners and morals, fountains, miracles, rivers, antiquities, arts—all described at length. If the reader still had the strength to proceed, of course. This book included poetic descriptions of cities, and it had that page so familiar to the twentieth century, a careful explanation of the coins in use in Rome, and their value. There was, toward the end, a thoughtful inclusion of a page of prayers for travelers, prayers specifically approved by the ruling pope, Pius V.

Careful measurement of every mile of the Via Appia and its sister Roman roads, not only in Italy but also across the Roman world, was a critical part of each map and each guidebook. The markers, the simple pacing and placement, were the crux of the matter, and one Roman set down on paper the tools and specifications for a mechanical aid to more accurate measurement.

He was Vitruvius, a military engineer who worked for both Julius Caesar and the Emperor Augustus. He was overseer for many of the public works of his time, and when he considered that he had made his contribution he settled down to write a ten-book work on architecture. Vitruvius knew the Greek written record. He had had practical experience in the field. His written work is occasionally unintelligible, usually innocent of true scientific knowledge, but a gold mine of information. From Book X, Chapter IX, of Vitruvius comes a detailed description of an invention which even the antic Rube Goldberg would have envied — the world's first, and most cumbrous, odometer.

> . . . a useful invention of the greatest ingenuity, transmitted by our predecessors, which enables us, while sitting in a carriage on the road or sailing by sea, to know how many miles of a journey we have accomplished. This will be possible as follows. Let the wheels of the carriage be each four feet in diameter, so that if a wheel has a mark made upon it, and begins to move forward from that mark in making its revolution on the surface of the road, it will have covered the definite distance of twelve and a half feet on reaching that mark at which it began to revolve.
>
> Having provided such wheels, let a drum with a single tooth projecting beyond the face of its circumference be firmly fastened to the inner side of the hub of the wheel. Then, above this, let a case be firmly fastened to the body of the carriage, containing a revolving drum set on edge and mounted on an axle; on the face of the drum there are four hundred teeth, placed at equal intervals, and engaging the tooth of the drum below. The upper drum has, moreover, one tooth fixed to its side and standing out farther than the other teeth.
>
> Then, above, let there be a horizontal drum, similarly toothed and contained in another case, with its teeth engaging the tooth fixed to the side of the second drum, and let as many holes be made in this (third) drum as will correspond to the number of miles — more or less, it does not matter — that a carriage can go in a day's journey. Let a small round stone be placed in every one of these holes, and in the receptacle or case containing that drum may fall one by one into a bronze vessel set underneath in the body of the carriage.
>
> Thus, as the wheel in going forward carries with it the lowest drum, and as the tooth of this at every revolution strikes against the teeth of the upper drum, and makes it move along, the result will be that the upper drum is carried round once for every four hundred revolutions of the lowest, and that the tooth fixed to its side pushes forward one tooth of the horizontal drum. Since, therefore, with four hundred revolutions of the lowest drum, the upper will revolve once, the progress made will be a distance of five thousand feet for one mile. Hence, every stone, making a ringing sound as it falls, will give warning that we have gone one mile. The number of stones gathered from beneath and counted, will show the number of miles in the day's journey.

This same device, Vitruvius assured all, could be adapted for sea voyages by means of an axle passed through the sides of the hull. Thus ends his description of "how to make things that may be provided for use and amusement in times that are peaceful and without fear." And next, a series of chapters on catapults or scorpiones, and other implements of siege and defense.

In the two millennia which have passed since Vitruvius worked this all out, and since the first Roman milestone was wrestled into position, the first public road map set proudly on display, billions of persons have casually, carelessly used and tossed away their equivalents. Many a map has proved deceptive in use, many a mileage marker slightly wrong. Yet on no other road in the world has there been lavished the amount of scholarship, the measuring and calculating, the arguing, the pacing back and forth, which has gone into efforts to establish with utter accuracy the precise route and length of the Via Appia.

Scholars have all but memorized the extant itineraries, and they mumble Horace's more obscure references in their sleep: "We next rolled downhill in carriages 24 miles to stay at a town whose name just won't scan." In the effort to find out where it was, and to measure the miles, archaeologists and other road lovers have climbed fences, waded streams, tripped over weed-covered rocks, cowered under summer storms, run from irate peasants' dogs and learned Latin.

They have learned reams and have also written them. Yet the miles won't come out right. One of the most devoted of the Appia's scholarly suitors, Italy's Giuseppe Lugli, in an effort to determine the exact location of the town of Caudium, whose destruction made it possible for the Via Appia to press from Capua to Beneventum, went to the mat with the mileage and lost:

> No matter how one tries to mark the distance between Capua and Benevento, the distance always comes out longer than the 32 miles indicated both on the Peutinger Table and the Antonine Itinerary.

> Twenty-five kilometers, that is 13 Roman miles, intervene between Santa Maria Capua Vetere [the site of ancient Capua] and Arpaia, on the site of the Caudine Forks . . . and a bit more than 26 kilometers from Arpaia to Benevento. By identifying Caudium with the present city of Montesarchio, and by placing the old crossroads of the road to the city with

the Via Appia itself a couple of kilometers to the south of the present crossroad, and by abolishing some of the curves in the modern road, one can still never arrive at the mere 11 Roman miles which both the Peutinger Table and the Antonine Itinerary establish for this stretch.

It cannot be done even if we correct the figure 11 to the figure 12, as it appears on the Bordeaux Pilgrim Itinerary. Along the entire route [Lugli concludes dispiritedly] one always lacks about five thousand paces.

Five lost miles. They wouldn't matter, perhaps, on another road. Lugli admits that part of the problem is that nobody knows just for sure where Caudium was, and he points out that Roman numerals can easily be garbled in copying. As copyists reproduced old maps and mileages, as they transcribed the itineraries through the centuries, a V could easily get switched to an X. Either could be made so carelessly that a reader didn't know which was meant. It is also difficult to avoid dropping a I now and again. Lugli, like other scholars, tried to make allowance for all this, but the figures still wouldn't come out.

It would be nice to know just where the discrepancy lies. But on the other hand, it is quite fitting that the Queen of Roads keeps some of her secrets still.

# VI
# HURRY, HURRY, HURRY

Just 100 kilometers below Rome on the modern Via Appia, which for much of this length lies on top of or very near to Appius Claudius' road, is Terracina, the Tarracina of the Romans. It is snuggled picturesquely between the craggy peaks of the Ausonian Hills and the Tyrrhenian Sea, for here both the mountainous spine of Italy and the Via Appia itself touch the shore for the first time south of Rome.

Once a seaport and a resort for Roman aristocrats, Terracina now sprawls low and summer-lazy near the water, its beaches and streets full of sunburned tourists and ice cream vendors, its sidewalk bars bordered with red and pink and white oleanders.

Towering over everything is 1,000-foot Mount Sant'Angelo, and clinging to it the massive masonry arches of the Temple of Jove Anxur, built in the first century B.C. Seen from below in the shimmering heat, or glimpsed at night when the arches are lighted from within, the temple looks like a *papier-mache* set for an epic by DeMille, or perhaps a backdrop for outdoor opera.

Seen up close, it is ponderously, enormously real. From each great arch opens a dizzying view up and down the coastline, back toward the Pontine Marshes, forward to the bluish peak of Mount Circeo

rising from the sea. Once the road went this way. Horace went this way: "We wormed our way onward, taking the rest of the day to arrive at the village of Anxur, loftily posed in its limestone cliffs."

Beside and below the solid shoulder of Mount Sant'Angelo is a smaller, reddish pinnacle of rocky outcrop standing with its feet all but in the bright blue water. Today's road skirts it to the right, going south, and passes also to the right of a little old arch much altered in medieval times.

This is a short stretch of road, less than half a mile, but it represents one of the most audacious and laborious feats of highway building in history, a triumph of the Appia. To make the road go this way, the red outcrop called Pesco Montano was cut by hand, straight down, for 120 feet to clear a passage between its rocky barrier and the sea.

The smooth cut is still clearly visible and so, up close, are the numbers. Nearest ground level, almost hidden behind some battered-looking cactus, is the figure CXX, and above it, also easily visible, are CX and C. The other numerals can be studied only by moving back and away from the wall, and by using binoculars. At the foot of the cut, though now buried, are two steplike embankments hacked out of the rock, about fourteen inches high and the same measure wide, designed to help hold the road and prevent deterioration of the cliff itself. Later road building and smoothing have hidden these steps.

The deepest cutting on the Appia, the Tarracina slash, was not made by Appius Claudius but by the Emperor Trajan about four hundred years later. It shortened the total distance from Rome to Capua by only one land mile, but in time it saved half a day. By Trajan's era the Romans were in a tearing hurry. They still loitered, in the Forum and in the baths, but when they left off loitering they were impatient to get on to their next appointments with the least possible delay.

Before Trajan's cut, the Appia abandoned its straight line just north of Tarracina, turned slightly inland toward the hills and then began a slow curving path upward. This original "high Appia" entered the walled city through a gate, part of which still stands, circled the Temple of Roma and Augustus, passed the Temple of Jove, and

*This is a view of Terracina as it appeared in the second half of the seventeenth century. Engraving by Braun in Florence; print courtesy of Autostrade S.p.A.*

opened into a large piazza, itself hacked out of the rock and smoothed with fill held in place by dressed masonry blocks.

This piazza, now some distance out of the populated center of the city, appears as a wide, grassy, flat place; only a few of the stones of retaining walls indicate that it ever was anything else. It was built to provide a stopping place, a halt to rest both man and beast, because on both sides of it the Appia was steep and difficult. Travelers going south had to climb almost a thousand feet from sea level to pass through Anxur, and there was no alternative route. This was the first *passaggio obbligato* on the Appia, the first section from which it was physically impossible to deviate from the roadbed. By the time it reached the city walls the road was about sixteen feet wide, but as it went up toward the city it was narrow and held by retaining walls. After it passed this rest stop, the Piazza dei Paladini, it went steeply downward, to almost regain sea level on the other side.

From the Piazza dei Paladini, looking south, one can still trace the track of the Appia, curving around the side of the mountain. There are a few small sections of roadbed with the typical polygonal gray stones in place, and scattered between the shacks of small farmers and squatters, mixed with broken chairs and tin chicken sheds and abandoned automobiles, massive broken stones with mossy inscriptions lie tumbled carelessly about. In the older parts of Terracina itself, up in the "high town," the stones of "high Appia" provide a parking lot in the main piazza. The principal cathedral is built over the ruins of a pagan temple. Fluted Roman columns are set into corners of later buildings, and near the piazza is one arch of a Roman forum, exposed when a 1943 bombardment blew up the accretions of centuries which had covered it.

Of the lower road which replaced this one for through traffic, very little remains except the massive rock cutting. There are a few stones of the road visible through a gate in a private garden near the sea, and that is all. The two branches of the Appia once joined each other again two or three miles inland of Pesco Montano, in a narrow strip of land between the Lake of Fondi and a peak called Pilucco.

Trajan contributed more than any man except Appius Claudius himself to the speed and efficiency of a road communication system which was the wonder of the ancient world. He and his predecessor,

*The present course of the road as it passes through Terracina. The ancient Temple of Jove Anxur is on top of the peak at left, the outcrop of Pesco Montano below it, and the smooth Roman cut visible in the lower right.*

*This watercolor by Carlo Labruzzi, done in the late eighteenth century, shows the "rest piazza" high above old Tarracina on the "high road" of the Appia. Print courtesy Edizioni Dell'Elefante, Rome.*

the Emperor Nerva, did the first real renovation of the Appia after its construction. They repaired sections through the marshes, added or replaced milestones, built bridges to replace the slow ferries which wasted hours of a traveler's time. And with one great gesture at Tarracina, Trajan removed from the road its single most difficult stretch. The cut shortened travel time not only for Capua-bound travelers but also for those headed toward the port of Puteoli and embarkation for Sicily or Africa. His other shortcut, the Appia Traiana from Beneventum to Brundisium, saved one full day to that port and the sea routes to Greece and Asia Minor. All the itineraries had to be recast, after his work, to correct the mileage and travel times.

Never from Trajan's time until the invention of the railroad could human beings move so rapidly, in all seasons, as they then could on the roads. Messengers rushing to take the news of Nero's death to Galba in Spain made 332 miles in thirty-six hours. Tiberius once rode

600 miles in three days and nights, and Caesar in a carriage covered 800 miles in eight days.

Such speed in that era was the equivalent of telegraphic service or of the Pony Express of the American West, which, if one can believe the stories, used to deliver the U.S. mail with a speed we could envy today. The same was true of the Roman postal system. In 54 B.C. a letter which Caesar dispatched to Britain from Rome arrived in only twenty-nine days. In 1834 Sir Robert Peel, rushing in person from Rome to London, required thirty days for the journey. By 1973 things were far less efficient. A letter from the U.S. Embassy in Rome took fifteen days, without the benefit of either postal strike or national holiday, to inch its way a whole twenty-five miles to its addressee.

In Roman times every ordinary foot traveler, who thanks to the Appia and its sister roads had few worries about being lost, bogged in mud or having to ford rivers, could make 20 to 30 miles a day. Wheeled vehicles did comparatively better or worse depending upon whether they were drawn by plodding oxen carrying heavy loads or fleet horses galloping along with light carriages. A rapid trip could be

*The way this bit of road looks now, with stones and some curbing still in place, but lost in weeds. The piazza foreground is still called the Piazza dei Paladini by the natives.*

a jolting one. Horace, having made fun of himself as a "slowpoke," added an implicit reason for his deliberateness: "The Appian Way is less rough if you take it in stages."

Least rough of all, from the standpoint of facilities and aid along the way, was the *cursus publicus,* or the official post, set up by Augustus. It was to serve the *res publica,* or the commonwealth, that the *mutationes* and *mansiones* were primarily designed. They were totally at the service of the imperial messengers and envoys, and they were obliged by imperial order to have both carriages and fresh steeds available day and night. *Mutationes* often had nothing but stalls and steeds, and enough slaves and workmen to make necessary repairs. *Mansiones* had spare vehicles, drivers, guides, porters, guards, and by law at least forty beasts, including horses, mules, donkeys. *Mansiones* were always on main roads, as often as possible in or near a sizable town.

Augustus based his *cursus publicus* upon earlier Persian and Greek models. The Persian kings regularly dispatched messengers on well-established routes and orderly time tables. The Greeks, whose system was less rigid, expected heroic feats of their running messengers. The 26-mile dash of Pheidippides from Marathon to Athens, bringing news of the Athenian victory over the Persians, gave the name of "marathon" forever to a moving event in the Olympic games and to all other feats of endurance. It was the Greek historian Herodotus who first penned, and saw turned to stone in all the centuries later, that tribute to the postmen and message bearers: "Neither snow, nor rain, nor gloom of night, stays these couriers from the swift completion of their appointed rounds."

Before the establishment of the *cursus publicus,* in Rome's earliest days and during the Republic, mail service was private. Anyone wishing to send a message could confide it, orally, to a trusted traveler headed in the proper direction, or could write it down and turn it over to a hired private postman. These men were called *tabellarii,* from the *tabellae,* or wax tablets, on which early communications were written with a stylus. When wax tablet and stylus gave way to parchment or papyrus scrolls, the name persisted. *Tabellarii* went most often on foot, and wore, as protection from sun and rain, a wide-brimmed headgear which Italians call the *petaso.* It looks familiar today because it is the very same hat which is always depicted on the head of Mercury, the wing-footed messenger of the gods.

Some *tabellarii* were retained permanently by a man of position or by a group of merchants. Others hung around the city gate, waiting for business, as scribes still congregate at the gates of Middle Eastern cities, and as taxis do around central points of arrival and departure all over the world. These messengers were hired by the day or by the mile. There was one free postal service, provided by the growing groups of Christian converts who trudged back and forth from the holy cities of the eastern Mediterranean to the new kingdom of Christ in Rome. All the great letters which constitute so much of the New Testament, the letters of Paul, of Peter, of John, were entrusted to the faithful who trod the Via Appia and the outlying roads of the Empire from Jerusalem to the "seven churches of Asia" in today's Turkey. The carrying of letters, of "the Word," became as much a hallmark of early Christianity as did the invocation of hospitality for the wanderers of the earth.

Julius Caesar organized his own corps of *tabellarii* to rush his personal and official correspondence back to Rome while he was conducting military campaigns abroad. These men must occasionally have carried letters from private citizens as well, because there is a letter from Cicero to his brother Quintus, who was serving with the Roman army in Gaul, which says that "When I arrive in Rome, I shall allow no letter-carrier of Caesar's to pass by without giving him a letter for you."

Private *tabellarii*, and later imperial ones as well, unless their messages were of extreme urgency, started from a central place as postmen do today and then separated according to their destinations and the shortest routes to them. They must have called sometimes at the houses of distinguished citizens who wrote many letters, because Cicero in another letter says with some annoyance that they were hurrying him. They wanted to get going, with the excuse that "their companions were waiting at the gate."

To travel in company, if they could, no doubt pleased the private postmen. They were not immune to the common hazards of the road and one of them once vanished completely in the wilds of Spain, "the forest of Castulo," where messengers were routinely stopped, searched, robbed and sometimes taken prisoner by bands of outlaws. Such inconveniences also occasionally made the postmen late. Seneca complained once that "I received [your letter] many months after it was sent off."

By Augustus' time the vague, disorganized private post was not adequate for a nation expanding in all directions. Not only personal letters but also letters of credit, commercial records, reports from captured territories, orders and receipts had to go through. Among the clamorers for a better service were the *publicani,* men who did business with the state as contractors for public works and/or supplies. Because senators in Rome were forbidden to engage in business, the *publicani* were drawn from the second social order, the equestrians, so called because though not rich enough to be senators, they were wealthy enough to own a horse. The collection of taxes and provision of supplies was farmed out to them in the provinces. Though Cicero referred to the *publicani* as "the flower of Roman knighthood, the strength and ornament of the State," their wider reputation was not so rosy. These are the "publicans" of Luke:

> Two men went up into the temple to pray; the one a Pharisee, and the other a publican. The Pharisee stood and prayed thus with himself, God, I thank thee, that I am not as other men are, extortioners, unjust, adulterers, or even as this publican. . . . And the publican, standing afar off, would not lift up so much as his eyes unto heaven, but smote upon his breast saying, God be merciful to me a sinner.

Poor taxpayers or unfortunate souls who had to deal with or borrow from the *publicani* tended to share Luke's opinion of them, not Cicero's. *Publicani* had urgent need of reliable, regular communication with Rome, and Augustus had need of *them.* At first Augustus' postal system seems to have been based on the establishment of runners along the road, men ready to rush off in relays to deliver either news or documents. Sometimes they carried the news only in their heads, like the runner from Marathon. There are no specific records of misinformation having arrived at Rome because of this method and its inherent possibilities of garbled words and names, panted hastily from one runner to another, but the possibility is infinite.

Next, for a time, the runners carried rolled-up scrolls and passed them, like the baton in a relay race, to the next postman. Augustus eventually changed this system too, in favor of the establishment of the *mutationes,* where the steeds could be changed instead of the messenger. Suetonius applauds the change: " . . . he kept in close touch with provincial affairs by relays of runners strung out at short intervals along the highways; later, he organized a chariot service, based on posting stations—which has proved the more satisfactory arrangement, because post-boys can be cross-examined on the situation as well as delivering written messages."

Augustus' messengers were drawn mainly from two groups of soldiers, young scouts or the centurions of legions, depending upon the urgency and responsibility of the mission. Private, nonimperial messengers often were drawn from the ranks of household slaves or freedmen for hire.

Both official messengers and some privileged private citizens, to whom the facilities of the *cursus publicus* were extended, had to carry a special document called a *diploma* or *diplomata*. The derivation of the word is "double folded," and it was a document never taken lightly by either issuer or holder. It required an imperial seal. Augustus began by using on his *diploma* seal the figure of the Sphinx. This seems an odd choice, an Egyptian symbol on an imperial Roman parchment, but perhaps Augustus wanted to relate to an empire older than his own. Or, perhaps, then as now, the Sphinx was an object of wonder. Later Augustus switched to a rendition of the head of Alexander the Great, another empire builder from another—Macedonian—foreign culture. Finally he settled upon a seal bearing his own image. Later emperors had no such trouble making up their minds: they all used their own images as seals, though some ceded their right of issuance to court clerks.

The *diploma* entitled its bearer not only to horses, vehicles and housing in the *mansiones,* it also entitled them to all this free. One of the few extant copies of such a document was recorded by a monk in Gaul in about A.D. 660. By this time *diplomae* had become known as *epistolae evictionis* because their bearers were entitled to clear the way of all impedimenta, including other clients, at both changing stations and post houses. According to the monk, a seventh-century *epistola evictionis* read as follows:

To all our officials at their posts of duty. Greetings:—

Know ye that we have delegated . . . . . . . , an illustrious gentleman, to be our legate and ambassador to. . . . . . . We therefore command you by these presents to aid his excellency, to provide and furnish his excellency with . . . . . . . horses, to collect such quantity of supplies as to him shall seem good and reasonable, in places proper and convenient; furnish . . . . . ordinary sumpter horses and. . . . .

From this point the document goes into a length of possible needs, each with a handy blank before it, to be filled in, presumably, by the bearer. It lists everything from "bread and hogsheads of wine" to sides of bacon, pounds of oil, of pickles, of honey, of cloves, to ricks of hay, oats and straw, and it concludes with the imperious words "Let everything be accomplished without delay."

Men have committed murder to lay their hands on documents less valuable than this, and it is inconceivable that their very existence failed to create both a black market and outright forgery. Cicero once sharply reproached a Roman magistrate whom he suspected of trafficking in *diplomae* for profit, and it is likely that in the earliest days of their use they were much more respected, and less grandiose, than they had become by the seventh century A.D.

Among honorable men in the early days of the Empire they were near-sacred. Pliny the Younger, to whom the world is indebted for its most vivid description of the destruction of Pompeii in 79 A.D., was serving as governor of the province of Bithynia, in Asia Minor, when he received word that his wife's uncle had died in Italy. As a provincial governor, Pliny had a *diploma*. Its rights did not extend to his wife, however, and even so august a citizen as Pliny was dubious about lending it to her so she could rush more quickly and easily back home to comfort her aunt. In the end he succumbed to wifely tears and implorations, and gave away his *diploma*. Then he sat right down and wrote a letter to the emperor. He explained the circumstances, apologized at length for his action, and was forgiven in a gentle letter.

"Thou didst well . . . in trusting to my good will," Trajan replied, "and in not waiting to consult me about furthering thy wife's journey by means of the diplomas which I granted to thy office, all the more as thy wife had to increase by speed the pleasure her arrival was to afford her aunt." In one more small way, the good Emperor Trajan had contributed to the ease and the speed of travel on the Via Appia.

The cost of all this special service was a source of constant turmoil. At first the expense was laid squarely upon the provincial administrations and regions through which the road went. Post station and *mutationes* directors passed the cost along to local taxpayers, and if they found themselves suddenly short of either horses or wine, they simply went to the nearest farm or resident and requisitioned what they needed. In the same way the costs of the passage of the *cursus clabularis,* the heavy cart carrying military hardware and equipment, were distributed. These vehicles, because of their slow and painful progress, were called *angariarae* and so, in time, were the administrators of the postal service itself, because of the heavy burden they put upon anyone who lived nearby.

At the end of the first century A.D. the Emperor Nerva transferred to the imperial treasury all the expenses of the *cursus publicus* and its way stations, and his successors Trajan and Hadrian continued the practice. Their efforts were often frustrated by local governors, however, who found tax collecting and requisitioning for the imperial post a handy means of skimming profits for themselves. The problems of payment had never been settled when the Empire fell, and the system fell with it.

While it lasted, however, the Roman postal system was a splendid institution. People wrote fewer letters then than now, but as historian Will Durant has pointed out, they wrote much better ones. Long, thoughtful, observant, carefully composed letters, saved centuries ago because they were literature, preserved today in anthologies and translations and compendiums, provide much of what the world knows of life when the couriers clattered down the road.

Letter writing then was an art, a diversion, a dedication, and perhaps because delivery was both personal and sometimes perilous, the writing of them was more prized. In the first century A.D. Seneca created a charming, spare vignette of a letter-writing traveler on the Via Appia: "Wearied with the discomfort rather than with the length of my journey, I have reached my Alban villa late at night. I find nothing in readiness except myself. So I am getting rid of fatigue at my writing table. . . ."

Written, rolled, sealed, letters like this then went off into the hands of the imperial deliverymen, waiting with valises packed, horses hitched, the emperor's orders in a special case. How grand it must have been to see them pass, cracking their whips to encourage the horses to haste: a fifth-century A.D. law forbade the use of "cudgels" for the same purpose. The clatter of hoofs or of thin swift carriage wheels carried for miles over the clear quiet landscape in which no automobile, no motorbike, no airplane intruded.

Ox-drawn vehicles, alerted by the commotion, moved placidly off to left or right to get out of the way. Horsemen reigned up and waited. Pedestrians bolted into the bushes. Elegantly costumed slaves, carrying on their shoulders the curtained litters of rich Roman ladies, stepped delicately aside with the superior but exasperated air of a chauffeur in uniform moving his Rolls-Royce from the path of a fire engine.

In the hurry, hurry, hurry of the Roman world, the post had to go through. The arrival of such a messenger or vehicle, at any outpost of the Empire, must have been like the sweaty, dusty, noisy, much-awaited arrival of a stagecoach in the American West, with every native within sight and sound congregated to see it. What tales would the driver have of troubles en route — robbers, hysterical maidens, bad guys riding out from behind the bushes?

Beyond all this, what a glorious, heady sense of contact with the larger world. No one could know what was inside the postman's bags, what news from far away. By the time of Trajan the Roman world stretched north through Spain and France to England. It included the Netherlands and parts of Germany, reached around the Mediterranean through Turkey and Palestine and the Arab nations of the Middle East. It spanned much of North Africa, and it had just taken over as a province a place called Dacia, part of modern Rumania. News could come from any one of these places: news of battles won, or beloved relatives lost. News of the welfare of colonists dispatched to help hold the line. News of triumph, news of disaster, other news, because the road went two ways, from home to the outposts and back again.

Athens to Rome was about 1,065 miles, partly by sea, but one letter carrier made it in twenty-one days. From Cilicia in the Middle East to Rome, a messenger took only forty-seven days to travel between 1,700 and 1,900 miles. From North Africa to Rome the distance was 400, 500 or 900 miles depending upon the route taken, but one man made it on the twenty-second day.

It seems odd that no ancient writer recorded, specifically, the scenes of chaos, excitement, abandon, upon the arrival of the post. It remained to Dante, in the thirteenth century, to capture the atmosphere: "As the multitude flock around a herald . . . to hear what news he brings, and in their haste tread one another down. . . ."

# VII
# THE MANY MEANS
# AND MISSIONS
# OF THE ROAD

Not everyone careened along the Appia at the speed of the post.
Hundreds of thousands moved more slowly, or more comfortably,
or more grandly. Romans were inquisitive by nature and migratory
by circumstance. By the time of the Empire they had set out to explore and settle a world whose horizons receded before them almost
faster than a good horse could gallop.

Travelers chose their vehicles according to personal taste, financial
resources and the nature of the mission on which they had em-
barked. Some walked, or rode horses and mules. Others were carried,
by fleet carriage or rumbling cart. Some went by chariot or by sedan
chair. Almost everyone, except soldiers and prisoners, had a slave or
two in attendance.

Some of these migrant processions became so ostentatious that the
writers, self-proclaimed watchdogs of public behavior, were outraged. Seneca protested that "Everyone now travels with Numidian

outriders preceding him, with a troop of slave-runners to clear the way. . . . Everyone now possesses mules that are laden with fragile crystal cups carved by skilled artists of great renown, for it is disgraceful for your baggage to be made up of that which can be rattled along without danger. Everyone has pages who ride with ointment covered faces; it is disgraceful for any of your attendant slave boys to show a healthy cheek, not covered with cosmetics."

Elaborate retinues were sometimes made mandatory by the rapid expansion of the Roman world. As tribes, cities, provinces fell to the legions south and east and then across the seas, civil and military governors found it prudent to travel in a style which would impress the subject peoples and would also protect them from recalcitrant or rebellious natives. The same retinue could carry with it both food and rudimentary lodging en route, thus avoiding the dangers of inns and other public facilities.

The Roman nobleman Milo, when making the short 21-mile trip on the Appia to his villa at Lanuvium, took along his wife, the household slaves, a few musicians to lighten the journey, and also coachmen and a bodyguard made up partly of sword-endowed gladiators.

Caligula lived up to his generally nasty reputation by taking troupes of dancers, courtesans and painted boys wherever he went. Nero, whose antics and excesses are entertaining to all who didn't have to live during his regime, customarily traveled with a train of a thousand carriages and mules shod with silver. His second wife, Poppaea, not to be outdone, had her steeds shod and harnessed with gold. She also had five hundred she-asses included in the retinue so that she could bathe nightly in their milk.

This kind of high-visibility trip on Rome's most traveled highway was, to some men, well worth the expense. Each elaborate procession, described and exaggerated and repeated by all who saw it pass or who heard about it later, was calculated to awe the peasantry, frighten potential enemies, create instant fame for the traveler and then pass into legend and folklore.

One of the best places for procession watching was just outside the walls of Rome. Here the tombs and monuments were worth a visit on any sunny holiday morning, and half the days of the year were holidays in ancient Rome. The idle, the curious, the tourists went out along the Appia with assurance of being dazzled by the monuments and with the hope of seeing a grand procession pass. Many of these sightseers trudged slowly on foot, their mantles pinned up at the shoulder to keep the hems out of the dust, their feet tucked into leather sandals with sturdy soles and laced uppers to protect their insteps and ankles. Some of the more prosperous rode, but they rode bareback. Until about 150 B.C. the use of covering for a horse's back was considered effeminate in Rome. Later, riders used lengths of cloth folded to a comfortable thickness, and later still the skins of lion or tiger. These pelts were both decorative and soft.

Women rode sideways, as much for comfort as for modesty. Romans had no equivalent to the modern saddle until the fourth century A.D. Riding sideways can be very comfortable. It allows a shift from north to south or east to west; it rests the legs and posterior; it is a riding posture often used today by aggressively male Turks who are forced to make long journeys on muleback.

Stirrups were not in general use in Rome until a century after the saddle. In their absence, men learned to mount their beasts by other means. Some steeds were trained to kneel on command, as a camel does. Agile horsemen leaped onto standing beasts with the aid of either a push from their lance shafts or a boost from friends or slaves. Along the Appia, as along other main roads, workmen installed mounting blocks of stone at intervals.

From any vantage point along the road, riders or walkers might see a nobleman trotting out from the city to his villa in the Alban Hills, or a bilious bibbler headed for the mud baths and curative waters of the hot-spring resorts to the south. Perhaps they would see a train of elegant embassy from across the sea, men glittering with the jewels of the Middle East, come to present their respects, or their complaints, or their tribute, to the rulers of Rome. Legations came from everywhere, their trains as elaborate as those of the Roman grandees. The philosopher Philo accompanied a Jewish delegation from Alexandria, Egypt, in the first century A.D. with a plea for the Emperor Caligula. Philo reported, with awe, that ambassadors from all the world were in waiting.

If perhaps the holiday sightseers were deprived of a procession, they could laugh at the ragtag passage of persons who felt they should take all their household goods with them when they moved.

Martial, whose comments could be cruel, wrote about the march of a man with his white-haired mother and his red-haired wife, taking with them "a three-legged truckle bed and a two-legged table, a lantern and a cracked chamberpot . . . making water through its broken side . . ."

Sometimes there was even the equivalent of a circus, because wild animals from Africa were shipped in thousands to Rome, to be killed in the Colosseum. They came by sea to Ostia, the port of Rome, to Tarentum, to Puteoli, and were trundled into the city in carts with heavy bars, attended by muscular slaves with whips and prods. Their passage, exotic though it would seem today, must have been common: when Titus opened the Colosseum in A.D. 80, five thousand beasts were slaughtered in a day. Even the enlightened Emperor Trajan conducted a series of games in A.D. 107 in which eleven thousand wild animals perished. Cicero wondered what pleasure it could be to any man of refinement, faced with the sight of beasts killing men or men bringing down magnificent beasts. His scruples were not widely shared, but to this day most Italians will flee in panic from a spitting cat or a barking dog, as if they suspected that the entire animal world may still harbor some resentment from the bad old days.

Not the least of the sights along the Appia was the passage of soldiers, marching off to distant provinces or returning from them. The soldiers marched grandly down it in ranks, with an officer strutting along the elevated sidewalk to keep an eye on his columns.

Rome's great road system is often described as military, but this is only partially true. When the soldiers made their first thrusts into new territory they could travel any track at all, any mule path or drovers' road or valley in the hills. They had no time, on early campaigns, to pause and build a road, as they did later all over Italy and the known world. It would have been far easier for them to move their equipment—the carts with baggage and supplies, the heavy catapults and battering rams—along a smooth road, but this movement was a later stage, a second stage in Rome's military domination.

Dinu Adamesteanu, an archaeologist in Italy, explains colorfully the relationship of the military to the road. "When the Roman army advanced, it cut through, *zan-zan*," he says, making a sharp chopping motion with his hand and forearm. "Then, when they had taken their objective, the rest of Roman influence came behind them. It spread out." Leaving his cutting hand still in the air, Adamesteanu moves his elbows outward, slowly. "It spread, like this. The Romans made colonies, made roads like the Appia, and then they made trade and commerce. Always they moved outward, outward, from the slash the legions made through the territory.

"The road came after the conquest. It was military, but it was a secondary military stage. The road made the conquest solid, bound it to Rome forever."

In the final analysis it was the vehicle, not the soldier or the conquest, which dictated the criteria of the road. Soldiers, or single travelers, had no particular need for a wide path, for a viaduct, or even for a bridge. When they arrived at a stream, they could wade, swim, ride logs or support themselves with inflated animal skins. But when vehicles began to follow the soldiers, to consolidate the conquest, they brought their own needs. To accommodate them, builders made viaducts across steep declivities, bridges across streams, retaining walls on the outside edges of mountain spurs.

The width, the surface, the gradient, all were dictated by the vehicle. Parts of the Appia were only eight feet wide, but most of it was built from ten to fifteen feet wide, specifically to accommodate wheels and carts. Though still a rudimentary science, vehicular engineering took note of the fact that wheeled vehicles were more efficient if they carried two persons side by side, and that draft animals worked better if harnessed in pairs or in a series of pairs. Thus the optimum width of a vehicle was established at about five feet, and the road was built to permit two vehicles of this width to pass.

Even the great cut at Tarracina was dictated in part by the needs of the vehicle. When the original "high Appia" went through, travel on the steep road up Mount Sant'Angelo was mostly military or commercial. The high, steep road could be navigated easily by troops or by the indigenous Roman vehicle known vaguely as the *vehiculum*, as general a term in Latin as "car" is in English, or the *currus*, a lighter, two-wheeled cart in which passengers rode standing up.

Four hundred years later, however, when Trajan made his time- and trouble-saving cut in the rock by the sea, vehicles were carrying the tender gentry instead of the rough soldiery or the indomitable merchant in search of his fortune. Both vehicles and passengers had become numerous, more sophisticated and less accustomed to submitting their fragile structures to the rattling of the rough old road.

Most of the newer, lighter carriages which supplemented the *vehiculum* and the *currus* on the roads were of Gallic design, from regions far north of Rome in what are now France, Belgium, the Netherlands, parts of Germany.

Rome imported not only the vehicles but also some of their specifications and nomenclature: Hilaire Belloc, a prolific Edwardian writer of history, satire and nonsense verse (*Cautionary Verses*), was also a road scholar. He pointed out that the word for the width of vehicles, "gauge," has no Latin equivalent. Belloc traced it to some old northern French versions of Latin, and found that it entered the English language in the Middle Ages when French was the educated tongue in England. Belloc believed, therefore, that "gauge" was of Gallic origin and that it entered Roman mind and usage, as a basic criterion for road construction, along with the Gallic carriage itself.

From the Gauls the Romans imported the design of the *cisium*, a trim two-wheeled cab which was light and swift and designed to carry two persons sitting, instead of standing. From them too came the *raeda*, an often splendidly decorated four-wheeled carriage with seats and luggage space enough for an entire family.

A *raeda* would have had difficulty climbing up the steep Appia track at Tarracina before Trajan's cut was made. But after that, hundreds of them must have swept grandly beside the sea, the wife and children excitedly looking from the view of the foaming surf on one side toward the Temple of Jove Anxur high above them on the other, the head of the household beaming at both the pleasure of his family and his own achievement in having bought, or hired, such a grand carriage.

Just past Trajan's cut the Appia turned inland to run through citrus-fruit orchards, gardens, rows of low bulbous cactus which Italians call "figs of India," and eucalyptus trees. Then it rose slightly to pass on the lee side of the Lake of Fundi, one of the largest coastal lakes of the peninsula.

Today in spring the air here is heavy with the scent of orange blossoms, as it was when the road first went through to reach Roman

*Portion of a frieze in the Roman Forum, showing a two wheeled cart pulled by horses*

Fundi. Fundi was a very old settlement which in 338 B.C. chose to join Rome and become an ally. It was a wise choice, for within three decades the road went through and carried with it all the commercial benefits of linkage with Rome. The route was chosen not so much to reward Fundi as to avoid a marsh which reached from the lake to the sea, but the result was the same. The marsh near Fundi was never drained in Roman times. Drainage work began there in the seventeenth century, under the aegis of the popes, and continued for almost three hundred years. It was wrecked by German troops in 1943, who broke the dams, returned the area to marsh and gave back to the low-lying plain the epidemic malaria from which the builders of both Fundi and the Via Appia had fled to the hills to avoid.

From Fundi the old road meandered gently up the Sant'Andrea Valley, with mountains on both sides, to reach a pass at the town of Itri. Itri's name comes from the Latin *iter*, "way" or "passage," and its location is smack on the single most logical and convenient place for the road to debouche from the hills and go down to the sea again at the site of the Roman city of Minturnae.

The modern Via Appia follows the same route, though it goes south on the left of the Sant'Andrea Valley between Fondi (as it is now called) and Itri. The original Appia went to the right of the valley. This ancient route, most of its stones and retaining walls intact, is clearly visible across the valley. It has been reduced to a mule path and it is marred by a line of concrete electricity poles, but it is there for more than three kilometers. The main street of modern Fondi is still called the Corso Appio Claudio, and as the present Appia enters Itri there is a long stretch of the old Appia, stones firmly in place, at the left edge of the highway. Also visible in Itri is the masonry of an ancient viaduct, built when the Appia was young, to lift carriages gently over a valley. Inclines of 15 or even 20 percent were sometimes permitted in the original Appia, because the gradient was tolerable to foot travelers or mule-drawn carts. But wherever possible, the builders eased the trip by viaduct, as they did in Aricia and in Itri.

It must have been a lovely ride, from Tarracina to Minturnae, in a *raeda*.

Even more sumptuous than the *raeda* was the *lectica*, a sort of horizontal sedan chair. This was not of Gallic origin, but rather of Oriental. It came into favor in Rome after the victory over King Antiochus of Syria in 190 B.C. Though it could be borne by horses, mules or donkeys, the *lectica* was most commonly carried on the shoulders of slaves. It became, quickly, a favorite of aristocratic ladies and wealthy, luxury-loving citizens. No wonder: it was fitted with a mattress for reclining, pillows and bolsters and cushions for achieving a range of comfortable horizontal-to-vertical positions, a leather top, draperies to the owner's taste, and side curtains which could be drawn against sun, dust or disrespectful glances from the peasantry.

*Lectica* carriers were selected for their height and handsomeness, the favorites being slaves from conquered provinces like Thrace, Bithynia, Syria. They hoisted the litter onto their shoulders on sturdy poles slipped through iron rings set in the rigid upper structure, and stepped along in their elaborate livery. Both brown and red were popular colors for livery, but a fine red wool from Canusium was considered the most chic.

In addition to the chair carriers themselves, the *lectica* was equipped with a crier who led the way, bawling out "Make way for my lord!" or "Clear the path for her ladyship!" and if her ladyship chose to travel by night there was a slave with a lantern marching bravely at the fore like a helpful London bobby leading motorists across Hyde Park Corner in a blinding fog.

The use of the *lectica* was frowned upon in some circles as far too frivolous and luxurious. Julius Caesar once set up elaborate restrictions which limited use of the *lectica* to certain persons, of a certain age, on certain days of the year. But this restriction, like so many others in both ancient and modern Rome, proved impossible to enforce owing to the overwhelming frequency of its daily infraction.

Caesar's rival Antony had no such qualms. He liked the *lectica,* and is alleged to have traveled once with eight of them: one for his own mistress and one each for the mistresses of the seven best friends who accompanied him.

There was, inevitably, snobbery at both ends of the scale of travel. Many overweening nobodies hired trains of carriages and part-time slaves to "raise a great dust" and satisfy their ego. This practice became so common that Romans made jokes about what would happen to the show-offs once they had completed their grand journeys. They would be so broke, the wags suggested, that they could never travel again except as gladiators or the paid fighters of wild animals in the arenas which lined the road they had once traveled with such great display and expense.

On the other end of the scale, many who could afford *lecticae* or processions chose to move with such modest accouterment that their progress along the road amounted to ostentation because of its austerity. One of these was Cato the Elder, a forbidding man who was accustomed to ride around on a mule even when he was a ruling magistrate of Rome in the second century B.C. Perhaps Cato shouldn't really count, for he was a man so critical of his fellows that he was nicknamed "Censorius." He hated innovations of all kinds, even for the sake of comfort.

Horace like going off quietly on a bobtailed mule. In one of his satires he made fun of the sort of man who went traveling "with five slaves walking behind . . . carrying jugs and chamberpots." As for himself, he said, "I can ride as far as Taranto, if I want to, on my little old donkey, the saddlebags chafing his flanks, the cowboy his back. And no one will call me a cheapskate."

Apuleius in the second century A.D. found other reasons for traveling simply and lightly: "Persons who had occasion to travel rapidly preferred to ride horseback than sit in a vehicle, on account of the annoyance of baggage, the weight of the coaches, the clogging of the wheels, the roughness of the roads, the piles of stones, the projecting roots of trees, the streams in the plains, and the declivities of the hills."

Then there were those who felt that they *should,* morally, eschew ostentation, the better to see the world and encounter their fellowmen. Seneca was one of these. He went off on a short trip with a friend carrying "no paraphernalia except what we wore on our persons" and with "very few slaves—one carriage load."

Seneca eventually took a seat in a farmer's cart, and like many a man after him discovered to his chagrin that the simple life is more appealing in theory than it is in practice. "Only by walking do the mules show that they are alive," he wrote. "The driver is barefoot, and not because it is summer either. I can scarcely force myself to wish that others shall think this cart mine . . . I blush in spite of

*A burdened horse, shown in the courtyard of the*
*archaeological museum in Capua.*

myself, proof that this conduct which I approve and applaud has not yet gained a firm and steadfast dwelling place within me."

Gallant to the end, Seneca knew that he was doing the correct thing even though he was miserable. To brighten his own spirits, and to defy anyone who might laugh at him for riding in a farmer's cart, he invoked the name and habits of Cato. "Oh how I would love to see him meet today on the road one of our coxcombs, with his outriders and Numidians, and a great cloud of dust before him! . . . Oh what a glory to the times in which he lived, for a general who had celebrated a triumph, a censor . . . to be content with a single nag, and with less than a whole nag at that. For part of the animal was preempted by the baggage. . . .

"Would you not therefore prefer Cato's steed, that single steed, saddleworn by Cato himself, to the coxcomb's whole retinue of plump ponies, Spanish cobs, and trotters?"

No answer to this stirring question is recorded, but it seems likely that it would have been a loud "No." Seneca's contemporaries, much as they loved to travel, had a notable reluctance to seek out discomfort when comfort was available.

The Emperor Claudius, for example, fitted up his favorite traveling carriage with a gaming table because he was so fond of dice. One of his successors, Commodus, had a vehicle with specially built swiveling seats so he could shift his position comfortably to take the sun, or get out of it, or simply alter his view of the passing scenery. Caesar carried on his expeditions tessellated marble slabs for the floor of his tent. His coeval Gaius Verres once carried along embossed silver plate. Other travel inventories included everything from zithers to money chests, masks for protecting the face from the sun, javelins and swords, and lard as a "preventive of weariness."

One of the largest vehicles on the Roman road was the *carruca dormitoria*, a primitive version of the camper or sleeping car. Closed, covered, heavy, and big enough to accommodate a bed inside, it could be used for transporting the sick, the wounded or the chronically sleepy. It was not customary at that time to travel by night, though one could arrange to do so by hiring fresh teams of beasts at the *mutationes* and by carrying in retinue an extra shift of slaves and drivers. Often the *dormitoria* doubled as an inn. It halted at night and its owner or renter simply slept in it, avoiding the inns and impositions of sudden descent upon friends or kinsmen along the way.

Along the 70-mile stretch of the Appia between Tarracina and Capua, there was little need for the *dormitoria* for overnight stops, for here were three *civitates,* small cities which could provide lodging. The first was the seaside city of Formiae, where the modern Appia still passes and where visitors are shown, on the outskirts, an enormous circular tower popularly called the Tomb of Cicero. Cicero had a villa here, and he was murdered here in 43 B.C. Having incurred the wrath of Antony because of his kind words for Caesar's assassins and his cruel words for Antony himself, Cicero was marked for murder. He tried to flee Rome by ship but got so seasick that he demanded to be put ashore at Formiae. When his executioners arrived, the poet stretched out his head to make it easier for them to lop it off. They took both his head and his writing hand—the right—back to Rome. Antony accepted the trophies with pleasure, and hung them in the Forum for the people to see. Judging by the circumstances of Cicero's death, it seems unlikely that his defenders would have been permitted to erect such a towering monument as "the Tomb of Cicero" near today's Formia. Yet the tower is there, and a villa attributed to him. Formia also has the ruins of a Roman theater, and on the sea, the moss-grown rocks of a fish hatchery which supplied the city in Cicero's time.

The second *civitas* along this reach of road was Minturnae. The Appia went straight through it, and remains of an aqueduct, an amphitheater, city gates, mosaic floors and columns are visible from the modern road just a few kilometers past Formia and a little town called Scauri. The Appia now runs straight through a broken section of aqueduct, with the amphitheater on the right, just before it crosses the Garagliano River, the Liris of the Romans.

The third *civitas* in this relatively short bit of road was Casilinum, today's Capua, where the Appia had to vault the Volturno River. The Volturno must have loomed like a Mississippi to the builders of the road, and they threw across it one of their finest bridges. After being restored repeatedly over the centuries, it was blown up in 1943. Now it is repaired and usable, but supplemented by a wider, modern, parallel bridge. Local traffic still crosses the Volturno on the old Appian bridge, but only the stubs of two rounded towers and a bit of retaining wall remain of the Roman construction.

Formiae, Minturnae and Casilinum were big enough to provide at their gates rental vehicles of all kinds, and beasts to pull them. Good horses were a luxury. Mules, donkeys, broken-down nags were the main horsepower of the road. Ponies, especially fat lively little Gallic ones, and dainty-hoofed wild asses, were affectations of the wealthy and were almost always privately owned.

Oxen provided the brute power which drew peasant carts and freight vehicles on the road: the *plaustrum,* which carried heavy merchandise; the two-wheeled *carrus,* which could drag along field artillery and military supplies; the *clabularis,* a sort of flour scoop on four wheels, open-sided, a curved rack in which the sick, wounded or discharged soldiers were laid out like limp sacks for the long trip home.

All classes, all professions, used the road. The Greek geographer Strabo went from the Black Sea to Ethiopia, from Armenia to Rome and back again in his search for information. Intelligent Roman youths went off to study at the schools of Alexandria and Carthage in Africa, Antioch in Syria, Tarsus in Cilicia. Cicero went to Greece on the Via Appia and then sent his son Marcus back there later, to study. This turned out to be an expensive gesture, not so much for the transport as for Marcus' passion—and lack of luck—at gambling. The physician Galen was always on the move in search of new medical information and local skills.

The most famous philosophers, according to Cicero, were constantly traveling, it being necessary in those vigorous times for philosophers to get out and look around instead of contemplating their navels.

There was also quite a lot of riffraff on the road. Quacks and fakers and purveyors of dubious potions and spells found it prudent to keep moving. One of them, Alexander Abonuteichus, turned up regularly in Rome behind his personally hired herald, one of the world's first advance men, who made a great noise and proclaimed to the gullible the reputation of his master.

Festivals, triumphs of generals, gladiatorial games in the arena, brought to Rome not only thousands of spectators but also a cloud of predators: petty thieves, pickpockets, acrobats, mimes, musicians, panders with troupes of girls. The girls, to the disgust of more strait-laced Romans, were as much in demand at great religious occasions as they were for savorers of the bloody gladiatorial events. Augurs trekked to Rome on these occasions, and fortunetellers, and what one Roman described as "swarms of artists, hovering about looking for a profitable place to land."

Though perhaps outnumbered by this shifting class of profiteers, the earnest merchant and the serious student counted most. They traveled soberly, joined by and saluting such other purposeful voyagers as voters, who had to get to Rome to cast their ballots, or provincial functionaries moving back and forth to receive and carry out administrative orders.

In summer the traffic was swollen by thousands who fled the city to escape heat and pestilence. Horace noted that people took good care not to stay in Rome during the burning months "which made so much work for the undertaker of funeral pomps and his black lictors."

Tired businessmen built villas in the country and rushed to them to forget the pressures of daily affairs. Lucretius in the first century A.D. described one of these commuters in terms which ring wryly familiar: "He rushes headlong to his villa as if hurrying to bring help to burning dwellings, [but] scarcely has he passed his threshold than he suddenly yawns, or falls into a heavy slumber, or seeks oblivion, or hastens back to town."

All travelers on the Appia were presented the marvelous scenery of the road as it skirted the Tyrrhenian Sea, and they must have marveled at the temples, arenas, bridges, viaducts, as the road reached Capua. But there were dull stretches. These contributed, almost by accident, to the increase of learning and to the invention of the world's first compact books.

Pliny the Elder, a prolific reader and writer, compiler of a priceless encyclopedia of natural history, used the boring bits of road to dictate to his secretary. His carriage was equipped with secretary, writing table, stylus, tablets, pens, parchment and texts which he was studying. On chilly days Pliny equipped the secretary with gloves, or with a long-sleeved toga considered too effeminate for ordinary men, so that the amanuensis could keep his hands and fingers sufficiently thawed to write legibly.

Along the same stretches of road where Pliny dictated, others read. Leisure for reading helped create the first pocket books, neatly bound parchment volumes which were far easier to handle on a trip than the long papyrus scrolls which were written on one side only and had to be held with both hands. Martial in the first century A.D. highly recommended these new compact volumes.

"Thou who dost wish my booklets to be with thee everywhere, and seekest them as companions on a long journey, buy them compressed into a small binding," he wrote. Then, generously, he added a plug for his fellow writer Cicero. If a sojourner took along one of the new compact volumes of Cicero, Martial said, he could have the exquisite pleasure of imagining that he actually was traveling in the company of that great man, all the way.

Just how easy it could have been to read, while jolting along the road on wooden wheels encased in iron rims, no ancient bookworm seems to have recorded. Not only were there no tires; the vehicles hadn't any kind of springs. The *lectica* provided the only jolt-free ride on the road.

Carriage harness was not too different from that of modern rigs. The Romans used both shafts and either pole or tongue, depending upon the number of beasts to be hitched, and they had brakes or drag chains to alleviate the strain of steep descents.

Some scholars have held that the four-wheeled Roman carts did not even have movable front axles, so that the beasts which pulled them had to drag the front wheels diagonally across the surface of the roadway when they came to a corner. Recent technical studies of Roman terminology and the description of vehicles have by now convinced most experts that the Romans were not so remiss. They had words which were the equivalent of "kingbolt" and "wheel plate," so it is likely that they knew the concept of movable axles and that their carriages could proceed, however jarringly, around curves and corners.

The friction of their passage, however, the passage of those relentless iron-rimmed wheels, hundreds and then thousands and then hundreds of thousands, eroded the strength of both the passengers and of the roadbed itself. A French traveler in the late 1600s complained of the road between Terracina and Itri because of its roughness ("We avoid it at the same time we admire it"), but already in Roman times the Appia had become a symbol not only of might and efficiency but also of erosion, of wear and tear.

No one wrote of this quality of the road more vividly than did the poet Ovid at the dawn of the Christian Era. Ovid, who had been a favorite of Roman society, was suddenly banished from the city for life by the Emperor Augustus in A.D. 9. The reason for his sentence has never been quite clear, though there was gossip at the time that it might have been his "indecent" love poetry.

Ovid was desolate in exile. Reaching for an image of erosion, of the wearing away of spirit and flesh far from his beloved Rome, he hit upon the example of the stones of the already three-hundred-year-old road, and in so doing he gave the Appia a new dimension:

> The plough is not more worn by constant use, nor the Via Appia ground by the curved wheels, than is my soul darkened by a series of misfortunes.

# VIII
# THE NETWORK

At first glance a map of the main roads of ancient Rome looks like a giant starfish, stark and clean on the landscape.

When details are added, however, the image changes to something more like an elongated sketch of the circulatory system of the human body, with Rome as its heart. The largest artery in the system is the Appia, but the growing body of Roman control was served by other main roads and by dozens of smaller ones. Many had existed for centuries, as footpaths or animal tracks; others were created to connect with the Appia as it was built. Sometimes the Appia itself split into alternate routes to service specific needs, or threw out from itself *deverticulum* roads as required.

The first 132 miles, from Rome to Capua, were crisscrossed from the beginning by small connecting *viae* to the nearby Via Latina, which ran roughly parallel to the Appia but farther inland. The Latina and the Appia met on the outskirts of Roman Casilinum and went to Capua together. There they were met by the Via Campana, which came up from the south, from the Greek-founded port of Puteoli near Naples and from Naples itself.

Capua was both target and terminus of Appius Claudius' road, but it didn't remain terminus for long. Within a decade, work began to reach Beneventum, and with Beneventum as a fortress to guard the route it was extended to Aeclanum and to Venusium in 291 B.C., and about fifty years later to the coast, at Brundisium.

Beneventum, which lay roughly halfway between Rome and Brundisium, had by the first century A.D. become a nodal point in the network, a collecting and rerouting place, the Chicago of its era, or the Jamaica, Long Island. At least five main roads met there. Most important was the Appia, which brought to Beneventum travelers from Rome, Aricia, Forum Appii, Tarracina, Fundi, Capua and points between, as well as those who had come up from the south on the Via Campana.

From Beneventum there was a choice of two roads to the east. One was the continuation of the Appia; the other was a road which went slightly north out of the city and then turned east to cross the mountains and connect the towns of Aecae, Herdonae, Canusium, Butuntum. This road arrived at the Adriatic Sea at Barium, then turned south to glide across the flat, easy plains of the seacoast and end at Brundisium from the north.

Strabo mentioned specifically the two routes by which one could go from Beneventum to Brundisium. In his time, and in Horace's, the "southern route," the original Appia, was preferred. The northern alternative was little more than a mule track, visible and passable, but far from comfortable. It was this mule track which Trajan improved and turned into the Via Appia Traiana. Though a few miles longer than the Appia, it took a shorter route through the mountains and had the advantage of easy going down that coastal plain. This was the one which cut one day's travel time from Beneventum to Brundisium.

There was also a third route east of Beneventum, for part of the distance, between Aeclanum and Canusium. Horace took it, through Trevicum and the present town of Ascoli Satriano, but the road does not appear in many itineraries.

For those wishing to go due south of Beneventum, a road ran through the modern towns of Altavilla, Avellino and Salerno to the sea, linking as it passed with connecting routes to the Appia and the Campana.

More important than any road in Beneventum's network except the Appia itself, however, was a track which started far north of the city in the territory of the Pentri tribes. This was the most celebrated of the great drovers' roads along which herdsmen encouraged their beasts from summer pasture in the hills down to Beneventum and from there east over the spine of the peninsula onto the benign, fertile plains of what Italians still call the *tavoliere di Puglia,* the tablelands of the province of Puglia.

Drovers' trails were often more than a hundred yards wide, great trampled tracks like scars across the countryside. Once the Romans had knitted Beneventum into the network, they set about to pave and improve the drovers' trail into a proper road. Work was done between 125 and 120 B.C. This road probably was called the Via Minucia, though it is not certain. Whatever it was called, it connected Beneventum with an enormous section of the inner peninsula and helped make the city a hub. The drovers' road probably was the oldest of all which eventually met there. There is no doubt that it was heavily used and well known when the town itself was called Malies, or Maloenton, a name which on the Roman tongue became Maluentum or Maleventum.

Though it may seem esoteric, the question of how a place called Maloenton could turn into Beneventum is one of the more charming scholarly puzzles presented by the Appia and its environs. Local legend has it that the town was founded by Diomedes, one of the Epigoni, a hero of the Trojan War. Diomedes escaped the general slaughter, set sail for home and was driven onto the Adriatic coast of Italy by a storm. There he founded the cities of Argyrippa and Maloenton, or Malies. Both modern Arpi and Benevento claim him as founder.

Diomedes may be a legend, but somebody founded a settlement at Beneventum in very ancient times. The site, on a broad plateau surrounded by hills and watered by two rivers called the Calore and the Sabato (the "heat" and the "Saturday," in Italian), was a natural spot for early habitation. Within it were little hills perfect for primitive defense positions, and around them the plateau stretched away for miles offering pasture and arable land, enough open space for defenders to sight an advancing enemy far away.

Remains of Bronze Age people from the eighth and seventh centuries B.C. have been excavated in the area. The first Roman reference to the place came in 297 B.C. when a consul was dispatched there,

*The Arch of Trajan, erected to commemorate the Via Appia Traiana.*

with an army, during the Samnite wars. The Romans called the people Hirpini, a tribe of the Samnite group. Coins found in the vicinity indicate that the Hirpini referred to their town as Malies, or Maloenton, in a Greek dialect. The term has been translated variously as a reference to some sort of plant, or as a word meaning "the return of the flocks."

PHOTO: ALINARI

136

Given the existence of that shepherd track from the north, and the fact that seasonally migrating herdsmen must have passed through Maloenton twice a year, going to and returning from winter pasture, the latter translation seems most logical. On Roman ears, the name fell as "Maleventum," much as the Indian name Che-kag-ong fell on the ears of seventeenth century explorers of North America as "Chicago."

In Latin, as in Italian, the prefix *male* means "bad," and the Romans couldn't abide such a description of anything they decided to make their own. So when they annexed the town as a colony in 268 B.C. they decreed in one grand gesture that its name should be called *bene,* "good." There is no indication that anything else was altered instantly, but perhaps Beneventum had a better image.

The above is the most often repeated explanation of the name change, but there are others. One is that in 275 B.C., seven years before it became a colony, Maleventum was the site of a Roman defeat of Pyrrhus, and that Rome renamed the town to celebrate the victory. The Greek historian Procopius in the sixth century A.D. provided an inventive explanation quite different from the others. Procopius said the name was changed to counteract an evil omen, an ill wind. There came out of Dalmatia, Yugoslavia, a *ventus* so ferocious, he said, that "when this begins to blow, it is impossible to find a man there who continues to travel on the road. . . . Such, indeed, is the force of the wind that it seizes a man on horseback together with his horse and carries him through the air to a great distance . . . And it so happens that Beneventus, being opposite to Dalmatia . . . and situated on a rather high ground gets some of the disadvantage of the same high wind." So the *male ventus* was decreed *bene ventus.*

Most famous of Benevento's stone memories of grand gone days is the Arch of Trajan, fifty-one feet high, decorated with sculptured scenes of the emperor's life. It was erected between A.D. 114 and 117 to commemorate both the man and the starting point of his new road, and it is as impressive as any of the triumphal arches of Rome itself. Trajan never saw the arch. He was killed in the eastern province of Cilicia, in a campaign against the Parthians, before the arch was finished.

.  .  .

*The bridge which originally carried the Via Appia into Beneventum, over the river Sabato. It still stands and carries traffic, though it is no longer on a main highway.*

Also in Benevento is a piece of the original paving of the Appia, and a statue of Diomedes, in the broad entrance of the Sannio Museum on a hill which probably was the acropolis in Roman times. There are remains of a small stone bridge called the Ponticello, by which the Appia Traiana left the city; a well-preserved second-century A.D. theater which once seated twenty thousand persons, and several bits of Roman wall and arched baths exposed by World War II bombings.

Most evocative of the remains is the bridge over the river Sabato, a humpbacked span of four arches set on heavy stone footings surmounted by brickwork. This was the bridge by which the original Appia entered the city. It is still used, though now it lies off all main routes to anywhere and is crossed only by pedestrians, tourists, bicyclists and a few neighborhood trucks. Its entrance, inside the city, is beside a dusty cement works. Now it is called the Ponte Leproso because in medieval times there was near it a hospital for loathsome or contagious diseases, perhaps leprosy.

No stones of the Appia remain on either side of the worn roadbed of the bridge, but the track is visible as it reaches off into the countryside. Some battered remnants of Roman construction are embedded in farmhouses, and five hundred yards beyond the bridge is the brick core of a Roman sepulcher, now adorned with a large plywood Jesus whose halo has a permanently burning single electric light bulb.

Much older than Jesus, or even the ruins on which his image has been installed, is a legend which may account for the name of the river, Sabato. According to this legend the witches of the whole area, from as far away as Naples, were accustomed to gather on a Sabbath night under a walnut tree on the riverbank. They met once a year and did wild dances under the tree. During their gyrations they cast spells, most particularly on beautiful young girls. A lively modern sculpture by Pericle Fazzini called "The Dance of the Witches" is exhibited in the Sannio Museum, and Benevento is in the heart of the producing area of the sweetish, yellow Italian liqueur called Strega—which means "witch."

When Rome began it was true that, as the world has said forever after, "all roads lead to Rome." The wandering tribesmen of pre-Rome were attracted to the site on the Tiber, the low-lying pasture lands, and by the little island, the Tiburtina, which formed a land bridge across the water. Much of the area was marshy, but from it rose the seven hills, easily defendable.

From all directions the tribes came, Etruscans from the north and west, Sabines from the east, Albans and Latini and Volsci from the south. They took the simplest, most natural routes and arrived at a common meeting ground on the bank of the river between the Aventine and Palatine hills. The place became a cattle market, still called the Foro Boario.

As the city grew, its heart remained in the market and the pattern of entrance and exit was established forever by the drovers' roads. Thus Rome is one of the few "Roman" cities in the world which has neither *cardus* nor *decumanus,* those rigid and geometrically laid out central thoroughfares designed to meet one another at right angles and form the framework of the classic grid pattern which became a trademark of Roman city planning. The mother city just developed, without plan, up and down the passageways of its peculiar hill-strewn and river-cut terrain, its whimsical and meandering form stamped into a permanent pattern by the bare feet and tough hoofs of its first residents and visitors.

When eventually the often-warring Etruscans, Sabines and Latins achieved an alliance inside the city, they moved the center slightly away from the river, north of the Palatine Hill, to the site of the Roman Forum. This area was both north and east of the old cattle market, and it forced a slight shift in most of the incoming tracks. The path which was to become the Appia could not be altered: it had always entered Rome to the east of the Tiber and thus had no need of the land bridge, the island. When the center moved to the Forum, the Appia was blocked from direct access by the mass of the Palatine Hill. Thus it never went straight into or out of the Forum, but instead skirted it to the south.

Far more important than a slight route dislocation when the center shifted was the dramatic change in the traffic pattern as a whole. What once had been an in-flowing pattern became a relentlessly outward one. Once all had sought Rome. Now Rome sought all: all the lands and peoples out beyond the city, all the excitement and the action, the opportunity for commerce and spoils, for knowledge and adventure on the edge of the Empire.

The footpaths of Rome's citizens and first immigrants were transformed to accommodate the outward flow as the city grew. Routes of dwellers to the south of Rome became the stabilized, marked, improved roads called Appia and Latina and Labicana. In 241 B.C. the censor Aurelius Cotta began improving a track the Etruscans had used to get south to Rome from their cities along the coast. It became the Via Aurelia, reaching north beyond Etruria to Pisa, Genoa and the Gallic tribes in France. Another Etruscan road became the Via Cassia, skirting the chain of volcanic lakes which stretches from Rome almost to Florence. The Sabines' salt road, from their hilly strongholds east of Rome to the sea, became the Via Salaria (from *sale*, salt, which they obtained from the sea).

In 220 B.C. Caius Flaminius opened the Via Flaminia north and east through the present towns of Narni, Terni and Spoleto. Many smaller, local roads were named for the towns to which they went: the Via Nomentana to Nomentum, the Tibertina to Tibur, the Tuscolana to Tusculum. When the great period of road building ended, there were nineteen, or twenty-one, or twenty-three, or twenty-seven specific road exits from Rome. Scholars cannot agree on the precise number.

So efficient was the concept of the road builders, so adapted to the needs and patterns of traffic that there were no major changes in the orientation of ancient Roman roads in Italy until the mid-twentieth century, when the great galumphing superhighways tore across the countryside. Even their routes didn't change the pattern very much: from high points on almost any *autostrada* the driver can see stretching somewhere near him the neat small line of some lesser asphalt road laid on foundations two thousand years old. The Aurelia is visible from parts of a northbound superhighway, still going past the Etruscan sites now called Cerveteri and Tarquinia; the Cassia crosses both Etruscan and Sabine country; the Salaria goes through the Sabine Hills; the Appia may be glimpsed from many a spot on the southern superroutes.

The old, now asphalt, roads bear neat numbers preceded by the initials SS for *strada statale,* state road. The Aurelia is SS 1, the Cassia SS 2, the Flaminia SS 3, the Appia SS 7. Many maps are marked only this way, but the Roman resident, native or foreign, almost always uses the old names if he wishes to make himself perfectly clear. "You take the Cassia . . ." he says, or "Leave Rome on the Appia, and then at Kilometer 35 you watch for . . ." Along these roads, Rome conquered the world. The principal ones, which have been called consular, or military, or praetorian, in an often-misleading effort to label them according to their uses or their builders, plunged to all the borders of the peninsula. When they arrived at water, their engineers paused briefly, built port facilities and leaped across to begin building on the other side. When they ran into enemies they subdued them, then put the vanquished to work extending the highways through what once had been their own lands.

The first highway the Romans built outside their own peninsula was an extension of the Via Appia called the Via Egnetia on the Balkan peninsula. Three Macedonian wars had won the territory for Rome, and in 145 B.C. the roadbuilders followed the legions. Straight across the sea from Brundisium they started toward Dyrrhachium and Thessalonica, and then Hebrus.

Spain, valued for its minerals, fell to the Romans and got a road from Gades (Cadiz) to Numantia and to the Pyrénées, where it joined a paved Roman road through Gaul to the mouth of the Rhône River.

It was an awesome performance. By A.D. 476, when the Roman Empire fell in the west, its roads crisscrossed Italy with more than 13,000 miles of highway. Rome had leaped its encircling waters to make 1,362 miles of road on the island of Sicily, 200 in Sardinia, 125 on Corsica. By land and across other seas it had knitted to Rome nations and peoples now encompassed by Yugoslavia, Rumania, Bulgaria, Greece, Turkey, Iran to the Caspian Sea and Iraq past the Euphrates. There were Roman roads to Jerusalem, to Antioch and Damascus and down through Israel and Jordan to Aquaba at the head of the Red Sea. There were roads across Spain, France, Switzerland, Holland, Belgium, West Germany and in the British Isles all the way to the Firth of Forth. In Africa, having used Sicily as a launching pad, Rome took the whole vast northern continental fringe and humbled Egypt. There were 1,500 miles of Roman road in Egypt, 9,348 in the rest of Africa from modern Tangiers and Algiers to ancient Carthage, across Tunisia and Libya to Alexandria.

Just how many miles there were is a figure impossible to calculate accurately so many centuries later. Scholars who study ancient itineraries, particularly the fourth-century Antonine one, arrive at a total of 372 main Roman roads, and a length of 53,658 Roman miles. These are enough miles to go one quarter of the way around the world, or twenty-two times across the United States.

In many areas, builders merely solidified, improved or enlarged, existing tracks as they had done at home. In England they raised embankments and dikes on the rain-soaked terrain and the existing tracks. Many Roman roads there were five to seven feet above the level of the farmlands through which they passed, and they bestowed the name "high road" upon many a provincial English main street still based on Roman construction.

In Greece, Persia, Egypt, most of the Middle East, the Romans found existing tracks. But it was the invader who stabilized them, organized them, threaded them patiently into the great network. Romans made roads as relentlessly and instinctively as the space spider Anita made cobwebs in the twentieth-century's orbiting Skylab. Neither Anita nor the Romans permitted any long-term disorientation, or inefficiency, just because they were far from home.

Also like Anita, the Romans worked to their own plan, for their own personal reasons. The road was a tool for conquest and profit; the interests of any city or citizen who lay between Rome and the ultimate objective were of no concern whatever. Many of the roads bypassed completely some settlements near its route. The road had a single-minded objective, and Rome saw no reason to detour simply for the convenience of adjacent communities.

Occasionally a by-passed city made such a row that Rome bent its own rules. When Trajan's time-saving new route was built from Beneventum to Brundisium, it cut off traffic from the thriving towns of Aeclanum and Venusium on the old Appia. Aeclanum, feeling itself thus unfairly isolated from the larger world, protested to the emperor himself. Venusium, hometown of Horace, had taken its lifeblood from the Appia for three hundred years and it, too, was outraged when long-distance traffic was diverted from the old Appia to the new. Between the two, they made such a fuss that Rome reacted, not by retracting any earlier decisions, but simply by building more roads. The Via Herdonitana and the Venusium-Herdoniae were constructed to plug the two cities back into the network between Beneventum and Herdoniae, an important city on the Appia Traiana. These new arteries both connected to the Via Herculia, which ran from Venusium straight down to Potentia, today's Potenza, west of the route of the Appia, to the Greek colony of Heraclea in the Italian instep. This interior route eventually linked with Milan and became an alternate highway on which a traveler could, if he wished, avoid Rome and the coast altogether.

Some cities larger than Aeclanum and Venusium were treated shabbily. An early extension of the Appia, for example, had gone from Brundisium to Hydruntum, a more southerly seaport. In passing, it helped make a city called Lupiae, modern Lecce, a thriving place, with a huge amphitheater, villas and outlying port facilities. When the port of Brundisium became big enough to provide the vital launching point for Greece and the East, the Brundisium–Hydruntum tract of the road was all but abandoned. Because it was no longer needed, Hydruntum was banished from the Roman mind, and Lupiae, caught in the middle, was left to wither.

Its Roman ruins and some later Baroque architecture nowadays attract visitors, and in the seventeenth century the citizens persuaded the city fathers of Brindisi to give them the broken pieces of the terminal marker columns of the Appia on the Adriatic, to help re-establish Lecce's position as a once-grand stop on the route of the road.

Rome had no interest whatever in connecting its far-flung cities or colonies one to another. Such linkage would have made it easier for them to band together and revolt against Rome. And that was definitely not the point. These were days when the thrust and impetus made all roads lead *from* Rome, but the network was also designed to lead straight back home again with no dalliance, political or military, along the way.

Yet ideas traveled along the network of roads, as did growing knowledge, and understanding. The roads created a kind of world citizenship, and in some periods, peace.

Professor W. M. Ramsay, a Biblical scholar, wrote that "Christianity spread first along the great roads that led to Rome, as every free and natural current of thought naturally did, owing to the circumstances of the period, and from the center was redistributed to the outlying parts of the Empire . . ."

In A.D. 70 a Roman general could address restive Gallic troops in reasonable, fellow-citizen terms: "All is common between us. You often command our legions, you govern these and other provinces. There is no privilege, no exclusion."

Aristides of Smyrna in the second century A.D. penned a paean to Rome as seen through her roads and the Roman peace. "Could not every man go whither he would, without fear? Are not all harbors busy, are not mountains safe as cities? Is there not the same charm in all fields, whence Dread has vanished? There are no streams impassable, no locked gulfs . . . Hellenes and barbarians may wander from their own homes to arrive at their own homes; the Cilician Gates, the narrow sandy roads to Egypt through Arabia, present no terrors of mountain pass, torrents or savages; to be the Emperor's subject, to be a Roman, is the one talisman."

Aristides was particularly enthusiastic because the Emperor Marcus Aurelius had just ordered the rebuilding of the writer's native city, Smyrna, after a disastrous earthquake had leveled it in A.D. 178, but he could hardly stop gushing: "You have measured the earth, bridged the rivers, made roads through the mountains, peopled the deserts, and enobled all things . . . opened every gate and given every man his freedom, to see all with his own eyes."

One of the most important contributions of the road network, for Western civilization, was the opportunity it afforded a man to "see with his own eyes." Tourism as we know it began with the Romans. Once the roads were there, and a relative security of passage, people went sightseeing by the thousands. Plutarch mentioned "globe-trotters" who spent their entire lives rushing around the world just to see what was there, and Seneca noted that "Many people make long voyages to see some remote sight."

Roman tourists were impelled by the same motives that apply today; they even saw many of the same things. They watched Egyptian peasants scramble barefoot up the sides of the pyramids, a feat more difficult then than now because most pyramids still had their outer covering of smooth, trimly fitted, very slippery stone.

As we go to Rome, they went to Troy, scene of the most familiar epic of their world. Homer was to the Romans what Shakespeare is to moderns. Roman tourists went to Athens to view the Acropolis, and to Delphi, where the great oracle lived. They saw the Colossos of Rhodes, and the canal at Corinth. They toured the temples as we tour museums, for temples then were repositories of the finest art, the books, the technological advances of the age.

Sites of myth and legend were most popular of all. Tourists were solemnly shown the prow of Odysseus' ship, or the very eggshell from which Helen of Troy was hatched, her mother having been visited by the god Zeus in the form of a swan.

Like Mark Twain, they were not always convinced. In the second century A.D. Lucian remarked, with no ill humor: "Abolish fabulous tales from Greece and the guides there would die of starvation." Lucian knew his tourists, however: "No one wants to hear the bald facts, even for nothing . . ."

Guideposts to foreign cities and sites existed very early. In the second century B.C. there were guides to Troy, to Sparta, to the Athenian Acropolis. Four hundred years later, the Greek geographer Pausanias had produced a detailed and quite reliable *Description of Greece*. Copies were rare and expensive. Most Roman tourists must have consulted them in libraries, then gone off on their journeys to fling themselves upon the mercies of local guides. The reputation of these worthies was not much higher than that of innkeepers back home. "Zeus protect me from your guides at Olympia, and you, Athena, from yours at Athens," one satirist wrote. Plutarch, a patient man, wrote a satire about a group of tourists in Delphi, and made one character remark: "'The guides went through their standard speech, paying no attention at all to our entreaties that he cut his talk short.'"

For every tourist who went out from Rome to see with his own eyes, there was someone going in the other direction along the network, aiming to see Rome or to emigrate to it. Though never an egalitarian society, Rome was an open one. There was no attempt to exclude foreigners of any origin; citizenship was extended freely. Even slaves were often granted freedom, or permitted to purchase it. From about 58 B.C. Rome provided a monthly ration of ten gallons of grain, free, to all who wanted it. This largesse was a ploy for popularity on the part of the rulers, and they added to it free entertainment in the arenas, the "bread and circuses" of fact and legend. It was the writer Juvenal who gave the system its name, *panem et circenses,* and he complained that it attracted idlers by the thousands. The Syrian river Orontes had, Juvenal said, "emptied itself in to the Tiber." Tacitus referred to Rome as "the cesspool of the world."

The thousands of foreigners, or new citizens, in the "cesspool" were invaluable to the expanding life of the city. Upper-class Romans disdained trade as beneath their dignity, and senators were expressly forbidden to engage in commerce. They were expected to have family lands and funds, and to remain always above the temptations of bribery or commerce.

Into the business breach rushed Romans of Greek, Levantine and African descent, men not hampered by aristocratic or wealthy plebeian origins, men content to make a little by trading a lot. They prospered, and they became the most numerous civilian users of the roads.

Roman subsoil contained no gold and no coal. It had a little silver, and small deposits of iron ore. Yet, fattened by the tribute of conquest, Romans were rich. In the halcyon days they ordered grain and oil from Africa, gems from the Middle East, woodwork from Sicily. In the area of today's central Turkey a whole school of Greek sculpture grew up in a city called Aphrodisias, to supply the demand of the Roman aristocracy for decorations for home, garden, grave. Greek marbles and Greek sculptors were imported to create statues and mobiles, funerary busts and filigrees, for the villas of the rich and the pleasure palaces of the emperors.

Merchants hawked abroad such Roman products as sulfur matches, pottery, wine, oil and glass. They exchanged wares from Britain to the Euphrates River, from the Nile to the Caucasus. The result was a richness of variety unmatched for centuries.

This volume of commercial traffic demanded a stabilized medium of exchange. Though Rome did not invent currency, it set up a system, as it had done with so many other usages and amenities of its world. The first Roman unit of exchange had been an animal, usually a cow or a sheep, which could be weighed and measured and then, most conveniently, made to move under its own power from seller to purchaser. This simple method was replaced by the use of metals, copper first. Each copper chunk had to be weighed and evaluated, a process called in Latin *aes tumare*, "to value copper." From it comes our word "estimate."

The transition from animals on the hoof to elementary coinage was eased by the device of stamping on the copper, in the early days, images of a cow, a sheep or some other beast.

Before long, even this currency was refined. Its basic unit became an *as*, one pound of copper. Very soon it was devalued. Pliny noted that even in the busy, ambitious, relatively honest years of the Republic, Rome was forced to reduce the value of the *as* from one full pound to only two ounces. He did not describe the effect of this stunning devaluation upon the life savings and daily budgets of retired citizens or workingmen on fixed incomes. He noted only that the public debt had been eliminated in one fell swoop.

Merchants and traders trekking along the roads found it inconvenient to carry even this devalued currency. Bulky copper ingots or bags of coins overloaded their beasts of burden, and were an invitation to armed robbery en route. To replace them, the Romans issued letters of credit. Wandering merchants could deposit money at home, obtain a receipt, and exchange it for cash or equivalent goods in any principal outpost of the Empire.

Trade and commerce required not only careful financial calculation but also acts of specific courage: the repeated embarkation upon water. Rome, unlike most of the great cities of the ancient world, lay inland. It had a port, but it was an inland city. Never did it quite shake off its fear and distrust of water. Even today, though its young athletes win gold medals in aquatic events in the Olympics, Rome has more residents who cannot swim than those who can. However crowded a Roman beach may be in August, there is always lots of room in the water. The natives are lying safely on the sand, stimulated by the ripples but unthreatened by the breakers.

No Roman expressed the common fear more eloquently than Seneca:

> You can persuade me into almost anything now, for I was recently persuaded to travel by water. We cast off when the sea was lazily smooth; the sky, to be sure, was heavy with nasty clouds. . . . Still I thought that the few miles between Puteoli and dead Parthenope [Naples] might be run off in quick time. . . . When we were so far out that it made little difference to me whether I returned or kept on, the calm weather . . . came to naught. . . . I began to ask the pilot to put me ashore somewhere; he replied that the coast was rough . . . but I was suffering too grievously to think of the danger. . . . Clad as I was in my cloak I let myself down into the sea . . . scrambling over the rocks, searching out the path . . .

Seneca saved his most devastating indictment of the sea for the end:

> You may be sure that the reason why Ulysses was ship-wrecked upon every possible occasion was not so much because the sea-god was angry with him from birth; he was simply subject to sea-sickness.

Even when the journey held no real peril at all, Romans didn't like boats, or ports, or sailors, or water. Horace took a little barge along the canal which ran parallel to the Appia in the Pontine Marshes, and he found this one little bit the most unhappy experience of the whole trip. "Never take a night boat, reader," he counseled. "You spend the first hour paying fares and hitching up the mules. Then fearless mosquitoes and resonant swamp frogs keep sleep safely at bay. A sailor and a passenger, soused with cheap wine, compete in songs to their absent girl friends. The mule driver finally drops off to sleep; the lazy driver lets the mules browse, fastens the rope to a rock, stretches out, and snores. Dawn was already at hand before we observed that the boat hadn't moved an inch."

Accounts like this did not encourage the Romans either to travel by sea or to become sailors. Neither did the seas. The placid Mediterranean, the Ionian, the Adriatic, could and did turn malevolent in minutes, with little warning. Tales of shipwreck, of death by drowning, were repeated wherever travelers gathered. Everybody from Diomedes to Ulysses to the apostle Paul had been shipwrecked or blown off course in efforts either to get to Rome or to avoid it.

Two hundred supply ships once foundered in the Roman port of Ostia in a gale. The Tiber repeatedly silted full and marooned ships bringing grain to the city. Sea travel was banned, except in emergencies, for almost half the year—from November through April—because of the vagaries of current, wind and weather. Ship captains and crews who dared dangerous passage in winter were given the equivalent of combat pay.

Romans who could escape sea service did so. The fleet's sailors were mainly Greeks, Phoenicians and Africans, men who didn't get seasick easily and who had made friends with water. Native Romans, safe on shore, perfected the commercial facilities of the ports and almost totally destroyed their own principal natural resource, forests, to build more ships for others to sail. The forests which once rose across the peninsula, up the slopes of the spiny ridge of the Apennines, down to the seas, were cut down by consuls, emperors, popes. Now the slopes are mostly rock, and good wood in the land of the Romans costs more than marble.

The principal Roman contribution to maritime matters was the perfection of the grapple, a tool for fastening suspendable landing ramps across which soldiers could move from one boat to another in combat. Roman soldiers liked it and used it to good effect.

The ship was, to Romans, only an instrument for moving from one road to another. It could all seem a dream today, except for the stones strewn across the lands of the Mediterranean. Roman roadbeds appear in the sand when the wind blows hard in North Africa. They emerge from the sea in Israel. They are dug up, lovingly, by archaeology students in England. There is a bridge still over a Roman road in the wilds of Eastern Turkey. It crosses a tributary of the Euphrates, the only viable bridge in the valley, still in use.

To get to these places the Romans had to swallow their fear of the sea, and set sail.

"IN ROME THE TRUE ARTIST IS THE ENGINEER."

Edith Hamilton, *The Roman Way*

"[THE APPIA STONES] WERE FASTENED TOGETHER SO SE-
CURELY AND THE JOINTS WERE SO FIRMLY CLOSED THAT
THEY GIVE THE APPEARANCE . . . NOT OF BEING FITTED
TOGETHER, BUT OF HAVING GROWN TOGETHER."

Procopius A.D. 490–562

# IX
# OF THE GROMA,
# AGRIMENSORES
# AND CONSTRUCTION

The Greek historian Procopius' respect for the excellent preservation
of the Via Appia almost nine hundred years after it was built has
been echoed through all the ensuing fourteen hundred years by both
tourists and engineers.

Some popular legends about the road—that it always went dead
straight, that it was as thick and rigid as a stone wall lying on its
side—were exploded the moment real research on it began more than
a century ago. It didn't always go straight. It made detours when
constrained to, up or down river valleys in search of a convenient
crossing, through mountain passes. Neither was it always of stone, or
always thick.

Building a long-distance road on the Italian peninsula was not at
all like laying one across the great plains of the United States. The
terrain of Italy is a rugged one, rearing and plunging alternately
toward the brilliant sky and the glittering sea, cut by the billions of

gallons of water which for thousands of years have rushed headlong from one to the other. It has been subject forever to earthquake and volcanic explosions, disturbances which both throw up obstacles to construction and then threaten, later, to shake it to pieces.

These physical circumstances impelled the Romans to build heavily when they could, imaginatively when they couldn't. They knew little about stress factors and load-weight distributions, and they had no real need for patterns of traffic dispersal. Their aim was simply to get where they wanted to go, by the simplest and most practical means.

Modern highway engineers are mildly critical of the steep gradients built into Roman roads, and of the sometimes very sharp curves. Yet once a bend was made, the Roman engineers contrived to bring the route unerringly back to a straight line on the other side, and they reduced gradients by viaducts and fill. A municipal Roman law regarding pavement sums up the national attitude toward roads simply and insouciantly. The work, decreed the *Lex Iulia Municipalis,* was to be done in *lapides perpetui.* In a word, for always. By most measurable human terms, the road builders succeeded.

Just how they did it has been a matter for endless speculation. One of the most important sources of information is Vitruvius, who worked in construction all his life. In his old age he received a pension, thanks to the intervention of the Emperor Augustus' sister Octavia, and settled down to pour out all his knowledge in the ten-book *De Architectura.* One of the subjects to which he devoted page after page was the matter of building a firm and "perpetual" sustaining floor for a large structure like an apartment house.

In this as in all man-made installations, including a road, one must begin with the earth itself. If the *terra* is sufficiently *firma,* Vitruvius pointed out, one needed only to level it to begin work. Upon this was laid a *statumen* of stones slightly larger than the size of a fist. The *statumen* was reinforced with a mixture of broken brick rubble and lime, and then "rammed": pounded with wooden hammers. Vitruvius recommended that it should be rammed until it was only three quarters of its original thickness.

On it went the *rudus,* a water-tight layer of random material bound with mortar. Above the *rudus* went the *nucleus,* a layer of gravel and concrete, and on top of that was the surface itself, called *pavimentum* or *summum dorsum,* made of cut and fitted lava rock, flint, marble, or other very hard material.

Scrupulous execution of this whole process would produce a floor, or a road, four or five feet deep, truly a wall lying down. Vitruvius' formula was studied and meticulously tested by one of the first students of the Roman roads, a French lawyer called Nicolas Bergier, in the seventeenth century. Bergier became fascinated by the remains of Roman roads near Rheims, and he devoted years to tracing them, analyzing their composition, studying the ancient sources. In 1622 he produced his monumental *History of the Great Roads of the Roman Empire.* The book influenced French highway engineering through all of the seventeenth and eighteenth centuries, and became a source for all later scholars of Roman roads.

Bergier knew perfectly well that Vitruvius' description was for floors, not for roads, but he had found four layers in the structure of some well-preserved Roman roads in France, so he adopted Vitruvius' nomenclature of *statumen, rudus, nucleus* and *pavimentum.*

Conflicting evidence came from Italy in 1813, shortly after a papal reconstruction of sections of the Via Appia across the Pontine Marshes. A Vatican chief engineer made a deep cutting across the bed of the old road and examined it carefully. At the bottom there was a layer of gravelly earth probably brought from the mountains just inland of the road. On top of this layer were big limestone curbing blocks set up to hold a fill of rock conglomerate. Over the conglomerate was a compact mass of stones of various sizes, all held in place by another curb. The smooth upper layer had vanished, having been removed successively by workmen who repaired and remade the road during the centuries.

There was no trace of cement of any kind, nor even of clear layers of mortared masonry. Yet this was a road through swamp, and parts of it had been supported by wooden piles driven laboriously well down into the muck. If the Romans hadn't used cement and mortar and sophisticated techniques here, where would they have used them?

The logical answer is that the road builders used a variety of techniques depending not only on the terrain but also on the state of their art when they were building, the condition of the national treasury, the availability of raw material and labor, and that old devil expediency. Most of the Roman roads, in Italy and abroad, were built between 300 B.C. and A.D. 200. It seems a short time in retrospect, but it was a long time—time enough for technological advance, for experiments with method and material.

Many sections of the Appia as it went southeast from Beneventum across the windswept reaches of Apulia required no more "construction" than a purposeful scraping away of vegetation which adhered to rocky outcrops on the surface. Once the slippery weeds and roots were removed, the rock itself was an all-weather road. On exposed rocky surfaces in Puglia the grooves and marks of Roman wheels still lie.

Other, less stable, sections could be made passable simply by adding a layer of gravel and holding it in place with stone curbs. Near Canusium on the Appia Traiana the Romans made cuts through the surface soil to find a solid base, and then buttressed with stone the walls of the cut. They did not normally, as earlier road builders had done, make artificial cart tracks in their roads, though on some mountain tracks they cut grooves so that traffic could attain purchase and guidance and not slide over a precipice or into a valley.

One research problem is that the Appia, like other ancient roads, has been pillaged for centuries by invading armies, later road gangs, and larcenous landowners who liked old stones, but there has been very little excavation with the simple aim of knowledge. A stretch of the Via Flaminia, built a few years later than the Appia, was taken apart 150 years ago. It proved to have been laid on eight inches of clay and rock, packed well together but not cemented. On top of it was a second layer of stones and chunks, held together with clayey soil, also about eight inches thick. The traveling surface had been made of big polygonal blocks of basalt.

A short bit of the Appia, where it crossed the present asphalt road just outside of Itri, was also taken up and examined. Its surface was basalt, the blocks carefully cut and firmly fixed between two rows of worked curbstones, but the surface lay crudely upon limestone wedges set in a bed of sand. No four layers here. Obviously they weren't needed; this road remained firm and secure until it was so rudely interrupted a couple of centuries ago by a modern highway.

When the Appia entered or left major cities, or crossed difficult terrain, it was more deeply and elaborately laid than elsewhere. These special stretches, fitted with beautifully cut blocks like those just south of Rome, have established in the modern mind the pattern, the typical appearance, of the Queen of Roads. This is the pavement so

*A section of the road between Fondi and Itri, south of Terracina. Beginning left foreground and reaching off into the valley is the route of the old Appia. At the right of the valley is the present road, SS 7, the modern Appia.*

much photographed, eulogized, analyzed. The native material is a gray volcanic stone which the Romans called *silex* and we call basalt. There were tons of it, mountains of it, on the slopes of extinct volcanoes near Rome. It is impervious to water and resistant to wear. Even the iron-shod wheels of ancient carts and carriages, so much more brutal than today's rubber tires, took centuries to wear a mark into it, and when they did, the mark came mainly at weak spots, joints or depressions.

Here pressure could crack; water, frost, ice could split the stone. Here puddles still collect on rainy days, while the surrounding surface washes clean and clear and glistens in the sunlight as it did when it was first set in place.

This was the surface, the joining, which Procopius admired. Special masons were hired to cut and fit it. The blocks were large, some three or four feet across, eight to twelve to twenty-four inches deep. Their bottoms were chipped in a diamond cut to seat them firmly into the foundation and to permit surfaces to touch smoothly. Cutting chips were used as both wedges and fill to hold the big blocks more securely.

Roads dressed this way were beautiful and almost indestructible. They were also very expensive, and they carried within their structure a defect: rigidity. "If so rigid a road became disturbed in any way, if the blocks slipped, then the surface could be worse than no pavement at all," says the Autostrade's Daniele Sterpos. "Two inches, four inches, five inches between blocks of paving could have destroyed the carriage wheels."

A French traveler of the seventeenth century, Maximillian Misson, noted the same defect. Misson was going from Rome to Capua on the Appia, and though he was aware of "the changes which the passage of time bring to the surface of the earth," he objected to the jolting ride between Terracina and Fondi. Here, he said, the surface was hard and impossibly rough because of the "separation of the bits of stone paving. . . . We take care to avoid this stretch at the same time we admire its *permanence.*"

Appius Claudius' original road was gravel until about 296–293 when a pair of aediles paved the first mile of it, to the Temple of Mars, with slabs of a speckled gray stone called *peperino*. Later on, basalt pavement was laid to Bovillae, and in about 191 B.C. the first mile was redone in the same material.

The best description of the work scene, the processes of construction, comes not from the engineer Vitruvius but from the poet Statius, the same man who named the Appia the Queen of Roads. Statius watched workmen building the Via Domitiana, which connected with the Appia in A.D. 95 near Roman Sinuessa, today's Mondragone, and from there ran near the coast to the port of Puteoli. The Domitiana may have been a special case, but every road in the Roman world was a special case. Statius' description is convincing:

> Oh! how many gangs are at work together! Some cut down the forest and strip the mountain-sides, some plane down beams and boulders with iron; others bind the stones together, and interweave the work with baked sand and dirty tufa; others by dint of toil dry up the thirsty pools, and lead far away the lesser streams.

Builders like these used footpaths and drovers' tracks to get themselves and their equipment to the construction site. From there they cleared the terrain, marked out the confines of the road, and ploughed parallel furrows to mark it. Hordes of laborers dug and leveled, and prepared drainage canals on both sides.

Roman road builders clearly had learned the importance of drainage, and how to grapple with it. They built water easements beside the roads, with inlets and outlets at regular intervals. They made cut log and stone dams to divert streams into new channels away from the roadbed. They directed spring water into fountains serving man and beast, and they devised a simple ingenious system for the convenience of the thirsty: the lead downspouts of Roman drinking fountains all have a hole at the top. Anyone wanting a drink has only to plug the spout with his finger, and the water will shoot upward out of the hole at handy drinking level.

Statius' description of the whole process says that once the terrain was leveled and the water diverted, workmen threw in a fill of resistant material—broken bricks, pebbles, gravel—and then gangs of "rammers" pounded with wooden mallets or pushed stone rollers to compress it. Each edge was secured with blocks of stone and hammered-in rock wedges.

Mortar was not a Roman invention. It was introduced by Greek engineers in the colonies of Magna Graecia in the Italian south, about the fourth century B.C. Greeks discovered that a lime mortar could be used to bind cheap materials like gravel into a hard surface. The Romans quickly learned the technique, and then organized it so efficiently that they produced both lime and lime mortar on a near-industrial scale, manufacturing as much as they wanted or needed for construction.

Shortly after this, they discovered that they had a natural mortar in their own soil, the powdery trass or volcanic tuff which blanketed the slopes of extinct volcanoes. It was first discovered near the old port of Puteoli, and therefore was called *puzzolana*, though it turned up later in abundance all across the Roman Campagna and in Sabine country. So excellent is this material that it is still used, though now called *pozzolana*. The Roman road builders could make any quality of cast concrete they required, just by adding differing kinds and qualities of gravel, chips and stone, and ramming the mixture to the desired thickness. A gravel-based concrete called *caementum* became popular for road building. Analysis of the material proves that mortar and stone mixed this way is as tough as today's Portland concrete.

American road builders were so impressed by the Roman exploit that the Department of Agriculture's Bureau of Public Roads commissioned a detailed research in the 1930s and then built a meticulous model of a Roman road. The original, eight feet long and four feet wide, is in a depository at the Smithsonian Institution in Washington. Copies in New York and Chicago museums have been removed from public view, but both photographs and diagrams exist.

In the reconstruction, three men stand in the foreground directing the work. One is the boss, probably a bureaucrat. One is the contractor, the third the *architectus.* He has rolled-up plans in his hand. Near him is an engineer aligning, with a *groma,* a directional stake being driven into the ground. Another man runs levels with a *chorobates.* Excavators on the roadbed use shovels and an instrument which was a combination mattock and pick. They load waste material into woven baskets carried by porters.

Mortar workers sit on low stools, wielding long trowels, supplied by carriers with two-man hods. Water to slake the lime comes from wooden troughs from a nearby stream, its supply supplemented by porters with earthenware water jugs on their heads.

Masons use chisels, mallets, wedges, adzes, saws, to work the stone. Heavy chunks are suspended from poles balanced on the shoulders of porters. Workmen use crowbars to manhandle rocks into position, and rakes to smooth the mortar.

The center of the roadbed, called the *agger* (from *aggerare*, to "pile up"), rises several inches above the height of the sides. This was primarily a drainage device, but it also served to change the height level of the inside hubs of chariots and carriages as they passed, to avoid collision.

Precise in every researchable detail, the Smithsonian model tactfully does not identify the workmen. Road building was hard, and its accomplishment fell to those least able to protest. Slaves, convicts, soldiers were most often committed to this kind of public service.

When Pliny the Younger was sent as warrior and governor to an eastern province of the Empire, he asked his emperor what to do about all the prisoners and convicts he collected. Trajan advised him to put them to work building roads. The idle and unemployed were sometimes hired for the same work.

Military annals and carved inscriptions indicate that the soldiers, however, were the mainstay of the road. Generals wrote that they put their troops to building roads, between battles, just to keep them out of mischief. When Trajan was emperor and Pliny the Younger was governor, Roman soldiers opened a road across the desert from the Nile to the Red Sea at Berenice. Men of the Seventh Legion left word that they had built a road south from the city of Salonae on the eastern shore of the Adriatic. The Third Augustan Legion made a road across Numidia in North Africa, from Carthage west to Lambaesis, and the *Legio II adiutrix* (reserve) carved its name proudly into direction stones of a road near Mursa in Pannonia, southwest of the Danube.

Soldiers carried shovels and trenching tools as part of their standard field equipment because it was Roman custom to build fortified camps wherever troops moved. They sometimes didn't take kindly to extracurricular activities like road building, however, and during the reign of Augustus they revolted repeatedly against this additional duty. Tacitus described an occasion on which the soldiers rebelled, handed their commander a pick and a shovel, and sat down to ask jeeringly how well he liked this aspect of military life.

The tradition of soldier–road builders died hard. In 1936, by the testimony of men who fought there, elite Alpine troops of Italy carried shovels with them to Ethiopia and were required to use them, between skirmishes, to help build roads designed to consolidate, in the ancient pattern, this new conquest by a wide new road.

During the last days of the Republic, workmen called *silicarii* (for that fine lava stone), were organized into gangs and housed in barracks along the roads they built and repaired. This, too, is a tradition which has not vanished from the nation. Strung along all state roads except the superhighways is a series of dark-red stucco structures marked "ANAS," for Azienda Nazionale Autonoma Strade, the highway department. Here, until recent years, workmen lived and kept their equipment, snuggled close to the reach of road for which they were responsible. Nowadays, when every laborer owns a car and wishes to live in the city, ANAS structures are being abandoned. Some are for sale. They remain, however, a familiar part of the landscape of the Roman roads.

Perhaps just because they were so good at it, Roman road builders have come under scholarly attack for having stolen other people's ideas, borrowed their techniques. No doubt they did borrow. Romans were insatiable cultural and technical blotters, soaking up everything they encountered. They learned from Persians, Greeks, Egyptians, Etruscans. Then they transformed the road from convenience into weapon and servant. They perfected the arch, the bridge, the viaduct, the tunnel, to make the road more effective. In so doing they made some mistakes, but their achievement was hailed by a modern scholar, R. J. Forbes, in 1934: "The fact remains that 15 centuries were to pass before engineering feats of similar skill and daring were performed."

Engineers were respected men in the Roman hierarchy, and high in their ranks was the surveyor, the land measurer. His role is described well in a charming contemporary book, *A Libation to the Gods*, written by E. M. Winslow, a professor of economics at the University of Iowa. Winslow was fascinated by the Roman aqueducts, and through them he came to understand that the surveyor was the sort of useful, practical, outdoor man whom the Romans could appreciate. The surveyor, Winslow noted, "did not even walk like other men, but appeared as a madman as he strode about in rough woods and thickets looking for the lost landmarks, stepping off the distances in the self-absorbed way of such devotees of accuracy."

Romans were respectful of accuracy, of measurement, calculation, assignment. Property rights were almost as inviolable as burial rights and plots. Both public and private lands, as well as the orientation and limits of cities and colonies, were matters of solemnity and contention.

In primitive times surveyors were augurs, those readers of signs and portents. Their services were required for the foundation of a city or the definition of a province because they could measure terrestrial space by sighting from a *lituus,* or augur's staff, from sky to earth. They calculated from the heavenly *templum* to a terrestrial one, by line of sight. The earthly *templum* was first conceived as a space measured off and sacred to the taking of auspices, especially the flights of birds. Its meaning broadened later to include city sites, but the augurs were still the magic men who could orient their sightings to the four cardinal points of the compass, and who could measure space and divide it amid great ceremony.

This all worked well for a while, but within a few hundred years the limits of city property, agrarian land, grazing boundaries and rights of way became too complicated for the augur. His pinnacle fell to rudimentary technology—to the *agrimensores* and their primary tool, the *groma*. Superstition, tradition, latent respect demanded the presence of augurs at religious rites which launched the measurement of territory, but the real layout work was gradually handed over to experts, *agrimensores*.

The existence of a professional class of these men is first recorded in the Po River valley about 200 B.C. By the fifth century A.D. Cassiodorus said that professors teaching surveying could always get a full audience for their lectures. Professors of arithmetic, geometry, astronomy and music were hard put to scrape up any audience at all. Romans chose applied science, technology, over "pure," or theoretical, science.

Their first identified surveyor was somebody called L. Decidius Saxa, who was hired by Mark Antony as *castrorum metator,* army camp surveyor. Antony's colleague Julius Caesar also used surveyors, but he seems to have depended upon trained centurions rather than professional civilians. He must have been impressed by Saxa's work, for it was Caesar who first organized a body of professional state surveyors for both civil and military work. Before Caesar, the *agrimensores* were free agents with no craft organization and no fixed criteria of skill. Caesar established a standard proficiency test, a fixed salary and a kind of union. From his time onward, *agrimensores* are mentioned as professionals.

Those not employed by the Roman state were free agents, available for hire by private citizens. They had to pass no test of competence, but they were much in demand to settle private disputes over

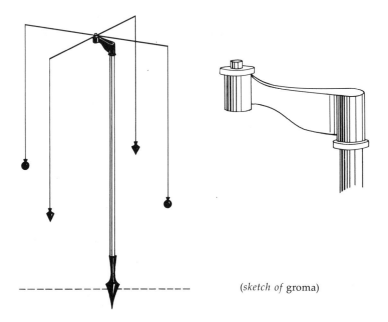

*(sketch of* groma)

boundaries. Their basic tool was the *groma*, which they learned from the Greeks with perhaps some help from the Etruscans: the Greek word for *groma*, because of peculiarities in the alphabets, would not have entered Latin in the form it did had it not been filtered through the Etruscans and their alphabet.

References to the *groma* in ancient books and descriptions made it clear that the instrument had been used to determine accurate right angles and straight lines, but until early in this century no modern scholar had seen one. Theories about the *groma*'s composition and precise use were based on educated speculation. Then finally in 1912 eleven pieces of bronze and iron turned up in the excavation of Pompeii, and in 1922 an Italian archaeologist, Della Corte, published drawings of the instrument and an explanation of how it worked. It had a metal point, like a lance point, which could be stuck into the ground. Into this was fitted an upright, probably of wood, which supported a swing arm about twelve inches long. This could be turned in a complete circle, like the arm support of some modern floor lamps. Fixed to the arm was a lightly balanced metal crosspiece, an X whose arms precisely divided a circle into four equal segments. From each arm end a thin cord or wire descended, weighted at the bottom with a lead or bronze plumb. A surveyor could set up this instrument, adjust the swing arm until he achieved his desired alignment, check its balance by the descent angle of the weighted cords, and get critical angles and precise directions.

Good as it was, the *groma* was unwieldy to operate and inconvenient to haul around. In untrained or well-bribed hands it was capable of gross error. The Greek scientist Heron in the late first century A.D. complained about its imperfections and produced an instrument called the *dioptra,* a sighting tool which worked on the same principle as today's transit, or theodolite. The modern transit is fixed on a tripod and uses a series of lenses to establish horizontal and vertical angles from the horizon of any fixed object. Heron's *dioptra* (named from the Greek *dia,* "through," and *opsomai,* "I shall see") may have measured only horizontal angles, but it embodied the same principles. Immediately the Romans adopted its use.

Once the road builders could calculate their lines and angles, they used a variety of devices for measuring, leveling, aligning. They made short linear measurements with long pieces of cane marked into feet. For longer ones they had lengths of measured chain, or stout cord and rope. These equivalents of tape measures they treated with waterproofing material so they would neither shrink nor stretch when subjected to weather and the stress of work in the field.

For long distances, the Romans sometimes measured by rolling a wheel over the ground. They measured the wheel's circumference, marked one point on it with chalk or a metal disk, and then counted the revolutions. Circumference times turns gave them accurate distance. Just how they did the arithmetic, using X's and V's and III's, nobody recorded. It must have been pure hell.

To lift heavy loads, they had the pulley and ropes, counterweighted levers and a complex turntable arrangement with which they could screw up, literally, enormous weights. They used stakes and flags to lay out lines, achieved long-distance leveling by judicious use of angle bars and plumb lines. For short, restricted level measurements they had a water level called the *libra.*

Simple and primitive as they were, these devices were so practical and so flexible that variations of them are in use today. In 1970 the authors watched with awe as five workmen constructed a country house without any architectural drawings whatever. The men paced off the linear limits, established verticals by driving nails into any handy crosspiece and then suspending from it a rock tied to a string. On one spectacular afternoon they tested the level of a floor by pouring water on it. Spilled water today does, it must be admitted, tend to accumulate under the sink or near the fireplace, but a series of exterior arches on the veranda, built entirely by instinct and eye, never reinforced, are beautifully proportioned. They have survived one earthquake, a dozen lightning bolts and several sonic booms. This is as it should be, for the arch was the greatest single triumph of the Roman engineer. Upon it he made the road, the bridge, the aqueduct, the vaulted ceilings of churches and palaces.

The first Roman bridges were made of wood, including the one which the brave Horatius held against marauding Etruscans. This was the Pons Sublicius, or Bridge of Piles, which was the first man-made link from one side of the Tiber to the other. On the Via Appia the first bridges were wood, often rigged with pulleys and weights so they could be drawn up at night or in case of attack.

Boats were anchored across streams or bays to serve as bridges and on one famous occasion the Emperor Caligula ordered his engineers to span the entire Bay of Baiae near Naples with boats. Upon this bridge he threw a celebration illuminated by lamps and flares, free drinks for all, and such a carousal that some of the boats overturned and guests were drowned in the bay. Caligula required so many boats for this party that Roman citizens went hungry for lack of cargo ships to import grain to the city.

The city of Venice still uses bridges of boats for special holidays. The bargelike craft are custom-built with attached wooden walkways for pedestrians, and they can be maneuvered into place to create the equivalent of avenues from the Piazza San Marco to the islands in the bay, or across the Grand Canal at any point.

Bridge building, like road building and the establishment of colonies, were near-sacred acts to the Romans. All were accompanied by priestly rites and sacrifices. Plutarch reported that earlier authors than he had linked the word *pons*, "bridge," to the titles *pontifex* and *pontifices* which the emperors affixed to their own names. The same title exists in *pontiff*, for the pope, but it began, according to Plutarch, as the designation of an order of priests charged with dedication, custody and maintenance of a bridge. This priestly control included designation of the materials used in bridges, and Roman tradition held that the priests had been warned by an oracle not to use either metal or stone in construction. By the same tradition, the destruction of a wooden bridge was considered not just unlawful but actually sacrilegious, an offense to the gods.

Some scholars believe, on the other hand, that the Roman use of wooden bridges was a matter of simple defense—they were easy to destroy, if necessary, to impede the advance of the enemy. Others say that the prefix *pons* came not from the word "bridge" but from the word *potens*, "powerful." All theories admit that the bridge was a thing of awe and respect.

The first stone bridge in Rome was the Pons Aemilius, begun in 179 b.c. and finished in 142, connecting the little island in the Tiber to the bank. It was partly swept away by a flood in 1598 and has ever since been called the Ponte Rotto, the Broken Bridge. Contemporary with it was a stone bridge on the Appia, the Pons Altus, or High Bridge, near Terracina, part of which still remains.

Oldest of the functioning stone bridges in Rome is the Ponte Milvio, built in 109 b.c. to carry the Via Flaminia across the river. It has been much rebuilt and restored, but several of its original arches, footings, abutments and lateral walls still help carry traffic out of Rome to the Via Flaminia and the Via Cassia. Most cars use an adjacent bridge which is far larger, newer and more fragile—the Ponte Flaminio. For all its monumental Fascist proportions and décor, the Flaminio is often closed for repairs while the narrow old Milvio by its side remains open, though nowadays only to one-way traffic. The Pons Milvium appears on a Roman coin of 17 b.c., now in the British Museum; on a fifteenth-century map of Rome; in an 1849 painting of the French siege of the city; in Piranesi prints; and in countless photographs of the past hundred years.

On the subject of bridge engineering, ancient authors are even more reticent than they are on road building. In his entire work on architecture Vitruvius didn't use the word *pons* once. Knowledge about the bridges comes from a study of the ones still in use, and the remains of ruined ones. It seems likely that the Romans honed their bridge-building skills first on dry land, in the construction of aqueducts and viaducts. A key step in the refinement of the masonry arch was construction of the Aqua Marcia in 144 B.C., an aqueduct which required six miles of stone arches to carry water. After it was completed successfully, with blocks of tufa, builders used the same techniques and material in the first stone city bridge.

By the beginning of imperial times, at the dawn of the Christian Era, they had mastered the arch and they began to employ it with dramatic success. Because the point of a bridge is to span flowing water without blocking it, the arch was essential. Romans tried always to cross the stream with one single arch if they could, supporting this central structure with smaller arches on either side to support the roadbed as it crossed the riverbanks and adjacent uneven territory.

If they could not make one arch do the job, the Romans then built smack in the river. Earlier bridge builders had devised the system of diverting a river while they bridged it, but the Romans scorned this time-consuming and less-direct method. They sank piles in the riverbed and made square cores into which they could pour stones and cement. Sometimes they used a lead collar to help keep out the water. They never were able to drain completely the holes and supports they constructed in streams to foot their arches: this technique was not mastered until about two centuries ago.

Once the footing core was completed, the Romans built arches on top of a curved wooden frame. They laid out wedge-shaped rock on the frame, then held it together with the keystone, or center block, in the arch. The moment this stone was set, the arch became self-supporting and the wooden frame could be moved and set up on two other footings nearby to construct another arch. Sometimes, to support the stones as the arch was going up, they left projecting blocks on the bridge piers, or else they sprang their arches from a short distance behind the outer wall of a pier, to let the centering structure rest on a ledge.

The oldest, most primitive arches are made from a few very long voussoirs, the technical name for the tapering or wedge-shaped pieces of which an arch is composed. The piers and abutments which sustained them are always of squared stone, although sometimes in both bridges and viaducts the workmen alternated rows of oblong stones set lengthwise and crosswise.

Some of the early bridges were not aligned properly with respect to water flow: the piers presented too much resistance and were battered down, or they were too wide and acted as dams which forced the water upward and over the bridge itself. To correct this defect, the bridge builders began to open "windows," carefully calculated holes in the superstructure of the bridge to let floodwater pass. One of these windows may be seen clearly today in the center of the Ponte Sisto over the Tiber just north of the island of Tiberina, where it has served for centuries as a flood gauge. When water reaches it, or above its lower edge, the local citizens know they're in for it and they can evacuate the area. Years of experience have taught the neighbors the peril level for each street and quarter in the surrounding territory.

All the uses of the arch, in aqueduct, viaduct and bridge are still visible along the Appia. After the viaduct of Ariccia is another one at Itri. There is a fine aqueduct across the modern road near Minturno. Bridges still exist along the road's length, though at least three of them were demolished in World War II. There are two outside Terracina, fragments of one in a much-reconstructed bridge in Capua, two in Benevento, one outside Canosa, a lovely half bridge, half viaduct near Minturno (see Appendix).

Elsewhere in Italy, on the other main Roman roads, are other bridges in which four, five, six arches still survive. One of the most dramatic, even in ruins, is the great span which Augustus built over the river Nera near today's Narni. The central arch of this bridge was almost a hundred feet high.

Procopius wrote of it: "Two slopes lead up . . . one cannot go along without crossing the bridge which is thrown across the river and serves for passage. Caesar Augustus constructed this bridge in times past, a sight worthy of great consideration because, of all the vaulted structures that we know, it is the highest."

The central arch, now ruined, had a span of more than 100 feet, its adjacent ones 55 to 65 feet. The entire bridge was 500 feet long, its roadbed 25 feet wide.

Bridge widths were variable, dictated by the volume of traffic. In difficult areas or straitened financial times, they were occasionally narrower than the road itself and designed to be crossed one way only, taking turns. Almost all of them were humped slightly in the middle. Some were equipped with footpaths along the sides, as were the roads, and drainage channels between roadbed and sidewalk.

In the time of Augustus an unprecedented amount of money was spent on bridges. They had become so important, so familiar that whole series of them were projected, planned, calculated along the length of a road to be either built or rebuilt. Augustus recorded proudly: "In my 7th consulship, I reconstructed the road from Rome to Rimini and all the bridges between the Milvium and the Minucius."

This was a project as sweeping as any superhighway of today, and into it was securely lodged that vaulting triumph of Roman engineering which some ancient writer described, endearingly, as "the little brother of the road," the bridge.

"AFTER JANUARY 1 NEXT NO ONE SHALL DRIVE A WAGON ALONG THE STREETS OF ROME . . . AFTER SUNRISE OR BEFORE THE TENTH HOUR OF THE DAY . . ."

Edict of Julius Caesar, 45 B.C.

"I FORBID ANYONE TO BUILD . . . [IN] A PUBLIC ROAD ANYTHING WHEREBY THAT STREET OR THAT ROAD MAY BE OR MAY BECOME WORSE."

Edict of the urban praetor, A.D. 129

# X
# RULES OF THE ROAD

The first Roman law involving roads and public right of way preceded even the Via Appia by 138 years. It was incorporated into the Twelve Tables, a compilation of the body of unwritten law, collected and codified in 451–450 B.C. by the decemvirs. Some ancient sources indicate that the laws were once inscribed on bronze tablets which did not survive the Gallic sack of Rome in 390 B.C., and that later they were carved on marble and set up in the Forum. So important were they to Roman life that generations of schoolboys committed them to memory.

Included in the Twelve Tables were key items about roads: the width of a public passageway should be eight Roman feet where it went straight, sixteen feet around corners. Roadways were to be kept in repair, though the Tables were not specific about who should be responsible for this. If they were not repaired, according to Table VII, then shepherds and graziers could not be fined for driving their flocks on the unrepaired road.

If rainwater or flood damaged a public thoroughfare, it was to be fixed according to the order of an official arbitrator. If a water course directed through a public place or for the public good damaged a

*169*

private person or his property, he had the right to sue for redress.

Legal widths and limits for highways changed during the centuries, but there was always careful distinction between *semitae*, or footpaths, *iter* for horsemen and walkers, *actus* for a carriage road, *calles* for drovers, and *aquae ductus*, the carrying of public water.

Best-known of the Roman road laws is the edict banning traffic from the city. Julius Caesar, who is usually credited with this stroke of genius, seems only to have repeated traffic bans passed by his predecessors. His edict was specific and detailed:

> . . . no one shall drive a wagon along the streets . . . in the suburbs where there is continuous housing after sunrise or before the tenth hour of the day, except whatever will be proper for the transportation . . . of material for building temples of the immortal gods, or for public works, or for removing from the city rubbish. . . . Whenever it is proper for the vestal virgins, the king of the sacrifices, or the *flamens* to ride in the city for the purpose of official sacrifices . . . whatever wagons are proper . . . for public games within Rome or within one mile of Rome or for the procession held at the time of the games in the Circus Maximus, it is not the intent of this law to prevent the use of such wagons during the day. . . .

Neither was it, Caesar took pains to point out, the intent of this law "to prevent ox wagons . . . from carrying out dung from within the city of Rome or within one mile of the city after sunrise until the tenth hour of the day."

Like all traffic laws, Caesar's required repeated explanation and tireless enforcement. The Emperor Claudius had to repeat everything in another edict when he took power, and he underlined that all persons wishing to pass through Rome in the daytime must do so either on foot or in a litter borne on the shoulders of slaves. Within a century Marcus Aurelius had to repeat the same orders. The writer Suetonius, in an effort to help, wrote that he personally considered driving inside the city to be a crude and ungentlemanly act.

When these traffic bans were obeyed, Roman days became peaceful interludes of business and pleasure. Nights were a hell of clomping beasts, screeching axles, swearing drivers, arguments over right of way, and fistfights in the streets. The satirist Juvenal asked despairingly: "Where is sleep possible?" Many a visitor to Rome has asked the same thing, even as neighing horses gave way to braying motorbikes, shouting muleteers to argumentative and eloquent cabdrivers.

There were no speed limits and no NO PARKING signs on the old roads. They were swollen at key places into piazzas to permit vehicles to stop and rest their beasts. At heavily traveled points on the Appia, workmen inserted blunt conical stones at curbside to prevent impetuous drivers from mounting the sidewalks to pass dangerously. In Rome, aediles in charge of construction prudently ordered continuous curbs and sidewalks in residential areas so owners of light gigs would have difficulty driving them straight through their front doors and into the atrium.

Nobody knows whether traffic on the Appia originally traveled on the right-hand side of the road or on the left. Albert C. Rose, in his study of the road and its vehicles in the 1930s, offered the logical theory that it varied depending on where the driver was sitting in relation to his hitch and his carriage. If he was on a box wagon, sitting to the extreme right in order to use his whip hand more effectively, he would either drive on the left or move left when he encountered oncoming traffic so he could see his own wheel hubs and those of the advancing vehicle and make sure that they cleared one another.

If, on the other hand, he was sitting on the left horse or over the left wheel of a lighter vehicle, he would drive on the right or move to the right for the same reason—to have a better view of the wheel hubs which had to pass on the road.

Just such simple, practical considerations may well have switched the direction of traffic in the American colonies from the English left to the American right, Rose explained. In the first days of America, traffic tended to proceed on the left in the English style. But in the 1750s came the heavy Conestoga covered freight wagons, which were driven by the postilion method—that is, with the driver riding the left horse of either a single team or a multiple team. The postilion, trying to calculate safe clearance on the roads, went logically to the right. As the Conestoga wagon moved west, it took the right-hand rule of the road with it.

Probably there was no rule in the Roman world. Horsemen traveling fast could thread their way easily through carts on the road. Chariots and carriages must have veered from side to side as automobiles do today on a rough country road, seeking to avoid potholes and bumps and washouts. When Roman rigs met oncoming

traffic they made quick adjustments, avoiding collision by any maneuver available. There is a literary hint, in Dante, that Italy even in the Middle Ages had no orderly, rigid two-way traffic law or even any memory of one. Dante describes religious pilgrims during a Jubilee Year in Rome trudging back and forth across the Ponte Sant'Angelo, which still spans the Tiber near the massive circular tomb of Hadrian, and he makes a *double entendre* on the fact that the faithful trudged in neat lanes of two-way traffic across the bridge, turning their backs alternately on God — the Vatican — and on the world — the rest of Rome. The fact that he chose two-way traffic as a symbol suggests that it was unusual, worthy of note, important enough to support a metaphor.

Even early in the twentieth century there was a dichotomy in the Italian traffic pattern. In rural areas it went along the left of the road — when it wasn't in the middle — and in cities it moved on the right. Mussolini decreed that all traffic should go on the right, but even he was not completely obeyed, any more than Julius Caesar was, or Augustus, or Marcus Aurelius. Italians in general, and Romans in particular, have throughout the centuries exhibited a consistent resistance to edicts, most especially to edicts on matters of traffic and taxes.

Today motorbikes, three-wheel farm trucks and other piston-driven vehicles are constrained to proceed on the right of the road, but many a slow country farm cart will turn up suddenly on the left. Peasants understand why: "Rules on where to go were invented when people invented cars, which go very fast and are made of metal," a *contadino* explained. "But you will notice that people when they walk are requested to go on the left so they can see what is coming that might hurt them. It is the same with the animals. The *asino*, the *mulo* or the *bue* does not wish to be murdered. So he walks on the left, like the *semplice cristiano*." *Semplice cristiano*, "simple Christian," is the Italian peasant expression for an ordinary human being.

Many Roman laws and edicts were designed to limit the road, to constrain its expansion. This seems odd indeed until one realizes that the drovers' road, the track, however well beaten and heavily used, could turn into a bog in heavy rains or a morass by constant usage.

*This stretch of the Appia, visible in the excavated site of Minturnae, demonstrates the hazards of meeting oncoming traffic on the narrow road. Stones placed on the curbs are funerary or dedicatory inscriptions found on the site.*

Travelers tended to skirt it, to left or right, to avoid being mired, and in the process they created a "road" literally hundreds of feet wide. This diversion represented to the Roman mind an intolerable invasion of either public or private terrain on both sides of the main track. So laws were framed, first, to insist upon construction of a hard, water-resistant, clearly defined surface along the most logical path, and second, the banishment of all beasts except those bearing persons or commercial goods, or pulling vehicles, from this central track.

Beasts of burden were much respected by Roman law, as they too were servants of the state. The Emperor Constantine in A.D. 316 issued a sweeping decree covering load limits and the protection of animals from cruelty:

> Considering that most [drivers] by means of strong and knotty cudgels oblige the public horses from the very beginning of their journey to use up whatever strength they have, we decree that no one shall use cudgels, but a switch or a whip with a goad, which, by means of a harmless tickle, may serve to admonish the lazy limbs but not to exact more than their strength can yield.

The same decree provided that two-wheeled carriages could be drawn by one, two or three beasts but that the load limit exclusive of the carriage weight should be 144 pounds. Four-wheeled carriages like the *raeda*, which had two seats and storage for luggage, should be drawn by eight horses in summer and ten in winter. They should carry no more than 718 pounds in excess of the carriage weight.

These were very light loads, by modern standards. During the French stagecoach era of 1875, horses or mules pulling much the same kind of vehicle were expected to manage loads of from 1,100 to 1,800 pounds. Roman freight vehicles, which traveled more slowly, were much less restricted, but even they carried lighter loads than their equivalents of later centuries.

The explanation, scholars believe, is that Roman horses were small in stature, their harness was not sophisticated enough to distribute the drag weight evenly, and their strength was briefly but unduly taxed by the occasional sharp gradient or difficult turn on the Roman roads. There was also the Roman passion for speed, which probably induced drivers to coax the utmost from their beasts.

No laws seem to have applied to the width or weight of the rolling stock on the roads, though vehicles were important enough to figure in civil suits and the probation of wills. The best-known instance of vehicle litigation, recorded in fragmentary texts of an early digest of Roman laws, concerns the inheritance rights of a woman from the estate of her late husband. She demanded to receive her own personal effects, and she asked the judge to rule upon her right to inherit one of the family's most valued possessions, the *carucca dormitoria,* or covered sleeping carriage. One of the best lawyers of the first century B.C., the pontifex Quintus Mucius Scaevola, ruled in her favor and awarded her the *carucca.*

Subsidiary road laws covered the tipping of state employees who assisted official travelers along the road — tips were sternly forbidden — and ordered severe penalties for such employees if they attempted to extract extra pay for services. There was a rural law which forbade women, while walking along public roads, to carry their distaffs uncovered. The distaff, a simple staff with a cleft end for holding wool or flax from which its user could draw thread for spinning by hand, would seem the most inoffensive of objects. Certainly it occasioned no peril to traffic. The origin of this odd law may lie in some now-forgotten superstition. Or, quite within the bounds of credibility, the uncovered cleft of the distaff could have been a sign of the availability of the woman who carried it. Covered distaffs apparently were permissible. The law may have been an early attempt to regulate the morals of the Roman traveling salesman.

"No sort of man, of any dignity, degree, or honor, must desist from the making and repairing of the ways and bridges," said a Roman edict of A.D. 394.

This spirit, this attitude, far more than any decrees about distaffs or road widths, or even load limits, constituted the rule of the Roman roads.

In Appius Claudius' time, public roads were the honored responsibility of elected censors. They used for funds the public treasury, supplemented by their own money. Although they could count on free labor provided by slaves, convicts or soldiers, they had to buy rights of way, materials, and pay the salaries of the contractors who moved onto the terrain to oversee construction.

Though it seems incredible today, the public treasury during the Republic was not fed primarily by taxes. Funds came from the agricultural fruits and the rental of public land, tribute from conquered provinces, the sale of slaves, fines levied upon moneylenders or graziers who invaded public lands. Livy noted that in 296 B.C. the brothers Gnaeus and Quintus Ogulnius, serving as aediles to police the city, victual the populace, maintain public works, "brought a number of usurers to trial and, confiscating their possessions, employed the share which came into the public treasury to put brazen thresholds in the Capitol, and silver vessels . . . in the shrine of Jupiter, and a statue of the god in a four-horse chariot on the roof." They also "made a paved walk of squared stone [on the Via Appia] from the Porta Capena to the Temple of Mars."

Just a few years later, still in Livy's words, "the aediles procured the conviction of a number of graziers, and with their fines paved the road from the Temple of Mars as far as Bovillae."

Other road money came, as the centuries passed, from a variety of sources. Censors, consuls, and praetors vied with one another in construction and repair. They raided the public treasury if they could, gouged provincial landowners if they could, levied fines if they could. Patriotic citizens left their worldly wealth, in wills, for road building. This was as honorable a gesture as it is today to endow a hospital or a chair of learning in a university.

In return, the benefactors got rewards in the form of commemorative medals, statues, stones, even sometimes the right to erect a memorial arch. Grand men like censors and consuls and, later, emperors bestowed their names upon the roads they built, and were entitled to public esteem forever after. Everyone from Caesar to Augustus, from Agrippa to Trajan, undertook the task and its honors as a sacred public service.

Some road building was assigned, willy-nilly, to rich senators, by strong emperors who explained to them that they could find no better use for their money, nor do anything to so endear them to their constituents. Occasionally the senators were not impressed. Augustus, having handed out road assignments to a select group and set an example by offering to pay for the renovation of the Via Flaminia himself, ended up having to pay for a lot of the other work as well because the senators reneged.

Victorious generals also were given the opportunity to build roads, as an unspoken price for having been accorded a "triumph." The triumph was a particularly Roman institution, a scene of splendor and pomp which is perhaps best reconstructed today in the trumpet blowing, marching, palm waving of the second act of *Aïda*, the famous triumphal march with Radames in his chariot and his captives in chains, the cheering populace on all sides.

The triumph was the highest honor accorded to a military commander, and it was not awarded lightly. It went only to a supreme commander—a dictator, consul, praetor—and the victory had to have been achieved in a genuine all-out war. No triumph was awarded a man who merely put down a revolt of slaves, or who fought his fellow citizens in civil combat. The Senate had to give its blessing to a triumph, and the general had to remain outside the walls of the city until the day of the great event. His command, the powers the people had given him to enable him to win the conflict, expired the moment he entered the free city of Rome. Echoes of this tradition still exist in London, where the Monarch of the Realm must pause, by ancient custom, before entering London to receive permission from the Lord Mayor to come into the city.

When all was in order and the time had come, the general and his troops entered Rome, marched to the Circus Maximus, down the Via Sacra in the Forum, and up to the Capitol. The streets were decorated with garlands; all temples were open. The victor was followed by trumpeters, by spoils of war carried in carts or on the soldiers' shoulders. There were painted images of the conquered country and models of captured forts, cities, ships. There were captives in chains, and white bulls intended for ritual sacrifice, their horns gilded. The general rode in a chariot, standing, wearing an elaborate tunic and toga, with a slave holding a golden crown over his head. According to Tertullian of Carthage, in the second century A.D., there were also Cassandra-like characters whose duty it was to call out at intervals, "Look behind you, and remember that you are mortal."

In the midst of such tumult and shouting, such garlands and banners and heat and hordes, it must have been difficult to think of either mortality or immortality. At first triumphs lasted for only one day, but they proved so pleasant to both recipients and participants that they grew into week-long festivals. The building or the repair of a road, using for funds part of the war booty captured abroad, was a small price for the triumphant general to pay.

During the later days of the Empire the triumph fell into disuse, partly because emperors claimed the glory for themselves on the theory that field generals commanded only as the emperor's lieutenants.

From the beginning of the Empire, emperors assumed responsibility for the roads. In 20 B.C., the same year he erected the *miliarium aureum* in the Forum, Augustus appointed himself head of the building and maintenance of state roads. Having thus assumed the responsibility, he immediately delegated it, and set up an official body known as *curationes viae*, curators of the roads. These men replaced the temporarily appointed *curatores viarum*, who had fulfilled the same function in earlier centuries.

Road maintenance and supervision had long been a responsibility and honor which fell to respected citizens. Julius Caesar was curator of the Via Appia when he served as aedile, and he spent on it vast sums of his own money. The reformer Gaius Gracchus in the second century B.C., who set up all those milestones, was hailed by Plutarch. "His most especial exertions were given to constructing the roads, which he was careful to make beautiful and pleasant, as well as convenient."

Augustus, in gathering power to the emperor and making the curators permanent instead of temporary, still used men of senatorial rank as *curatores* and he was polite enough to pretend that the Senate had concurred in his choice: his orders and documents rhetorically carried the words *Ex senatus consulto.* Later emperors didn't bother with this. They simply decreed what work was to be done, and told the Senate afterward. It remained generally the practice to appoint important men as supervisors, but after the death of Trajan in A.D. 117 the road he had ordered, the Appia Traiana, was supervised by a man who had only equestrian rank. This was a cut below a senator, in the Roman social and political order. Senators were drawn from the major landowning families and theoretically had to be the masters of a million sestertii in taxable property. After them came the knights, or *equites*, traditionally drawn from citizens rich enough to own a horse. Before long the equestrian class was expanded to anyone who had about half a million sestertii, whether he owned a horse or not. It even ceased to matter whether the man could ride a horse.

This tacit downgrading of the Appia Traiana by appointment of a curator of the equestrian order may have been merely an exhibition of Roman pride. The Traiana, though a major road, was measured from Beneventum, not from Rome, and its mileage calculated from there. This simple fact lowered its importance in Roman eyes, because the original Appia set forth from Rome and was measured on all its length from there.

The early emperors, having inherited from Augustus the responsibility for the roads, were conscientious. From the final decades of the first century A.D. for more than a hundred years Nerva, Trajan, Hadrian and Septimius Severus worked hard on them, building and repairing.

Repair was a constant problem. Though often built with *lapides perpetui,* the roads were battered by more aggressive forces than today. Iron-rimmed wheels and iron-shod hoofs attacked the surface fiercely. Cracks and crevices were endemic, and the Romans appear to have had no concept of stripping at intervals with some rubbery substance which could absorb the expansion and contraction of rigid surfaces in heat and cold. If they built too loosely, the road broke up and disintegrated in frost and rain. If they built too tightly, heat expansion buckled the surface. Despite all this, some roads in Italy required rebuilding only once in a hundred years, and a technical study of the Roman roads in Spain indicated that most of them lasted seventy years before repairs were required. In difficult stretches like that of the Appia across the marshes and the mountains, major repairs were required every thirty to forty years.

During the Republic, roads were considered far too important to entrust to even the most reliable provincial functionaries or landowners. All direction, planning and funding were done from Rome. The imperial system, which used permanent bureaucrats as curators, and which had heavier expenses on an expanded network, required help from the provinces and from landowners along the routes.

When Hadrian repaved sixteen miles of the road, he erected milestones indicating that he had paid 1,147,000 sestertii for the work and that the owners of adjacent lands had contributed 569,100. This was a more honest milestone legend than many others: even the subtleties of the Latin language were bent to the ends of more self-aggrandizing emperors. In the middle and late Empire, each milestone or commemorative marker carried the name of the emperor and only a grammarian could have noticed that the name was written in the nominative case if the major funds for the road had come from the emperor or the public treasury. If local authorities, or local landowners, had borne the fiscal burden, the emperor's name was written in the dative case.

Despite Hadrian's exact notation of the sestertii spent, in sixteen miles, it is almost impossible to render the sum into present monetary value. Some twentieth-century economists have tried, and have estimated that the cost of rebuilding one mile of the Appia in Hadrian's time would have been $5,000. The figure should be regarded with suspicion. Whatever it cost, the repair or rebuilding of a Roman road, especially in places where it was thick and rigid, probably was more than the original cost.

In general the quality of the work reflected the character and conscientiousness of the rulers, but graft in high places and cheating contractors were always the problem. Livy reported a scandal in the late first century B.C. when a member of the triumvirate, Marcus Aemilius Lepidus, diverted public funds to cover some private expenses at Tarracina. He had been put in charge of building a mole in the port and he seems to have accomplished the task. But Livy says that the "work brought him censure, because he owned property there and he had included, with expenditures chargeable to the state, some private expenses."

In A.D. 21 Tacitus recorded an argument over the roads which involved the Senate and the Emperor Claudius. Senator G. Domitius Corbulo had raised the matter as a subject for debate. The highways, he charged, were in a bad condition throughout the Italian peninsula. In some cases they were impassable. He attributed the mischief to fraudulent practices of contractors and to lack of attention on the part of responsible magistrates.

Corbulo then got tough with the contractors, levying punitive fines. Tacitus felt that he had gone too far, that he had exceeded the interests of the public good by "ruining" individuals and confiscating their property. In the end Claudius interceded and punished

*The statue of the Appia's single most famous chronicler, the poet Horace, stands in the main square of his hometown, Venosa—only a few yards from the Communist party's headquarters.*

the obstreperous Senator Corbulo by making him pay back, from his own fortune, some of the punitive fines he had extracted.

Despite a chronic need for road money, the Romans resisted the device of using taxes and tolls. A senator called L. Scribonius Curo, in 50 B.C., proposed and argued earnestly for a law levying taxes on vehicles, but he was defeated. Until the Empire fell, Roman public roads in Italy were free of tolls. One of the reasons for Romans' frenetic activity abroad, their rapid expansion, may have been the need to ensure toll-free passage of their troops and commerce toward the cities with which they wished to trade. Desert peoples in the Middle East and North Africa were particularly prone to halt travelers and extract exorbitant tolls. The Romans thus had to subdue the territories in order to secure their markets and trade, the passage of traffic. One of the principal provisions written into any Roman pact of peace or compromise was the free, unhampered passage of persons and vehicles through the foreign territory.

There is some evidence that a narrow road across a swamp near Silvium, today's Gravina di Puglia, may have been a toll road, but it is far from clear. If it was, it was a small connecting road which led from the Appia to a very ancient city near Silvium and thus it was not part of the public-road system. Not until the Empire fell could private citizens attempt to extract tolls by closing the roads, as the Caetani family did on the Appia at the site of the Tomb of Cecilia Metella. Even there they were frustrated because travelers simply detoured along other existing tracks or new roads to avoid passing through the toll gates and controls. In the Middle Ages, when there was no effective central control, brigands or landowners or enterprising freebooters could set up barriers on any of the roads and exact payment from tourists.

Throughout the early days, however, Rome remained convinced that the roads, like air and water, were public and inviolable. Some financial contribution might be required from time to time, but their free and unobstructed use was unquestioned. Romans were stern with offenders or cheaters. When Cato was consul, he dealt summarily with such people. Plutarch noted admiringly that "He caused the pipes, through which some persons brought the public water into their houses and gardens, to be cut, and threw down all buildings which jutted out into the common streets. He beat down also the price in contracts for public works to the lowest . . ."

When public interest clashed with private, the public won, though there is evidence that the law was reasonable in dealing with such things as rights of way across private property. In the case of road building, the state preferred to buy the entire property of any owner who opposed the road's passage. Then, having made the road, the state sold off surplus portions of the land to defray the expense of the original purchase.

There seems to be no specific case of a man who fought a road and won, but there is the record of a man who blocked the passage of an aqueduct. His name was L. Licinius Crassus, and he refused to permit the construction of masonry arches across his property to permit the passage of a new waterway. Unfortunately the location of his property is obscure, and even the name of the aqueduct. It was neither Appius Claudius' aqueduct nor the equally old Anio Vetus. Perhaps Crassus' intransigence halted its construction and therefore it never existed.

Though they eschewed tolls and vehicle taxes, Romans did exact customs duties. They set up barriers and customs houses at all sea-ports and provincial boundaries, and there stationed customs men whose honesty the travelers seldom trusted. The practice of exacting customs charges on commercial traffic inside Italy persisted until the early 1970s when the European Common Market's decision to levy an across-the-board "value added tax" eliminated such old-fashioned levies as the *dazio,* or customs duty, on goods passing from one Italian province to another.

In Roman times, persons landing at Brundisium, Barium and Hydruntum to take the Via Appia were required to exhibit to the customs officer all their possessions. As a general rule wagons, beasts of burden, personal clothing, supplies required for the trip itself, were exempt from duty. Anything the traveler had acquired abroad for resale, including slaves, was taxable. Items acquired for the use of the state were free, but their bearer was required to produce an official list and the inspector checked it against the purchases to make sure they matched. Any articles not included on the list were confiscated.

Roman bureaucrats, soldiers and some eminent persons traveled without inspection of either themselves or their baggage. Flagrant advantage was taken of these exemptions. There exists a letter sent from Rome to the secretary of a finance minister of Egypt in 257 B.C.:

> Send . . . a bathing costume as quickly as possible, of goatskin if possible or, if not, of sheepskin. You mentioned you were surprised that I did not realize these things are subject to duty. I knew it, all right, but you are perfectly able to arrange to send them without any risk.

Emperors could bestow duty-free passage upon friends or favorites. Trajan gave such rights to his friend Polemo of Smyrna, and stipulated carefully that the exemption should apply for both land and sea travel. Hadrian gave a waiver of customs to all his descendants.

Ordinary travelers smuggled outrageously, and considered customs officers nosy and obnoxious if not downright corrupt. Plutarch grumbled that "We object to customs officials, not when they examine open wares, but when they finger the insides of bags, and yet this is their job."

It was not part of their job to extract items of value and pocket them, during the course of these investigations, yet many of them did.

Customs rates began at about 2 or 2½ percent of the value of items either undeclared or for resale. Records exist of this rate in Gaul and the Near East. Other accounts mention 5 percent in Sicily, Illyricum and parts of Africa. Luxury goods were taxed more highly. "Many purchases which were not necessities, but were luxuries like eunuchs and handsome boys, were dutiable even though the purchaser kept them for his individual use," one account reads.

Customs duties of from 8 to 25 percent were levied on such obvious nonnecessities as perfume, spices, silk and gems. Pearls were high-duty items, and Roman matrons were particularly addicted to them. Julius Caesar was alleged to have paid the equivalent of $300,000 for a single pearl for a favorite lady, and Pliny the Elder once lamented that "Our dames must have their ears behanged with [pearls]. There is no remedy."

One inevitable confrontation between the passion for pearls and the Roman law on customs duty was recorded. The language of the first-century writer is sober, the scene comic. One of the few restrictions on the activities of customs inspectors was that they could not inspect the persons of "matrons." Plutarch said that "the official is entitled to examine the baggage and confiscate all undeclared dutiable goods: he may not touch women."

On one memorable day, at a border not identified, there appeared a Roman matron with four hundred pearls concealed in her bosom. The statistic alone conjures a picture of either four hundred very small pearls or else an impressively ample bosom. The presiding official, while busily rooting about in the matron's baggage, inquired whether or not she had something to declare. The lady remarked grandly that if he had any doubts, she would permit him to search her. Embarrassed, the customs man refused, and the matron passed the barrier—only to be confronted on the other side by the same official, who demanded that she hand over the pearls.

Despite diligent search, the authors have been unable to establish the outcome. It would be delicious to know. Was it the lady, or the pearls?

# XI
# THE BLOODY ROAD


From the beginning, the Appia received infusions of blood. Vendettas, assassinations, dramatic public punishments, invasions, wars coursed up and down its stones.

No assassin in those days would deliberately choose a dark alley as the site of his evil act, and no public enemy brought to justice would have met it in the sterile privacy of a little square room containing an electric chair. If murder or retribution were to have value they had to be committed in a public place: in a forum, on the steps of a temple, or on that majestic road, in order to focus upon the event the full attention of the Roman world.

It is difficult, now, to imagine the situation. It would be as if to site upon, say, the New Jersey Turnpike between New York City and Philadelphia the events of Bunker Hill, of Appomattox, of Little Rock and Kent State, Ford's Theater and Pearl Harbor. To say nothing of Woodstock and the National Cathedral, for minstrels and mimes performed and met on the road; royal brides traveled it to meet their bridegrooms.

Almost every event of national or international import, every rising of the poor and beset, every armed incursion and insurrection sent its temporary force up and down the road like the invading inrush, the sighing outwash of a wave upon the sand of a beach. It went on like this for two thousand years.

Perhaps the single most celebrated bloodletting on the road took place in 52 B.C. when the followers of a Roman nobleman named Milo murdered a descendant of Appius Claudius himself, a shifty and swashbuckling fellow called Publius Clodius Pulcher. It was a routine murder for the time, growing out of an atmosphere of civil disorder and the bloody competition between cliques of nobles. It was raised to the status of international event because it upset a delicate balance of power in Rome, because it invoked the name of Appius Claudius, and most of all because Milo was defended by Cicero, the greatest orator of his time.

Yet it happened almost by accident. On January 18, 52 B.C., Titus Annius Milo, a former tribune who had been a candidate for the consulship the year before, spent the morning in the Senate and then decided to go to Lanuvium to attend affairs there. He went home at noon, changed into traveling clothes, told his wife to get ready for a journey and set forth with her in a carriage. The route to Lanuvium was the Via Appia. Because danger lay everywhere for a man of strong opinions and high visibility, Milo took along with him three hundred armed men. Some were slaves, some were gladiators including two famous ones, Audamo and Birria.

Purely by chance, Milo's sworn enemy Publius Clodius Pulcher chose the same day and almost the same hour to depart from the Appian town of Aricia where he, too, had business. He was returning to Rome, with three friends, all on horseback; he also had a retinue, two columns of armed men, possibly more than Milo had.

These convoys met and passed each other on the Appia near Bovillae, between two and three o'clock in the afternoon. At first nothing happened. It isn't likely that the two noblemen saluted each other, and witnesses reported that their touchy escorts of warriors exchanged insults as they passed. By the time the stragglers of both columns met, face to face on the narrow road, tempers flared and a scuffle broke out. It is possible that Milo, riding ahead in his carriage, didn't even know it. Clodius, on horseback, either saw or heard it and reigned up as if to go back and enter the dispute. At this moment the gladiator Birria, perhaps fearing for his master,

*Reconstruction by Canina (c. 1850) of the section of the road near the Clodius villa where Milo murdered Clodius, as he imagined it looked in Roman times. To liven things up a bit, he added the battle between the defenders and supporters of Milo and Clodius. Courtesy German Archaeological Institute, Rome.*

jumped on Clodius and ran him through the shoulder with his sword. Instantly the other slaves and gladiators clashed. In the confusion, Clodius' servants carried him to a tavern in Bovillae.

When runners reached Milo with the news, he too stopped and turned back. Clodius and his followers would never, he knew, forgive the assault whether Clodius lived or died. It might be prudent to finish off his enemy once and for all, and worry later about a murder charge. He ordered his men to search for the wounded Clodius. They ransacked the tavern, dragged out the bleeding man, hacked at him with swords and knives, and left his body on the Appia.

There was so much traffic on the road that the corpse was found almost immediately. A Roman senator, Sestus Teidius, returning from his country villa to the city, ordered his servants to lift the bloody remains into his own litter and carry them to Clodius' home. Before dark the body arrived in Rome and was laid out in the atrium. The news flew through the narrow streets. Clodius had curried favor with the plebeians by renouncing his connection with the aristocratic branch of the family and running for office as a pleb. Crowds of plebs and slaves, hearing of his death, rushed to the Clodian home and then, goaded by the sobs and shrieks of the dead man's wife and female relatives, dispersed through the city to kill. Their excuse, later, was that they were hunting for the murderer Milo and for all who supported him.

At the time, Rome was governed by a shaky triumvirate of Caesar, Pompey and Crassus. Caesar and Crassus were both in the provinces, leading armies, and Pompey was caretaker in Italy, scheming for power but not yet ready, or quite able, to seize it. The city was left in the hands of warring street gangs loyal to the ambitious Clodius or the equally ambitious Milo.

The outrages committed by Clodius' followers caused so much chaos in the city that the Senate first ordered an interregnum, then docilely put the power in Pompey's hands. He was made consul-without-colleague, a title his advisers thought would sound better than dictator.

This was a break for Milo, and incidentally for literature, because when Pompey scheduled a trial within three months, Cicero decided to defend Milo. Cicero had good reason to detest the dead Clodius: Clodius had once assaulted him in the street and had conspired with Julius Caesar to pass a law condemning the writer to exile. That exile ended when Pompey came to power.

Milo's case came up duly within three months. Cicero was ready, but his oral defense was strangely weak. He excused it afterward by saying that the presence of soldiers in the court, the shouts of unruly spectators, his certainty that Milo would be found guilty in spite of everything had stopped his lips. Perhaps this was true, or perhaps he later polished his preliminary defense to publish it as *Pro Milone,* one of the masterpieces of eloquence and lucidity in the Latin language.

One of the persons who thought Cicero had improved his oration when he wrote it down was Milo himself, who was found guilty and exiled to Massilia, today's Marseilles, for four years. From here he wrote his defender: "O Cicero! If you had only spoken as you have written, I should not now be eating the very excellent fish of Marseilles."

Neither Milo's fate nor the legal points raised by Cicero are so interesting in the present context as are the glimpses Cicero gives of the attitude toward, the position of, the Via Appia in the whole affair. It was only a road, but it had become a thing of reverence and mystique, its builder after more than two hundred years a near-saint. Clodius' supporters cried shame at the villainy of a man who would kill a member of the Claudian *gens* on the very road which another of the *gens* had built. They regarded it, or pretended to, as an offense as great, to us, as if a descendant of Lincoln had been murdered right in the lap of the grand brooding figure sitting in the Lincoln Memorial. But the Clodians overstated their case, and Cicero in *Pro Milone* called their bluff.

Publius Clodius Pulcher and his sister Clodia were among the bad apples of the Claudian tree. Clodius was a roisterer and murderer, his sister so licentious that being seen with her could shame a man. As for the road itself, Cicero wrote that "the great Appius Claudius the Blind" had built it to serve the people, not to give his descendants the right to perform brigandage and murder upon it. This referred to the murder of a Roman cavalier committed by Clodius on the Via Appia at an earlier date. "When this same Clodius, still on the Appia, killed the worthy Roman Marcus Papirius, this was not a crime to be punished," wrote Cicero. "Yet now the name of that same Appia comes up again amid so many tragic laments. That road which first, the fruit and work of an honest and innocent man, was not even named, today makes everyone speak of it because it drank the blood of this brigand and traitor to his country."

Finally, as Cicero was at pains to point out, Publius Claudius Pulcher and his sister had both deliberately changed their names from Claudius to Clodius to disassociate themselves, specifically and irrevocably, from Appius Claudius' branch of the family.

This interesting name change illustrates the Roman talent for maintaining both a rigid system and useful devices for altering it. Citizens had, in the classical period, three names. The first, the *praenomen*, was the given name. There was little choice in the selection: there were about fifteen traditional *praenomina* ranging from Appius through Lucius, Marcus, Publius to Servius, Tiberius, Titus and Vibius. Next came the *nomen*, or family name, given to every member of the family. There were thousands of these names.

There was no handy or traditional list of female *praenomina.* Because girls had to be called something, however, they were often given a feminized version of the *nomen,* or family name — Julia for *gens* Julius, Claudia for *gens* Claudius, etc.

*Gens* names proliferated in a way which would drive a modern census taker mad. If a Roman emperor granted citizenship to a province far away, every person in it was entitled to take his family name. Many people who live today in the vast area the Romans called Gaul are called Julius as the result of just such a bestowal of civic rights and names.

Slaves had only one name, but when they became freedmen by either fiat or payment, they could take both the *praenomen* and the *nomen* of their former masters. Often their old name, the slave name, became the *cognomen,* the final of their three names.

It is the *cognomen* which is most fascinating, because it was Roman habit to make this a description, a characterization, of the person in question. Plutarch recorded that surnames given in mockery were very common: one of the Metelli *gens* was called Diadematus because he suffered from a running sore on his head and went around wearing a bandage jeeringly designated a "diadem" by his fellow citizens. Dark-skinned persons might get nicknamed "Niger," and redheads "Rufus."

Appius Claudius Caecus was blind, and his relative Publius Clodius Pulcher handsome, or so at least his name implies. The usage persists in Rome and in Italian provincial villages, where townsfolk have official baptismal names but are commonly referred to by descriptive nicknames echoing the old *cognomina*: "the short," "the often-inebriated," "the crippled," "the wanderer."

More than two hundred years before the murder of Clodius, the Appia had experienced its first big happening. That was in 281 B.C., when Pyrrhus, king of Epirus, threatened Rome from the south. He and his army moved from territory in northwestern Greece and southern Albania, and a Roman army under the consul L. Emilio Barbula marched out on the Appia to Capua and the province of Apulia to do battle. Outlying cities in the Italian peninsula frequently changed sides, in these early wars, if they felt themselves in danger of extinction at the hands of invaders. Their infidelity was sensible and protective: they were immediately exposed, and far from the center of power. During the campaign against Pyrrhus, the Romans realized for the first time that a road was not only useful for transporting troops and supplies but also a magnificent tool for securing the loyalty of the outpost cities. It maintained commercial ties which would otherwise have withered in war; it encouraged the outposts to remain loyal to Rome.

Once they had noted the utility of the ribbon of Appian road, the Romans instantly made plans to extend it farther, drive it on, to link with other strongholds all the way to the Adriatic Sea.

The first test of this philosophy came with Hannibal. He invaded Italy, as everyone knows, over the Alps with those famous elephants. Rome tried to curb the terror engendered by these enormous beasts by scornfully calling them "Lucanian cows." Hannibal conquered the whole north of the peninsula and then, after the battle of Lake Trasimeno, crossed to the Adriatic, marched across to the Volturno River and occupied the fertile plains of Falerno and Campania. He even cut the Via Appia, moving across it to the sea at Sinuessa to hold the breadbasket and supply line of Rome itself.

It was 217 B.C. Rome was in panic. Reports of horrid portents came from everywhere. It was reliably reported that the statue of Mars on the Via Appia and images of the wolf had sweated. At Capua, observers said that the sky seemed to catch fire, and that a moon fell in a shower of rain. Peasants reported that their goats had grown sheep's wool; a hen had turned into a cock, and a cock into a hen.

Hurriedly, Roman troops fortified Casilinum where the Appia crossed the Volturno, to cut off Hannibal's retreat in that direction. They rushed troops to a narrow defile above Tarracina to pinch him off in the north. Then they settled down to starve him out. The breadbasket Hannibal occupied was lush, but not lush enough for an entire army to feed upon for months.

Hannibal escaped the trap by one of the most famous ruses in military history: he tied twigs and branches around the horns of cattle, set them afire and shooed the beasts off in the direction of the garrison in the pass above Tarracina. Just what the Roman soldiers thought they were, as they advanced in the night, can only be imagined. They didn't wait long enough to find out. They fled, and Hannibal and his soldiers got away.

The next year he came back, entered Capua and cut the road. After that it was easy for him to persuade Capua to defect to his side, and quickly he took Casilinum. Romans could no longer travel safely to Beneventum and beyond, could not reach their Adriatic ports except by sea. Hannibal eventually was stopped, and he retired from Italy, but the lesson was clear to the generals: to hold the cities and the colonies, they must hold the road.

Two centuries after Hannibal, the Appia was the scene of a solemn happening. The first emperor, the beloved Augustus, died in Nola, east of Naples, in 14 A.D. and was carried home to Rome on the Via Appia. As word of his death spread through his domain, the citizens turned out in thousands to pay him homage. His body was borne on the shoulders of the most august citizens of the realm, all the long weary miles from Nola to Rome, in a cortege which must have been as moving, as packed with mourners, as the long, slow passage of Lincoln's funeral train across the United States, worlds away and centuries later.

Senators, hearing of Augustus' death and eager to make their homage personal and specific, rushed from Rome in fast carriages to compete with local dignitaries for the honor of bearing the remains of the man they called "the restorer of the nation." So vivid was the competition for pallbearer that their posts had to be divided carefully between senators representing neighboring municipalities and those of old, veteran colonies.

Unlike most travelers on the road at this time, Augustus' cortege moved only by night. The decision was made partly because of daytime heat—Augustus died on August 19—and partly because of a desire to permit as many persons as possible to view the remains. Each day the cortege halted and the body was laid out in the town hall or principal temple of the city through which it passed.

The specific homage of Rome itself began at Bovillae. Here, near the tavern where the bad Clodius was slain half a century before, the knights and horsemen of the city met the slowly moving procession and escorted it past the tombs and monuments, across the neat stones, through the Servian Wall, to the entrance of Augustus' house. Crowds of ordinary people surged ahead of the procession and behind it, jammed the sidewalks, vied with one another in the volume of their wails, the copiousness of their tears.

In a rather melodramatic deathbed speech in Nola, Augustus had asked, "Have I played my part in the farce of life creditably enough?" and implicitly answered his own question: "If I have pleased you, kindly signify appreciation with a warm goodbye."

It was a very warm goodbye. Senators competed with one another thinking up extraordinary ways to honor their lost leader. One suggested that the name "August" be summarily transferred to the month of September, because Augustus had been born in September but died in the month by then called August. It would be more respectful, he thought, to give Augustus' name to the month of his birth rather than that of his death. Another proposal would have declared the entire period between his birth and death "the Augustan Age," and thus entered it officially in the calendar. These ideas came to naught, but Augustus was given two funeral eulogies and a magnificent pyre on the Campus Martius. Afterward, barefoot knights with unbelted tunics carried the ashes to his family mausoleum between the Via Flaminia and the Tiber River. Some witnesses swore that they had seen Augustus' spirit soaring upward out of the flames of his cremation fire.

Quite another mood pervaded the Via Appia and its procession watchers twenty-three years later when the Emperor Tiberius died. Tiberius had spent the last ten years of his reign on Capri, indulging some exotic personal tastes and governing the realm by dispatching messengers up and down the Appia to Rome with orders for his underlings.

In the very year he died he once impulsively set forth for Rome, but stopped seven miles outside the city. He was already past Bovillae and could see from there the walls of Rome. The writer Suetonius says that Tiberius stopped here because of the death of a pet snake which he used to feed with his own hands. He was about to feed it on this day when he found the snake had been half eaten by a swarm of ants, and a portent warned him "Beware the power of the mob." Tiberius turned right around and headed back for Capri, where he felt secure. This time he didn't make it. He fell ill at Misenum, north of Naples, and there he died.

As his followers and soldiers prepared to take him back to Rome, the citizens of Misenum shouted that he should be taken instead to the amphitheater at Atella and there be half burned. Atella was the scene of popular, vulgar farce, and to half burn the body of an emperor in a place like this would have been ignominy beyond belief.

In Rome, meanwhile, news of Tiberius' death caused such joy that the people ran around shouting, "To the Tiber with Tiberius!" Suetonius, who clearly didn't like Tiberius either, implies that there was even a plot to drag the emperor's body off its litter and dump it onto the Stairs of Mourning, where were deposited the remains of strangled criminals. In spite of Suetonius' prejudice and the citizens' joy at Tiberius' death, the body of the emperor was duly cremated and the ashes put to rest according to Roman rite.

Neither Misenum, where Tiberius died, nor Nola, where Augustus died, is on the Appia. Both their stories became twined into the fabric of the road because of the funeral processions along it, and Nola was linked in half a dozen ways. A very ancient city, it became a Roman stronghold and base of operations in the wars against Carthage. Hannibal laid siege to it three times, but failed to take it. Nola may perhaps have been no bigger then than now in population, about 25,000, but in those days it had a defense wall three miles in circumference, two grand amphitheaters, twelve city gates, many temples.

Here in the fourth century A.D. lived a bishop called Paulinus who came from Bordeaux and who is believed to have invented bells. He made bells in Nola and sent them out along the Appia to eager buyers. For years they were called *nolae,* for the town, or *campanae,* for Campania, the region. Bells are still called *campane* in Italian.

More than by the bishop or the bells, more even than by Hannibal and Augustus, Nola is linked to the fate and history of the Via Appia by the story of Spartacus and the rebellious slaves. There was a gladiators' school near the Via Appia at Capua, run by a certain Lentulus Batiates. Batiates' pupils were all slaves or convicted criminals, who were trained for certain death in the arenas or at entertainments in private villas, fighting either each other or wild animals. In A.D. 73 a group of two hundred gladiators plotted to escape from Batiates' ill-treatment and their own fate. Word of the plot got out, however, and only seventy-eight of the slaves managed to get away, armed with meat cleavers and spits from the kitchen. Along the road outside the school they happened upon a group of wagons carrying other gladiators to another city, and seized their weapons.

First the men occupied a slope of Vesuvius. Some say they camped inside its crater; they had of course no way of knowing that in less than a decade this seemingly docile mountain would blow up with such shattering force as to make itself, and the victim cities of Pompeii and Herculaneum, immortal.

Plutarch says that the escaped slaves elected three leaders, the first of whom was Spartacus, a Thracian, who was "a man not only of high spirit and valiant . . . in gentleness superior to his condition, and more of a Grecian than the people of his country usually are." It was said of Spartacus that when he was taken to Rome to be sold, a serpent coiled around his face as he slept but did not hurt him. His wife, who must have been sold into slavery at the same time, was described by Plutarch as a "prophetess." She announced that this was a sign of her husband's formidable power and good fortune.

Powerful he certainly was. Spartacus and his little band lived by raiding the towns near Vesuvius. Nola was one of the first, in 73. As word of their success spread across Italy, dissatisfied slaves from everywhere slipped away at night to join the rebellion. Within months Spartacus had 70,000 men. They manufactured their own weapons, organized into companies and columns, trained until they were a superb fighting force. They beat off every Roman expedition sent against them. And they kept moving. Having sacked Nola and humbled it, they didn't linger and turn it into a camp, despite its fortifications.

Rome panicked as it seldom had since the days of Hannibal. This time the threat was not only outside the gates but also agonizingly inside the house. How could this opulent society, spoiled, served, pampered, exist if the slaves defected?

As the revolt grew, Spartacus' forces rose to 120,000 men and he refused further recruits. A larger army would have been unmanageable. He marched his victorious horde north, by-passing Rome completely, apparently heading for the Alps and dispersal. Once this far from Rome, he reasoned, his men could break up and return to their homes, free and able to make a new life.

Some of his army was rabble, however, and men of lesser stature than Spartacus found it agreeable to live by the sword. Instead of dispersing, they sacked and pillaged in the north. A Roman army of at least 40,000 men was dispatched against them, and Spartacus turned south toward the instep, perhaps hoping to escape by sea to

Sicily or Africa. His troops marched the entire length of the peninsula, were caught by Crassus and his army, and decimated.

Spartacus himself, according to witnesses, provoked his own death
by plunging into the middle of hand-to-hand combat. He cut down
two centurions, was wounded, continued to fight standing up as long
as he could, and fought from his knees when he could no longer
stand. Crassus' troops hacked his body to pieces so it could not be
recognized or identified.

No one knows how many slaves died in this battle. Some escaped,
took to the hills and forest, and vanished. Six thousand captives
taken by the Romans were ceremoniously crucified along the Via
Appia, all the way from Capua to Rome. Their bodies were left for
months, nailed to wooden crosses erected on the road. Here they
rotted and disintegrated, smelled and fell in bits onto the road, pro-
viding gruesome warning against further rebellion.

Ritual torture and execution along the road persisted for centuries.
In A.D. 298 word of a miracle spread through the Roman world and
excited the populace. In an age of augurs, portents and miraculous
events the authorities felt it necessary to quiet the restive citizens
with a diversion. What could be more diverting than torture and
death? The so-called Twelve Martyrs of Hadrumentum were seized in
North Africa, taken by sea to Italy and marched along the Appia to
be executed, a few at a time, in full view of the populace. Two versions of this gruesome event exist, but according to both, four of the
martyrs were executed at Potentia, which was not on the Appia but
near it, three at Venusium, and on the evening of the next day, three
more at Velinianum. The final two were tortured for two days at Sen-
tentianum, then killed. One scholar explains that the execution of the
martyrs took place at such obscure cities as the last two because they
were "on an important highway" and thus would be noticed, and
spoken about, by thousands.

Even philosophers could get into trouble on the Appia, sometimes
just because of the way they wore their hair, or because of their
dress . . .

Philosophy was an import to Rome, and it came mostly from
Greece. Greek philosophers spouting Epicureanism, or Stoicism, or
Platonism, had been around the Forum for years before a trio of
them, Carneades, Diogenes of Babylonia and Critolaus, turned up in

155 B.C. Though Diogenes' name is much better known than the others, it seems that Carneades was in his time considered the more brilliant lecturer. Talking and listening were always favorite Roman occupations, so half the city turned up to hear the Greek philosophers. One day Carneades gave a long public address in praise of justice—a subject very popular in the Forum because the Romans happily considered themselves among the most just of the world's men. The next day, however, Carneades returned, found an even larger audience, and then proceeded to prove, in best Greek logical style, exactly the opposite of what he had proved the day before. This time he said that justice, however noble it might be, was in fact an impossible dream. War, he said, was a form of injustice, and therefore the Romans, if they wanted to be truly just men, should restore to their previous owners the lands they had conquered. But if they pursued justice to such extreme ends as this, would they not be foolish? And could folly be regarded as a virtue?

The pragmatic Romans, totally unaccustomed to Greek polemics, to the intellectual exercise of expounding an unassailable philosophical point and then, quite calmly, destroying it completely by using the same system of logic, were flummoxed. The exercise sounded like double-talk to the spectators, and like some kind of mysterious subversion to the rulers. All three Greek philosophers were sent packing, and so deep a suspicion lingered in the official mind that in the reigns of Nero and Domitian in the first century A.D. all philosophers, and even anyone wearing the short "philosopher's cloak," were suspect. Nero even banned them from the confines of Rome, on the grounds that they were dangerous, secret wizards.

There is no evidence that a philosopher was ever slaughtered on the Appia, but Philostratus of Lemnos, a Greek who taught in Rome in the third century A.D., left a record of a near-miss. It involved a philosopher called Apollonius who adhered to the Pythagorean philosophy that the entire universe is a manifestation of various combinations of mathematical ratios. He also claimed that he could communicate with the gods through assiduous practice of ascetic discipline. Armed with these ideas, he turned up on the Appia in the middle of the first century A.D., attended by thirty-four disciples. All, according to Philostratus, were "recognizable by their short cloaks, their bare feet, and their flowing hair."

Just outside Aricia, Apollonius was met by a panicky fellow practitioner of the philosophers' art called Philolaus. Philolaus berated him: "You are trailing after you a band of philosophers, and here you are a target for ill-will, blissfully unaware that the officers posted at the gates by Nero will arrest you all even before you enter the city."

Apollonius did what a good philosopher should do: he turned to his followers and asked if anyone of them wished, under the circumstances, to leave the group. Within minutes his thirty-four disciples shrank to eight, and with these he entered Rome. As it happened, the guards asked no questions whatever and Apollonius was permitted to remain in the city.

In the sixth century A.D., personal dramas along the Appia were eclipsed, as they had not been for centuries, by wars and invasions so overwhelming that anyone's fate or blood, including the noblest of the Romans, was lost in the common bath.

In that century the Goths from the north invaded Italy and besieged Rome. They were, as barbarians go, a fairly civilized group, and Rome might have done well to make peace and ally with them to avoid the infinitely worse fate which eventually occurred. But Rome did not. In the course of the prolonged Gothic wars, with the Goths camped outside the city and the Romans entrenched within, in the year 546 the military lessons learned against Hannibal were well remembered and the Via Appia was open. General Belisarius rushed from Byzantium to the rescue of Rome, landed at Naples and marched his army up the Appia.

Procopius, who traveled with him, wrote that "Belisarius commanded all the Romans to remove their women and children to Naples, and also such of their domestics as they thought would not be needed for the guarding of the wall, his purpose being, naturally, to forestall a scarcity of provisions. . . . And a great throng set out for Campania. Now some, who had the good fortune to secure such boats as were lying at anchor in the harbor of Rome, secured passage, but the rest went on foot by this road which is called the Appian way . . ."

After the Goths came the Longobards, who captured Beneventum

*A beguiling funerary* stele *found near Capua. It was*
*commissioned and paid for by a freed slave for his former*
*masters: the scene at bottom shows them setting him free,*
*at top the masters rendered in severe formality on their funeral stone.*

and Capua around 593 and cut the road. Almost a hundred years later Charlemagne liberated the territory by taking Beneventum, Capua and Tarracina. Blood on the stones again.

None of these wars left such a scar on the national memory as did the ninth-century incursion of the Arabians, whom Italians call Saracens. The Saracens, waving the sword of Islam, exploded out of their desert reaches to humble every nation in sight, and they almost won all of Europe. They struck Italy around 827, from Sicily, and the shock was so strong that even the calm, contained twentieth-century road scholar Daniele Sterpos achieves a note of cultural outrage, of unforgivable offense, when writing of their arrival: "On the grand Roma-Capua of antiquity, on the Via Appia, the infidels came in a wave not far from Urbe [Rome] itself, at Aricia, which they assaulted and destroyed . . ."

The infidels also sacked and burned Roman Capua, laid waste to the amphitheater which lay beside the Appia, shattered and looted the tombs by the side of the road. Capua ceased to exist, in 841 or 842. The survivors of this cataclysm wanted to preserve the ancient name, and to attach it once more to its region. When the worst was over they moved a few miles north and established a new Capua "at the site of Roman Casilinum, at the bridge which is called Casilinum over the Volturno."

In so doing they saved the name Capua, but they created a cartographic confusion which plagues absent-minded scholars and exasperated tourists. The town now called Capua on Italian maps lies on the site of ancient Casilinum, and the town which once was Capua has risen again and became Santa Maria Capua Vetere. Anyone reading ancient references, or searching for Roman ruins, is constrained to remember the name change and to conduct himself accordingly.

Unmoved by the patriotism of the residents of ruined Capua, the Saracens advanced again. They considered it prudent to by-pass the Appia between Capua and Rome, so they made camp by the sea and invaded the heart of the former empire from the sea, from the Roman port of Ostia. Once there, they were hungry for new territory to plunder, so they moved south from Rome on the Appia to Fundi and Formiae. They captured both, and obliterated Formiae. After their passage there was no city on the site for centuries, only a fortified remnant on the hills called Castellone or Castel Nuovo, and a second stronghold on the sea called Mola di Gaeta.

By 868 the Saracens held almost all the once-Roman lands to the south of the city. In that year even Tres Tabernae, the last station on the Appia still being used, fell. From this moment for almost a millennium the section of road through the Pontine Marshes was abandoned, left to the encroaching muck and water of the swamps. Even after the Saracens retired, Rome had neither the strength nor the funds to mend this most impressive but fragile stretch of road.

Sometime after A.D. 1000, therefore, traffic shifted inland from the Appia, avoiding the swamps and passing near today's Sermoneta and Sezze in the valley which goes to Priverno, turning toward the coast again after the swamps were far behind. There had been an ancient track there for centuries, as witnessed by the writer Lucilius, who in the second century B.C. traveled from Rome to Puteoli, via Capua, and mentioned that he had passed by Setia (Sezze), i.e., inland from the course of the Appia. Even so, Lucilius found his journey "slippery and slimy." The Sezze route joined the Appia near Terracina.

After 1000, travelers had a choice of the detoured Appia or the almost intact Via Latina farther inland. In the twelfth century an abbot of Iceland, one Nikolas Saemundarson, trekked from his parish to the Holy Land and left a record of the route. He went, he said, by "the marvelous work of a road called Appia" which crossed the mountains, passed by Terracina, Fondi, and across the river Garigliano, and delivered him to Capua in two days. Travel time, even with the detour out of the Pontine Marshes into the foothills, had been cut in half since the time of Procopius.

Indication that the detour was still in use in the seventeenth century comes from the travel journal of an adventurous English explorer, John Raymond. He said that on the Appia, near Priverno, he had seen some "bandits brought to justice," their bodies left on display beside the road just as were those of Spartacus' slaves.

In the fifteenth century of Leonardo da Vinci the old route was a sad water-invaded ruin, and Leonardo sketched it. Italy was at war again, with the city-states of Milan, Florence, Genoa and Mantua pitted against Venice, Naples, Ludwig of Savoy and others. Neutral: the Pope, Ferrara and Bologna. Alarums and confusions ran up and down the Appia, but there was little combat because in 1451 Italy was having a plague. All public gatherings, including wars, were considered unhealthy.

In the sixteenth century the armies of Austria and Spain tramped up and down the road, snapping at each other over the prostrate body of Italy, and hordes of tourists used the Appia to seek papal indulgences and blessings in the jubilee years of 1575, 1600 and 1625.

These were years in which foreign struggles washed over the road and the descendants of the Romans seemed too divided, too tired, too weak to resist. They stirred themselves in the eighteenth century when the French Revolution broke out. Rome, led by Pope Pius VI, was totally against the "rising of the rabble" in France, and Italians later gathered around the banner of Austria to oppose the rise and the regime of the young general Napoleon Bonaparte. All that effort achieved was an invasion by Bonaparte's troops and a papal exit into exile.

With the Pope gone, a new Roman republic was declared, but there were insurgents inside the city and outside it. On the Via Appia the citizens of Albano armed and prepared to march on Rome. Further south, Velletri armed. The town of Ariccia was ready to rush into combat, until the clergy convinced the residents that battle would be fruitless.

Napoleon's man in Rome was General Joachim Murat. In 1798 he led French troops out of the city along the Appia, through the Porta San Sebastiano, to subdue the insurgents of Albano. Along that same route, the same year, went a prelate called Ercole Consalvi, a strong and vocal man who would live to become chief minister of the Papal States after the fall of Napoleon. In 1798, however, Consalvi had been ordered deported by the French. He left on an April morning, riding in his own little gig with one horse, accompanied by a military guard, a cart with eighteen galley slaves, and a carriage carrying four political prisoners. According to his *Memoirs,* Consalvi didn't mind much "the excellent road to Albano" until his fine gig mysteriously broke both shafts and his religious excellency was unceremoniously transferred to the more substantial carriage of the political prisoners.

Consalvi's French escort, not overly impressed by the personage or position of the prelate, kept him together with the prisoners and the galley slaves for meal stops and overnight lodgings, and when the convoy arrived at Terracina they turned the whole lot over to the local French commandant. This gentleman ordered them to get out and start walking. He didn't care much where they walked—just away from the Papal States. If they returned, he said, they would be killed.

This was a dilemma. Terracina was in a no man's land between the occupied Papal States and the independent Kingdom of Naples. The Kingdom had made a treaty with Napoleon. Would its soldiers welcome persons expelled from the Papal States? Consalvi convinced the French commandant that there might be some unpleasantness, and he persuaded the commandant to send the galley slaves ahead to test the climate. The *Memoirs* are couched in formal language, but the scene must have been one of wild disorder. The slaves advanced cautiously, and were met by Neapolitan soldiers with cocked rifles. Quickly calculating the odds, the slaves, with no prior parley, scattered and headed for the hills. Desperately, frantically, they clawed their way through the brush and behind the rocks. Their end is not a matter of record. Having thus demonstrated to the French the perils of passage across the border, Consalvi was permitted to remain in Terracina. Later he got a safe-conduct pass to Naples, where he waited out the war.

A random result of the French occupation of Rome was that the Via Appia carried more traffic than it had ever seen before. Armies marched to and from Naples, Rome, even Paris. Enormous military carts carried cannon and ammunition, food, commercial goods. France, having subdued Italy, was still fighting Great Britain, and the English were masters of the sea. Never before had the seas of Italy been so totally closed to traffic; never before had it been necessary to let everything go by road.

This crisis passed with Waterloo, and the end of Napoleon. Only once more did the old stones tremble under the wheels of horse-drawn military carts. This was during the Risorgimento, which brought the peninsula the first unity it had known since the glorious days when Rome ruled the world. It came at about the same time as the American Civil War. Garibaldi led his troops triumphantly up from Naples on the Via Appia in 1861 to take Rome and to create the modern state of Italy.

War and bloodshed, vendetta and sacrifice were not invented by the Romans or first practiced on their roads. The Etruscans, who ruled Rome for more than one hundred years, used sacrifice, quite possibly human, as part of their religious rites. Half a century ago an American scholar, Tenney Frank, found ruins in the Forum which he believed belong to an altar of 489 B.C., the first fumbling beginnings of the Roman Republic. Under it was "a peculiar old drain . . . a vaulted passageway with a narrow ledge at one side where a small runnel lay. The drain was not meant for a large volume of water; the runnel was only a few inches wide. There are many such channels here and there in the Forum, and I venture the conjecture that most of them were made to carry away the blood of victims slain at altars."

These are cool, scholarly words, but they cause a shudder all the same. It is difficult to understand such ritual bloodshed. It is easier, embarrassingly easier, to understand the excuse for it: superstition and fear, plain and fancy patriotism, self-interest. These are lame excuses, but they have been found acceptable, in Rome and elsewhere, for millennia.

Milo's murder of Clodius was the single most clamorous bloodletting on the Appia, but the most significant may have been Horatius' slaying of his sister, near the Porta Capena, in about 640 B.C. Horatius was one of the brothers who had fought the Curiatii along the route which was to become the road, and he was the only survivor. As he returned to Rome triumphant, according to an account of Livy, he was met by his sister, who had been betrothed to one of the slain Curiatii:

> When she recognized on her brother's shoulders the military cloak of her betrothed, which she herself had woven, she loosed her hair and, weeping, called on her dead lover's name. It enraged the fiery youth to hear his sister's lamentations in the hour of his own victory and the nation's great rejoicing. So drawing his sword and at the same time angrily upbraiding her, he ran her through the body. "Begone," he cried, "to your betrothed, with your ill-timed love, since you have forgot your brothers, both the dead and the living, and forgot your country. So perish every Roman woman who mourns a foe."

This was for the moment too harsh and unfeeling a punishment for even the Romans to stomach, and Horatius was brought to trial. He was convicted, and as he was about to be bound he cried "I appeal." Appeal was granted, and during these proceedings Horatius' father came forward to say that his daughter had been justly slain. She had, he said, betrayed her country by mourning her betrothed, who was an enemy.

Horatius' father then applied the touch which must remain the envy of all the sophists of his world and ours. He implored the court not to make him childless by the execution of his one remaining offspring, blinking the fact that this one had murdered his only daughter. "You have seen me such a little while before surrounded by a goodly number," said Horatius' father. The Roman court and the Roman people collapsed, by Livy's account:

> They could not withstand the father's tears, or the courage of Horatius himself, steadfast in every peril. They acquitted him, more in admiration of his valor than from the justice of his cause.

Bloody murder excused, washed away in floods of tears and a surfeit of patriotism.

# XII
# ARCHAEOLOGY
# AND THE ROAD

The two quotations above embody a modern dichotomy in the long search to pry from the soil of Italy all the secrets of the Via Appia.

Just as aerial photography, along with sophisticated instruments like magnetometers, electronic sounding devices, stratigraphic drills, have given valuable tools to archaeologists, so have farmers been presented with mechanized equipment and sharp, deep ploughs which can turn up earth undisturbed for millennia. Road builders, land developers and construction contractors have dynamite and bull-dozers and millions of dollars for ripping through a buried landscape before the perennially hard up and meticulous student can get to the site.

These are recent problems, and perhaps in the long run they are unimportant, but the archaeological search for the Appia has come to the very fine print of the story. Scholars who once might have over-looked inscriptions now are sifting pebbles.

For the first thousand years of its life, the Appia required no re-search, except perhaps for a decent lodging place, or a shortcut some resourceful local citizen had discovered. In all those years, most of it was still in use. By the time archaeologists, as distinct from tourists, treasure hunters or even historians, applied themselves to the road a century ago, only the broad outlines remained. Details had been obliterated by time and abuse. So the search was on and it continues today: the Appia is like a Christmas stocking—the deeper one probes, the more fascinating it becomes. Most intriguing of all is that last item, almost too small to see, hidden in the hard-to-reach depth of the toe. The achievement of this last bit can become an obsession.

All that we know or identify today—apart from the simple physical remains of paving and bridge, amphitheater and milestone—we owe to the archaeologists and their allies the historians, architects, sculptors, philologists who have pieced together the coherent story of the road and its buildings.

Like all good detectives, they used every clue to hand: written records, maps, coins, inscriptions, folk memory, place names. They also used aerial photographs, chemical tests, simple old picks and shovels, and their own heads, hands and feet. In the beginning, for all of them, was the word: the surviving ancient itineraries, and works of all the writers from Horace to Cicero to Livy, Suetonius, Frontinus, Strabo, Procopius, both Plinys, and all the rest. Each precious word about its appearance, its dates, its route and construction had to be extracted and collated, then compared. These references could be matched to details in the itineraries, which do not always agree, to establish sites and names of cities, relay stations, distances between them, dates and locations of diversions in the road. Because so many Roman cities have simply vanished, distances between them are crucial to a search for their sites.

With all this preliminary study completed, the archaeologists turned to more detailed clues, provided by milestones and the thousands of other inscribed slabs and columns, sepulchral monuments, votive inscriptions, commemorative stones. Many of these are written in the equivalent of shorthand because of stonecutters' abbreviations, others are so eroded as to be almost illegible. Dozens of scholars worked at deciphering them; they became the major life work of the German classical historian Theodor Mommsen. Mommsen's monumental *Corpus Inscriptionum Latinarum* helped win him the Nobel prize for literature in 1902, and it remains the most complete and authoritative work of its kind. It is supplemented by the five-volume *La Campagna Romana,* by Giuseppe Tomassetti, an Italian scholar who studied Latin documents as Mommsen did inscriptions.

Other clues lay in place names. Repeated references to a stop called Forum Appii on the ancient itineraries convinced scholars that this settlement, which has disappeared, must have been founded by Appius Claudius or his workmen when the Via Appia went through, else it would not have borne his name. *Forum* originally meant only an open space, or the forecourt of a family tomb, or a space for political meetings, though later it became any gathering place. Echoes of the name exist in a settlement called Borgo Faiti, and a Foro Appio marked on highly detailed military maps.

Mesa, in the Pontine Marshes, built as a post station in the eighteenth century when flooded parts of the Appia were rebuilt, is reminiscent of the Roman *mutationes* Ad Medias, "in the middle," somewhere near the same place.

Folk memories die hard, and names persist even when they are corrupted. A good example, though not on the Appia, is the Via dell'Origlio, a road south of Orbetello which coincides with a long-abandoned stretch of the Via Aurelia. Italy is dotted with *masserie,* or clustered farmhouses, which have strange names like Quarto or Sesto or Ponte Rotto. Quarto and Sesto mean "fourth" and "sixth," respectively, and hint that once this spot was known by the milestone number on some well-known, well-traveled road. Ponte Rotto, "broken bridge," reflects memories of some structure which may no longer exist at all but which once marked the region in the minds of all who knew it.

Some folk designations can be deceptive. To many a peasant a Ponte Rotto is just that—last year's footbridge which collapsed in a flood, or some bridge of twenty, two hundred or two thousand years ago. Similarly, any old piece of road ("old" in this case being older than the experience of the person describing it) is often in the countryside called generically "the Appia" or "the Via Selciata," the paved road.

More reliable than place names for the vanished tracts of the Appia are the crumbling foundations of medieval defense towers or churches, even though they could not possibly be more than eight or nine hundred years old. Because the road was used well into the

Middle Ages, even in places where it had been reduced to a mule track, the neighbors tended to site their shrines and lookout towers along it. Thus much later buildings mark the track. Many medieval churches stand on ruins of Roman temples, the sites having remained holy despite shifts in political and religious loyalty.

Then there are the maps. The scale and the distortions inherent in the strange projection of the Peutinger Table make it of little use in determining fine details of the route, but by the sixteenth century there were fairly reliable maps of specific regions, including one of the province of Campania south of Rome which included many miles of the Appia. This map was produced in 1548 by the chief huntsman to Pope Leo X. Huntsman Domenico Boccamazza, who had tramped or galloped up and down the territory in search of game for His Holiness, kept his eye not only on the quarry but also, alertly, on the surrounding terrain. His map is remarkably accurate, full of clues to the location of pieces of road now invisible under fields, farms or later highways.

After Boccamazza came the men whose impressions of Rome and its monuments, the evocative remains of the Via Appia, live most vividly in the modern mind—the artists and engravers. First and best-known of them was Giambattista Piranesi, author of the Piranesi prints which hang in well-appointed offices and studies across Europe and the United States. Piranesi was born in 1720 at Maestre, a suburb of Venice, and grew up in the tradition of the Palladian architecture that has left its stamp on Jefferson's house at Monticello and half the courthouses and public libraries of American cities.

Piranesi, however, yearned for Rome, and when he was twenty he went there as official artist of the Venetian Embassy to the Papal States. There he fell hopelessly in love with ancient ruins. His architect's eye studied and measured and reconstructed, his artist's skill produced a series of meticulous and powerful engravings which called the attention of the whole world to the grandeur that once was Rome. To him, as to Luigi Canina a century later, archaeologists owe many indications of how things once looked, how to identify their remains centuries later.

Shortly after Piranesi came another artist, Carlo Labruzzi, who accompanied the English classical dilettante Sir Richard Colt Hoare on a tour of the Appia in 1789. This was the era of the romantic traveler, the brooder over shattered statues and crumbling walls, a time when rich Englishmen built fake Greek and Roman ruins on their estates, the better to brood by on long summer evenings.

Sir Richard was an ardent admirer of Horace, and he longed to follow the Appia as Horace had done. He was rich enough to indulge his passion, and scholarly enough to prepare himself for the trip by studying the contemporary works of a French abbé who had searched Italy for Horace's villa, and a detailed investigation of the Via Appia completed in 1745 by one of the early Italian road scholars, Francesco Maria Pratilli.

In Rome, Sir Richard retained the talented twenty-four-year-old painter Labruzzi to accompany him, and the pair set forth in a two-horse carriage with a folding hood. They stopped everywhere Horace had stopped, searching for the quiet inn at Ariccia, the fortress at Terracina, Cicero's villa at Formia. Because they traveled in November and December, they were halted at both Minturno and Benevento by bad weather. Then Labruzzi got sick, and Sir Richard had to give up at Benevento. Labruzzi completed 226 drawings, an incredible average of four a day. His delicate, evocative sketches and engravings eventually found their way to antiquarians' collections and classical institutes, and added, as did the Piranesi prints, to the body of solid reference on the appearance of Appian monuments and traces of road.

After them came another Anglo-Italian team, Sir William Gell and Antonio Nibby. They tracked the Appia all over the Campania, found and marked its feeder roads, used triangulation and modern measurements to produce the first scientifically accurate map of the region. Nibby's contribution to topography is recognized in a street named for him in a relatively new section of Rome. Fittingly, Rome headquarters of Autostrade S.p.A., the company which built Italy's postwar superhighways, is at No. 10, Via Antonio Nibby.

In the mid-nineteenth century there was a flurry of archaeological excavation on the Appia. It began under an enlightened pope, Pius IX. He was fascinated by the tumbled remains along the first few miles of the Appia near Rome, and ordered excavation and restoration of the road from the Tomb of Cecilia Metella to the ruins of Bovillae. From December 1850 until May 1851, 150 workmen dug. Then the unhealthy air of the region forced them to stop. They had uncovered an area almost two miles long, seventy yards wide, five feet deep, and found perfectly preserved roadbed, sidewalks, an incredible number of monuments—four hundred in that short stretch—and so many inscriptions that they lost count.

Work commenced later under the direction of Luigi Canina, commissioned by the Pope to draw and measure everything found. Canina's drawings joined those of Piranesi and Labruzzi in the precious archives of scholars and archaeologists, but his greater contribution was a proposal that the excavated fragments be left *in situ*. He seems to have been the first archaeologist in Italy who wanted to reconstruct and leave the remains where they had been placed instead of hauling them away to a new site or to a museum. Canina reset funerary busts, inscriptions, statues into their niches, on their bases, or into original walls if he could. When niches and bases and walls were missing, he supervised construction of new supports for the old fragments.

After the unification of Italy, in 1861, the flurry of archaeological interest increased. The glorious past was important then to the heady present, the first unification of Italy since Roman times. One scholar excavated and identified the Porta Capena in 1867; in the same year the man who was to become master of Roman and Appian topography, Rodolfo Lanciani, turned twenty and began his first work, the study of remains of a monumental structure built by Trajan.

With Lanciani began one of those remarkable dynasties of scholars of different personalities and different nationalities who passed to one another all that they knew. Linked by personal affection and absorption in their subject, they became marvelously expanding sources of related knowledge. Lanciani, born in Rome in 1847, studied engineering and the classics. He did excavations in Rome, Tivoli—the Tibur of the Romans—and Ostia; he won a prize for his examination of and commentaries on the works of Frontinus; he spent eight years collecting and checking a *Forma Urbis Romae*, forty-six sheets of topographical research which traced the full story of the city's ancient, medieval and modern monuments. He followed this prodigious work with four volumes on the history of the excavations in Rome. Much of his work is available in English, and it is delightful reading.

One of Lanciani's most devoted students was a young Englishman, Thomas Ashby, whose family moved to Rome when Thomas was sixteen. With Lanciani and his own father, young Ashby developed a

*Remains of a "Roman edifice," found in Brindisi during*
*excavation for an apartment house in 1959.*

love for the Roman countryside and a passion for archaeology. When the British School at Rome was founded for the study of classical art and architecture and archaeology, Thomas Ashby was its first pupil. He became its director in 1906.

When Lanciani died there was Ashby to carry on, and when Ashby died in 1931 there was Giuseppe Lugli, who had known and worked with both men. Lugli became spiritual father to the present generation of Italian topographers, road archaeologists, historians.

His generation was trained, as some of its predecessors had not been, in the multifaceted discipline of archaeology, the many strands of evidence which can be wound into a cord of continuity. His contemporaries knew something of architecture, of geology, of chemistry, of sequence dating through pottery sherds. They could date structures not by reading names or numbers on a stone, but by studying workmanship, style, technical detail. They could figure out which sections of the Appia dated from Appius Claudius' time, or Augustus', or Nerva's. They could assign a year to a viaduct by its stones and structure, dissect a bridge and report that the central arch was original, the side ones later, the upper structure medieval. Because all Roman roads and bridges built in the same era look alike, their dating and dissection helped to establish which ones had lain on the original Appia, which were on connecting roads linking it to the Latina, or the Domitiana, or the Traiana.

Slowly, carefully, they picked at the knots to unravel the mysteries, reconstruct the network. Up and down the road they went, correcting previous errors, enlarging upon earlier observations, finding remains overlooked by those who had gone before.

Study of the Appia never was the sole province of the Italians or the British. Learned works on Italy's geography and monuments were written in the 1600s by Frenchmen, Swedes, Jesuit fathers from Holland, Germans. In the late nineteenth and early twentieth centuries a dozen nations established permanent academies and institutes in Rome for training their scholars in architecture, classical art, Latin and archaeology: American, British, French, German, Swedish. Tenney Frank of the American Academy in Rome did pioneering work in dating of Roman monuments by study of their materials and construction details. Sweden's King Gustav Adolf, who died in 1973, was an avid amateur archaeologist and supporter of the Swedish school. He spent most of his vacations digging in Italy.

Members, fellows, students at foreign institutes are required to be tireless researchers, good walkers, stout fellows and linguists. Some exhibit quite special talents. There was Dr. Esther B. Van Deman of the American Academy, for example, who spent thirty years investigating old bridges and aqueducts and who is reliably reported to have been the only archaeologist in all of Rome—perhaps in all the world—who could date a brick in an ancient structure by the taste of the mortar which held it in place.

Dr. Van Deman collaborated for years with Thomas Ashby, but she was not much involved with Ashby's study of the Via Appia Traiana. For that research, Ashby relied on another colleague, Robert Gardner. Together the two tramped the entire length of the original Appia and the Appia Traiana. The latter was a more complex assignment because there was no certain literary or physical evidence of the road's route across the Apennines. Horace and Strabo both described a route here, but they had, on the evidence, gone different ways. Other ancient itineraries were conflicting. Ashby and Gardner walked and walked and walked, studying maps and topographical evidence to find the telltale river valleys which were natural routes of passage, looking for the marks of carriage wheels, checking place names, hunting for worked stones. In 1916 they published the first comprehensive account of the specific route of the Appia Traiana—with gaps.

When Ashby and Gardner, Nibby and Gell, Sir Richard Colt Hoare and Labruzzi jogged or hiked over the old road, the automobile had not yet conquered all, industrial smog had not blurred the landscape. They could stand on a rise and see for miles. They could hear peasants hacking at their fields with hoes, and the ubiquitous bleat of sheep on the hillside. Their progress was slow over the landscape, but exciting. One of Ashby's successors as director of the British School at Rome, Dr. J. B. Ward-Perkins, evoked their era in an introduction to the 1970 edition of Ashby's book *The Roman Campagna in Classical Times:* "The tales they tell tend to have a quality slightly larger than life—of nights spent in remote country railway stations after missing the last train home; of the sinking hearts with which, at the end of a long day's tramp, they greeted the appearance on some distant horizon of some antiquity still to be explored. . . ."

Their successor Lugli still tramped the countryside, but by his time there were aerial photographs to direct his feet. Lugli was the first of the road scholars to use photos as a common, available aid. Even back in Lanciani's time, 1909, photographs taken from a balloon over the coastline had helped to delineate the ground plan of Ostia, the port of ancient Rome. Though as old as Pompeii, Ostia never became quite so famous because its end was not so dramatic. Silt and mosquitoes and malaria brought down Ostia, but the outlines of its silt-buried walls and buildings were clear from the air in 1909.

Despite this early and dramatic proof of the value of aerial photographs there was no effort to adapt them to orderly archaeology until the end of World War II. The British led the way. When the war in Europe ended suddenly in the spring of 1945 an RAF officer, John Bradford, found himself with nothing much to do. He was stationed in Foggia near the Adriatic sea, along with a friend and fellow RAF man, Peter Williams-Hunt. Both had been trained as archaeologists before the war, so to amuse themselves in peacetime they requested permission to make flights over the flatlands of Puglia and photograph them with the aim not of destruction but of research.

Both officers knew that the key to archaeological detection by air is in vegetation. Ancient drainage ditches, canals and moats fill up in the centuries with earth and refuse and support a rich, lush vegetable growth which shows dark in photographs. Grass and scrub struggling to survive in the few inches of soil which covers buried masonry walls or arches are lower, sparser, and look lighter from the air. Photographs taken at low, oblique light just after sunrise or before sunset accentuate the contrast.

The technique can be refined by mounting two cameras parallel to each other, in the same plane. This system obtains overlapping pictures of the ground which, viewed with stereoscopic instruments, yield three-dimensional photographs of dazzling detail and clarity. Bradford and Williams-Hunt didn't care much, in 1945, what they discovered. They were happy just to have something to do between the end of the war and the beginning of a new life. To their amazement, their aerials of the Adriatic plains revealed traces of two thousand settlements, many of them Neolithic, the existence of which had only been conjectured before they took pictures.

Bradford remembered the millions of aerials made during reconnaissance flights of British and American aircraft over Italy during the war. These, too, could be invaluable to archaeologists. In the euphoric atmosphere of war's end, it was not difficult to persuade military authorities to make sets of negatives and prints of all Italy available. These are in Italian archives today, as well as in British, American and Swedish schools; others are in the hands of U.S. universities which conduct archaeological research in Italy.

Italy's Ministry of Public Instruction, which is responsible not only for schools but also for excavations, museums and preservation of antique remains, established a technical branch called Aerofototeca to make its own aerial photographs. One of its earliest and most enthusiastic officials was Rumanian-born archaeologist Dinu Adamesteanu, who flew all over Italy in the fifties and became an expert at photo interpretation.

It is difficult for an amateur to interpret aerials, but with Adamesteanu as a guide the dim, pale circles become medieval forts or Roman city walls, Neolithic villages, Greek cities, prehistoric hutment sites. Thin, dark lines turn into canals and drainage ditches. Things totally invisible on the ground leap to life under his blunt, square thumb as it moves across the print. His rumbling voice trembles with excitement: "Here it goes, the Via Appia, can you see? Below this town and then straight, straight, to here, see it now?" It is a thin, pale line and one would never have seen it without his help. In the case of some recent photos it must be a quick look, an effort to memorize, because some of the aerials are used by NATO forces and not cleared for reproduction for people writing books about the route of the Appia.

Among the clearest patterns which trace across the photos are the remains of "centuriation," the precise square or rectangular division of land into individual agricultural holdings or a Roman colony's streets and blocks. This is the neat grid, born of the Roman urge to order, passed to the layout of army camps and roads, inherited by much of the New World as city planning.

Circles and arcs exist in nature, in the shape of a rainbow or a tree trunk, the rising sun and the setting moon. Nature makes no straight lines or square corners, however. These are inventions of man. Traces of lines, and angles, even if buried under the earth, are therefore clues to archaeologists of the presence of man and more specifically, in Italy, of the presence of the Romans or their neighbors the Etruscans.

The Via Appia shows in many aerials as the pale, wide slash which was once the *decumanus,* or central street, of a centuriation, a land division for a colony. Colonization followed conquest, and the road followed colonization. Identification of centuriated sites helps archaeologists to slip into its proper niche the town site, the road, and fit each into the jigsaw puzzle of routes, dates and construction.

Roman colonies were not made by wagonloads of pioneers who set forth bravely on their own initiative to build homes and a new life beyond the fringes of civilization. They were new settlements created as an official act of the state, settled by persons whom the state selected. Sometimes the state accepted volunteers, sometimes it simply drafted the colonists. Colonies, first in Italy and then abroad, were established with the primary aim of holding new-won territory loyal to Rome. Often they were small: in the early days, three hundred Roman citizens were chosen and each was given two *iugera* of tillable land. A *iugerum* was the amount of land which a yoke of two oxen could plough in a day. Two *iugera,* about 1¼ acres, were the traditional and hereditary land parcel of a Roman citizen.

Official measurement and formation of a *colonia* was an affair of solemnity. The decision to found a colony was made at various times by the Assembly, the Senate, the tribunes or the dictators, and commissioners were appointed to supervise proceedings. Once the site was chosen, surveyors moved in with their trusty *groma* and surveyed and subdivided.

When all was in order, the colonists marched to the site in military style under a banner called the *vexillum.* Auspices were taken, animals were sacrificed as burnt offerings to the gods. The chief commissioner put on ritual dress and marked the boundaries of the colony by plowing a shallow furrow, with a bronze plow, where the city wall should rise. At each place where there was to be a gate, he lifted the plow. Drawing the plow were oxen, a white steer harnessed to the right, a white heifer to the left. Use of bronze for the plow seems to have been a hangover from Etruscan practices in Italy, and their taboo against iron. Rome's first bridges, it may be recalled, were built entirely of wood because of this same ritual taboo.

Once all this was done, the settlers were allotted their land. Plots were determined in a lottery called *sortes,* possibly to avoid charges that one lot was better than another, more likely to break up cliques of persons who might have selected adjacent plots and then banded together to form an interior power bloc in the colony.

Then boundary stones were set up, and a *forma,* or official plan, of the colony made in bronze to show forever the centuriation and allotments. When the *forma* was completed, it was set up in the forum of the colony, and the *groma* ceremoniously removed.

Colonies differed in size and composition. Some were made up entirely of Roman citizens, others of "Latins," or indigenous residents who had not been awarded the privilege of Roman citizenship. Sometimes the settlers were imposed upon an existing town which Rome had just conquered; then both centuriation and colonization were accomplished around the fringes of the built-up area. In virgin territory, conquered but unpopulated, colonists were supported in their first perilous months with food from Rome, military aid to protect them until they could build their own defense walls.

They were linked irrevocably with the roads, set as strongholds along the way or as advance posts to which the roads could proceed. During the regime of the reforming Gracchi brothers in the second century B.C., thousands of poor and homeless residents of Rome were resettled in colonies. This took them off the dole and encouraged them to go it alone as shepherds and farmers. Ten Roman roads already existed before the Gracchan reforms, but between the years 133 and 109, eight new roads were built to link the Gracchan agrarian colonies into the network.

Colonies at vital and/or dangerous spots were almost always composed of Roman citizens. Inland and remote colonies were Latin. Often the latter were given more land than the traditional two *iugera.* Under Lucius Cornelius Sulla in the first century B.C., and for years afterward, colonies were established for veteran Roman soldiers as a form of pension. Many of these were abroad, populated by ex-soldiers and wives taken from the local population.

Often colonies were exempt from taxes and awarded a high degree of local autonomy. Colonists along the coasts, assigned to guard the ports, were excused from military duty on the grounds that their location and vigilance were service enough.

During the Empire the right to establish colonies was taken away from the Senate and representatives of the people of Rome and put into the hands of the emperors. They sometimes granted as much as

200 *iugera* to an individual, and they used the system in the way which has become so fiercely resented in modern times—as colonialism in other people's lands, for the purpose of exploit.

Wherever or however they were established, whether they consisted only of towns or also of tracts of agricultural land, the process of centuriation continued. The Roman term was *limitatio,* but the word doesn't translate gracefully into English, so the term *centuria,* a square of land covering 200 *iugera,* has been adopted. A centuriated area, whether buried city or measured farmland, shows its grid until it is covered totally by later building, and it affords key reference points for archaeologists.

The same vegetation which is so helpful from the air is a source of frustration on the ground. Crops, weeds, creepers cover the stone and hide remains of bridges and columns. Only in the dead of winter, when whipping winds, torrential rains, sudden snowstorms even in March make travel both dangerous and difficult in stretches of the Appia as it crosses the Apennines, are the ruins visible. For this reason archaeologists venture out in the worst possible weather, in bitter cold, to explore while they can see. They also develop sudden urges for long walks cross-country in the raw days of late autumn and early spring. This is when the new deep plows go into action, when a sharp-eyed scholar can find, turned up in fresh furrows, bits of broken pottery or tiny terra-cotta votive heads, or coins.

Small boys are particularly adept at spotting bits. A generation of them has come along in the past ten years, trained by local archaeologists and museum directors not to smash their finds for fun but to bring them in for examination. Coins are their specialty. An Italian urchin is able to identify a bent, dirty, eroded Roman coin on a trampled hillside as unerringly as an American child would spot a half dollar shining on the sidewalk.

Coins are much prized by the archaeological detectives. They are easily datable, often carry specific information, and are so small that they are likely to have been overlooked by treasure hunters, passersby or even earlier archaeologists. Furthermore, only certain cities in certain eras were given the right of coinage—Capua had a mint, very early—and caches of currencies provide valuable clues as to trade in early times and the routes on which it traveled.

The first medium of exchange in Rome was oxen and sheep, but coins were made as early as 450 B.C. The Latin word for money, *pecunia,* was derived from *pecus,* sheep or cattle. The first bits of unwrought copper which became media of exchange were marked with figures of animals, but by the time the Appia was born, coinage customarily bore images of gods. One of the most popular was Janus the two-faced, shown looking both ways and immortalized in Januarius, the first month of the year.

Unlike many Roman gods who bore a resemblance to Greek counterparts, Janus was indigenous, a purely Roman god who opened the gates of heaven when he went about his affairs in the morning, and closed them when he returned at night. He became the god of comings and goings, of entrance and exit, of doors and gates and passages. In ancient Rome, doors and covered passages were called *ianuae,* and arches *iani.*

In the era of the great roads, Janus' two-headed image was symbolically fitting for coins, and was often used. So were wheels, of four or six or eight spokes, and teams of prancing horses drawing two- and four-wheeled chariots. Colonies which had received the right of coinage were fond of showing the plow and ritual furrow of their founding, or gateways which they had built. Colonies abroad often used the names of Roman officials or of the legions whose veterans had peopled the place.

Typical of the detailed study, of the specialization which has become the pattern of road archaeology in Italy today is a work published in December 1972 by Giovanna Alvisi of Aerofototeca. Miss Alvisi settled upon one small section of the northern part of the modern province of Puglia, a geographical area which the Greeks had called Daunia. Her aim was to find traces of all the Roman roads in the territory. Portions of the Appia from west of Aeclanum to Venusium lay within it, as did bits of the Appia Traiana from east of Beneventum to Rubi, today's Ruvo di Puglia. The same section contains traces of the feeder roads connected to the Appia, and to Greek tracks which preceded all of them.

Miss Alvisi studied all the ancient texts, the pioneering work of Ashby, the researches of Pratilli and Lugli, and itineraries from Horace through the Middle Ages. She had aerial photos, made by Bradford in the forties, and more recent ones from her own office.

She lamented how much change had come in the terrain between 1945 and today, because of deep plowing, road building and private construction.

Despite all these mechanical aids and past researches, Miss Alvisi was careful to mark her maps, and indicate in her text, tracts over which she "had not walked personally." Without the walk, the clambering through fields and underbrush, the careful parting of branches for a close look, no researcher can be sure he has found a trace of the road.

No big surprises remain now. Most of the tracing has been done, most of the correcting and updating and double-checking. Yet here and there a tiny blank spot remains; a doubt is not entirely resolved.

One of these is the site of the Caudine Forks, where in 321 B.C. a Roman army suffered such a disastrous humiliation that the nation never forgot it. At that time Rome was battering at the boundaries of the Samnites, who had shoved at Rome in 354 B.C., getting dangerously close to the area of Latium where Rome had established control, and in 321 the Roman consuls decided to shove back, aiming at taking Maleventum, a principal Samnite city.

Just a few miles west of today's Benevento, in a narrow valley which even now seems wild and forbidding, locked between rugged hills reaching up 2,000 or 3,000 feet, the armies met. Samnite intelligence apparently was better than Roman, and legend says the Romans were further confused by Samnite soldiers disguised as shepherds who told them that the enemy had withdrawn and proceeded eastward. The Romans advanced in the valley without even the precaution of reconnoiter. There they found their way blocked by huge stones and felled trees, the Samnite soldiers well placed along the slopes of the encasing hills. According to Livy, the Roman army realized the hopelessness of its situation and surrendered. According to Cicero, it fought and was defeated. In either case, the soldiers, the consuls who led them and the dignitaries who accompanied the troops were forced to pass "under the yoke," an arch of hostile spears, as a token of submission.

Though the consuls surrendered, the Senate in Rome refused to ratify the decision. War with the Samnites continued until 290 B.C. Rome won, but the humiliation of the Caudine Forks lingered. One of the aims of the Via Appia was to press through their country—through Maleventum/Beneventum, Aeclanum, and the town the Romans called Venusium. At the latter site they forcibly dispossessed the Samnite residents to make way for a Roman colony.

No doubt it would have appealed to Rome to thrust the Via Appia straight through the battle site of Caudine Forks, once the Samnites had been driven back. There was in reality little choice of routes, owing to the nature of the terrain. Ancient texts about the battle are discrepant, physical descriptions vague, and scholars are not sure whether the present route of the Appia either follows the old track completely or truly goes through the Caudine Forks. There is in the valley of Arpaia, where the modern road goes, a town called Forchia which may be an echo of the Forks. But there is another valley, just north of a place called Sant'Agata de'Goti, which corresponds more closely to the description given by Livy. The matter is unresolved, though scholars agree that Roman Caudium, which came to dominate the pass, was on or near the present site of Montesarchio, which rises on a dramatic rocky outcrop at the eastern end of the complex of narrow valleys.

Another intriguing blank spot lies smack on the original route of the Appia between Benevento and Taranto. All the ancient itineraries and diaries say that the Appia went from Beneventum to Aeclanum, Aquilonia, Horace's hometown of Venusium, then to a place called Ad Pinum, another named Silvium, and thence to Tarentum and Brundisium. Ad Pinum has been identified satisfactorily near a place now called Posta della Morte, but Silvium remains something of a mystery, as does the route of the road between Venusium and Tarentum.

Geography and geology are fundamental here. There was no necessity for heavy road construction because the area was rocky and very dry—*siticulosa Apulia*, the writers called it. Bedrock lay close to the surface after Venusium, and "construction" required little more than clearing off surface vegetation, marking out a boundary, perhaps hacking shallow channels to divert drainage from rare rainstorms. In general the route must have been determined by geological peculiarities which haven't changed in two millennia. Venosa and the present town of Gravina di Puglia, even Taranto, lie between the spine of the Apennines on the west and the Murge on the east. The Murge is a high, massive limestone tableland thrown up millions of

years ago in a geological upheaval. Between it and the mountains is a depression, a trough. This is a natural trackway which was, like the one which came down from the north into Beneventum and there turned east toward the Adriatic, a drovers' road used for centuries before the Appia was built. Logically, the later road would have followed it, or part of it, but the traces are dim.

Careful calculation of distances recorded on the itineraries put the site of vanished Silvium about halfway between Venusium and Tarentum. On this spot, or near it, is the town of Gravina di Puglia.

*The excavation at Minturnae as it looked in the summer of 1973 — and the weeds are winning.*

It is in the right place, and it is very old, but it is not ancient. Gravina appears in the written record only in the ninth century, when a bishop went from there to a council in Rome. The name Gravina is derived from the Italian word for mattock or pickax; it refers to a high slash or scarp cut at the city's edge by a tributary of the Bradano River, marking the western border of the high Murge.

Gravina has neither Roman ruins nor clear traces of the road; yet it must have passed very near here. All recent Appia scholars have attacked the problem of Silvium and the road, and within the decade the British School at Rome has excavated an extremely ancient flat-topped promontory across the river from Gravina, a place known variously as Botromagno or Petramagna.

Their studies show that Botromagno was a large inhabited center as early as the eighth century B.C. It may have been the Sidion, or Side, of the Greeks, a form of which name appears on one coin in the British Museum. To Roman ears this could have sounded like Silvium. Artifacts dug up on the top of the promontory and from cemeteries at its foot indicate convincingly, however, that the city was completely abandoned by the first century A.D.

The British School's Dr. Ward-Perkins believes that the hilltop residents of Sidion, or Side, or Silvium, may have moved from their easily defended city down to the flat, lured from their lair as it were by the relative security and freedom of movement created by Roman dominion, the road and the *Pax Romana.* They wanted to be nearer to the road, its commerce, its entertaining comings and goings. Similar shifts occurred in other areas of Italy, he points out, as inhabitants of hilltop fortresses profited from the new security to move into lower, more benign surroundings.

This does not resolve completely the problem of the Silvium of the Roman itineraries, nor the precise route where the road passed. Today there are four roads across the flat, featureless plain between Venosa and Gravina. In 1968, 1969, 1970 and 1971 an American archaeologist working under the auspices of the British School and with the consent of Italian authorities picked his way up and down all four roads hunting for clues as to which could have been the Appia. Though the distance between Venosa and Gravina is less than 35 miles, the total area covered to investigate all four possible routes is more than 270 miles, a formidable assignment in which even so large an item as a road is transformed into a needle by the sheer size of the haystack.

Patiently, the American scholar S. P. Vinson trekked over the countryside with helpers who included the most skillful of the local graverobbers. This man, who has an uncanny eye for the location of ancient remains, was recast as an archaeologist to help the experts. Vinson recorded his finds along all four roads, dividing pottery remnants and other artifacts into periods which range from Neolithic through the Bronze Age, Hellenistic, Republican Roman, Imperial . . . and plotted them on charts. One or two routes could be ruled out quickly, either because they revealed so few Roman-era remains or else because geological surveys and local records indicated that they had been subject to flooding centuries ago and therefore would not have been chosen, in this region of generally sparse surface water, as a road site.

In the end Vinson settled tentatively on the southernmost of the four tracks. This one leaves modern Venosa just north of the present route 168, well south of the main road, No. 97. It passes Posta della Morte, which was Roman Ad Pinum, runs north of Mount Serico, passes the remains of Botromagno to the south and enters Gravina from southwest. This route coincides with theories held earlier by archaeologist Lugli, and with aerial traces found by Adamesteanu. Nobody is irrevocably convinced that this is it, including Vinson himself, but the Italian Superintendency of Antiquities, the British School and Vinson agree it probably is.

Silvium remains more of a problem. Perhaps it was on the site of Botromagno. Perhaps it moved to the plain. There are faint traces of plains settlements in many places but few substantial ruins. The Samnite wars, the Pyrrhic wars, the struggles against Hannibal raged back and forth across this area. Doggedly the residents rebuilt. Then suddenly in the time of Augustus, the beginning of the Empire, the number of inhabited sites diminished. This should have been an area of relative peace and prosperity. Did the sites diminish because there simply was no one left to build?

Certain knowledge of how this clue fits, of where proof of the site of Silvium lies, still uncovered, is among those last little rewards, tucked into the toe of the stocking, waiting for archaeologists to find someday and produce to whoops of joy and triumph.

"A MAN WAS DIGGING OUT THE PAVEMENT AND DE-
STROYING THE ROAD . . . THE POPE SHARPLY REBUKED
HIM . . ."

Pius II, *Memoirs of a Renaissance Pope*

"TODAY THE WONDERFUL ROMAN ROAD SYSTEM IS
BROKEN TO PIECES. DESOLATION AND NEGLECT . . .
HAVE TAKEN THEIR TOLL; BUT. . . MAN'S WANTON
DESTRUCTION HAS TAKEN A WORSE TOLL."

From Ferdinando Castagnoli's introduction
to Daniele Sterpos, *The Roman Road in Italy*

# XIII
# THE MIRACLE
# OF SURVIVAL

More than any city except Rome itself, Brundisium belonged to the
Appia. It was the nearest port to Greece and the lands of the Bible, to
the Turkish peninsula and the site of Troy, to the Byzantine capital of
Constantinople. Brundisium was seagirt symbol of the wide Roman
world, both terminus of and gateway to the proudest road of the
proudest empire.

What arenas and forums and baths must once have stood there,
what columns and arches and aqueducts vaulting across the coastal
plain. How many seaside villas and palaces, docks, monuments, great
masonry moles into the sea, tombs along the road.

The final 15 kilometers to Brindisi on the modern Via Appia,
highway 7, are marked on some maps from Mesagne to the sea "Via
Appia Antica." The road goes straight and true and enters Brindisi
by the medieval Mesagne gate, but there are no traces anywhere of
antiquity—no tombs, no monuments, no paving or curbing. There is
only that evocative straightness to indicate that this was the route.

Inside the city, one of the two marble columns which marked the end of the road soars 60 feet tall on top of its square base, imperiously staring across half a mile of polluted harbor water toward the 170-foot monument Mussolini built in 1933 to the glory of the Italian sailor. A flight of wide stone steps, fifty-two of them, leads upward from the gently sloshing water of the port to the little piazza where the Roman column stands. Beside it is the truncated base of its twin, which fell down in 1528 and was re-erected in the city of Lecce in 1666.

Stone tritons guard it, and sculptured likenesses of Jove, Neptune, Mars and Pallas Athena decorate it. Mildly dirty children play around it, climb on its protective iron railing and explain to tourists in an Esperanto-like patois composed of near-equal parts of Italian, English, German and Greek that this is the terminal point of the Via Appia Antica. Sea travelers arriving from or leaving for Greece and Turkey see the column across the water as tourists have for two thousand years, but now it looks hemmed in, dwarfed by the rigid geometry of TV aerials sprouting from the roofs of nearby buildings.

That, sadly, is almost all that is left of Brundisium. Near the column a marble plaque commemorates the poet Virgil, who died here on September 21, 19 B.C., on his way home from Greece, and there is a bronze bust of him in a park near the port. Near Porta Mesagne are remains of walls of an enormous Roman water storage tank and settling basin, where water was led in and allowed to stand to settle out silt and mud before it was routed into the city water pipes. The tank is now used by a *trattoria,* its brick roof supports covered with climbing plants. Still visible in the floor are the channels which were water ducts.

Under the entrance of an apartment house near the Piazza Vittoria are the big blocks and neat brickwork of an unidentified "Roman edifice" which turned up in 1959 during foundation excavations. Having been carefully exposed and preserved, the remains were then left, unmarked and unlabeled, and the hole in which they are exposed accumulates garbage and debris from the street and apartment tenants. Frolicking children point out that the stones are "very old" and "very important"; one small expert, tracing with a grubby finger the remains of green paint on ancient marble, informed us that these were traces of Roman blood shed in the defense of some treasure whose precise nature is unclear to him.

*A particularly imperious Roman eagle, dug up near Brindisi and exhibited in the courtyard of the town's archaeological museum.*

There is also an archaeological museum in Brindisi, housed in a pleasant *palazzo* with a columned patio. Inside is a collection of funerary fragments, broken columns, bronzes and vases and terra-cotta figurines. In the courtyard lie massive Roman ship's anchors, and a stern sculptured Roman eagle on a pillar. The eagle was assigned as a special badge to Roman legions by the consul Gaius Marius in 104 B.C. Before that, the legions had had four symbols—minotaur, horse, boar and eagle—but after Gaius Marius it was the eagle which they carried into action. The one sculptured into stone at Brindisi is so imperious and lively a bird that it looks as if it might suddenly fly off, pillar and all, to the lands of the East.

One final monument deserves attention. It is just a small seventeenth-century fountain, near where the Appia passed, in the Piazza Vittoria. It was erected in 1618 by citizens of Brindisi to a Spanish governor, Don Pedro Aloysio de Torres, and it isn't very pretty. But its base is made of battered Roman-era stones collected in the vicinity, and the simple dedication tells volumes about time, and vicissitudes, and Roman works. The citizens thank Don Pedro "because he brought water back to the city, having reconstructed an ancient Roman aqueduct."

That nothing more remains in Brindisi is a pity; that anything remains at all is a miracle. The settlement was founded at an unknown date by a people called the Messapici. In the seventh century B.C. it was a port for local traders with Greece, and with Greek colonies to the southwest on the Italian peninsula. The Greeks called it Brentesion. Rome conquered it in 266 B.C. and changed its name to Brundisium. In 244 it became a Roman colony. Shortly thereafter the Via Appia arrived at its gates, and three hundred years later the Appia Traiana entered it from the north, giving it a double link into the network.

Long before Trajan's road arrived, Brundisium had proved loyal in the civil wars and invasions of Hannibal, and Rome gratefully awarded it not only the title "city," *municipium,* but also the special privileges and attractions of a free port.

These were its glory days. All major traffic to and from Rome and the east passed through Brundisium. Its rivals Tarentum and Barium, Hydruntum and Lupiae declined as it rose. Julius Caesar rushed here in 49 B.C. trying to head off his rival Pompey, but Pompey got away. Octavian came later to make peace with Mark Antony, though the peace didn't last very long. Trajan, Vespasian, Marcus Aurelius, Septimius Severus came and went from Brundisium as did writers, philosophers, apostles.

Then came the bad days. As the Roman Empire disintegrated, Brundisium was captured, sacked and occupied by Goths and Byzantines, Longobards and Saracens. The Emperor Louis II, grandson of Charlemagne, destroyed it in A.D. 868. Normans under Robert Guiscard conquered it in 1071. It came back to life during the Crusades as a port of embarkation for Christian soldiers off to do battle with the infidel. In the thirteenth century Frederick II, king of Germany and Holy Roman emperor, built a fort and revived the city. He was followed by the Angevin monarchs of France, who established an arsenal and enlarged the port but who made the city suffer during their internal dynastic struggles.

Spanish rulers from Aragon took over next and almost ended the city's life forever by blocking the channel to the open sea. They did it to ward off the Turks, who threatened to conquer all of Europe, but the closed channel created marshes and stagnant pools, suffocating maritime life. From 1496 to 1509 Brindisi was in the hands of the Venetians. Then the Spanish took it back again. It was in that period that citizens erected the fountain to the Spanish governor who gave them back drinkable water.

As if all this hadn't been enough, Brindisi was shaken to bits by earthquakes in 1456 and 1743. Not until 1775, under Ferdinand IV of Bourbon, was the vital channel reopened to the sea. Brindisi began to revive, but it didn't really catch its breath until the Suez Canal opened in 1869. That new traffic route brought a renaissance to all of the Adriatic. From 1869 until 1914 Brindisi was an important embarkation point for the Indies, and afterward it was an Italian naval base. In World War II it was bombed and bombarded, and in September 1943 it became briefly the seat of the Italian government when King Victor Emmanuel III and Marshal Badoglio took refuge there as Mussolini's government collapsed.

Little wonder that nothing much remains of the grandeur that was Roman Brundisium.

Similar tribulations, though not often so internationally complex, were visited upon other cities and sections of the road. Appian monuments near Rome, and Rome itself, were devastated by Visigoths under Alaric in A.D. 410, Vandals under Genseric in 455, Saracens in the middle 800s. These marauders ripped from tombs and monuments the precious metals which adorned them and broke through the masonry looking for treasure.

Barbarians are routinely and traditionally blamed for most of the destruction of ancient monuments, but they are blamed unfairly. Rodolfo Lanciani wrote in *The Destruction of Ancient Rome* that the barbarians should be left in peace, for "their part in the destruction of Rome [is] hardly worth considering when compared with the guilt of others. By 'others' I mean the Romans themselves, of the Imperial, Byzantine, Medieval, and Renaissance periods."

One "barbaric" king, Theodoric of the Ostrogoths, ruled Italy from 493 to 526 and was so horrified by the Romans' casual destruction of beautiful old marbles that he restored an earlier office of *curator statuarum*, "keeper of statues," to try to save what he could from the destructive hands of masons, limemakers and stonecutters. He also commissioned work on the Via Appia and had large sections of it restored across the Pontine Marshes. It was partly thanks to Theodoric that Procopius found the road in such good condition in 535, and could write admiringly that "the breadth of this road is such that two wagons going in opposite directions can pass one another, and it is one of the noteworthy sights of the world . . ."

After Theodoric no king or pope, emperor or nobleman for centuries considered preservation of the road, or of its monuments, important.

Early Christians melted down "pagan" bronze works of art to turn them to their own uses. Marble statues were knocked to bits to make lime, or carted off as decoration—no longer as religious symbols—to villas and gardens. Temples were taken apart so the stones could be reused, in churches or private homes. Lanciani was able to trace one block of marble from the pedestal of a statue erected in A.D. 193 in a town hall near Rome to the Baths of Caracalla in 285. From there it was removed unceremoniously by a prefect of Rome in 365 and turned into a monument in honor of Valentinian I. It disappeared completely in 1548, probably into a lime kiln of Pope Paul III.

In the fourth century A.D. vast stores of unworked marble were left untouched on the Tiber's special marble wharves and on a canal leading to today's Fiumicino Airport because builders in Rome found it far simpler to rob the monuments of the Republic and the early Empire than to go get fresh marble and start from the beginning.

The Emperor Constans II of Constantinople in the seventh century ordered removal of the gilt bronze roof coverings of both the Pantheon and the Capitol for his own uses. Anything he overlooked was taken a thousand years later by Pope Urban VIII, who used the rest of the Pantheon's bronze to fashion the canopy of the high altar of St. Peter's and to make cannons for the nearby Castel Sant'Angelo. This circular building had begun life as the great tomb of Hadrian, but it had long since been transformed into a combination papal fortress and what the English call a "bolt-hole," a handy hiding place for precipitous flight when flight was prudent. Hadrian's tomb had already been plundered: in A.D. 536 its military garrison had beaten off an attack of the Goths by hurling down on their heads the magnificent Greek marbles which adorned the mausoleum.

As the centuries passed, the mindless destruction went on. In the countryside, peasants in need of material to make shelter for themselves pulled down the Appia's monuments and dug up its paving stones. Venusium's Roman amphitheater was almost entirely destroyed between the eleventh and thirteenth centuries to build an Abbey of the Trinity, and the road itself vanished with the houses, the forum, the baths, into a tumbled bumpy landscape of rock-strewn grazing land.

Barons of wealthy families appropriated any reach of road, any solid structure which they could use to convert into strongholds and toll roads. The Caetani straddled the Appia just outside Rome; the Savelli took over the great round theater of Marcellus; the Frangipani laid hands on the Arch of Titus and even the Colosseum. When the popes abandoned Rome to move to Avignon in the fourteenth century, things got worse. For seventy years there was no central authority. Destruction ran wild, aided by an earthquake in 1349.

Outside of Italy, the Roman road network which had spread across the continent was destroyed deliberately because people who lived near the roads considered them nothing more than a handy means of transport for wandering robber bands and conquering armies.

By the middle of the fifteenth century there was a pope in Rome of notable knowledge, culture and conscience. His name was Aeneas Sylvius Piccolomini, Pius II. Statesman, humanist, poet, he left a written work of *Commentaries* which forms the only true autobiography ever left by a pope. He was horrified by the wanton destruction.

In Book XI he speaks of the Appia, framing his remarks in the awkward third person in which he wrote all the *Commentaries:*

> Meantime Pius, after celebrating in St. Peter's the feast of the Ascension of Our Lord, was invited . . . to visit the monastery of St. Paul in Albano that he might make himself acquainted with those ancient sites. . . . Going out by the Porta Appia on the road toward Naples, he viewed on the way many ruins, chief among them the hippodrome near St. Sebastian's [this was the circus of Maxentius], a huge shattered obelisk which once served as a goal post for two and four-horse chariot races, and the noble tomb of Cecilia Metella now called "bull's head."

> He came on many ruined villas and an aqueduct borne on lofty arches but broken in many places. In the groves near Albano they found the Appian Way paved with very hard black stones and on either side the huge bulk of towerlike tombs stripped of their marbles.

Further on, the Pope describes a trip from Albano to Lake Nemi:

> He went by the Appian Way, the pavement of which is still visible. The road was in many places more beautiful than at the height of the Roman Empire since it was shaded on the sides and overhead by leafy filbert trees . . .

On this trip Pius II was infuriated by what he saw. He had admired Roman road construction, the way the ancients had "cut away the mountain" on one side, and on the other constructed "a retaining wall of huge squared stones." But

> here a man was digging out the pavement and destroying the road, breaking up the great rocks into small pieces to build a house near Nemi. The Pope sharply rebuked him and instructed Prince Colonna, the owner of Nemi, not to allow the public road, which was the Pope's responsibility, to be touched thereafter.

Five hundred years later, in the summer of 1972, the road the Pope ordered not to be touched was torn up for one kilometer through the heart of the town of Albano, to permit work on water, gas and electric lines during a resurfacing project. In the process almost all of the Appian paving stones which had lain under the modern road for centuries were shoved aside, dumped as fill, or stolen by people who know that stones from the Appia will fetch a fine price from antiquities lovers or villa owners who cherish nice courtyards made from historic basalt blocks.

Pius II was a man of his century: the fifteenth century was a splendid moment in the Renaissance, a burst of enlightenment, learning, artistic appreciation. But it contributed mightily to the destruction of the Appia and its monuments. The intellectuals and art lovers went about seizing capitals, columns, friezes, inscriptions, to add to their own new palaces and art collections. The more a once-grand structure was picked away and carried off, the more rapidly its framework deteriorated. Pius II spoke up again:

> It delights me, O Rome, to look on thy ruins, from whose wreck thy former glory still appears. But these, thy people, burn the hard marbles torn from thy old walls to make lime. If this sacrilegious people continue thus for three hundred years more, there will remain no vestige of greatness.

Less than a century later the painter Raphael was complaining of the same thing, in a letter to Pope Leo X:

> I should even go so far as to say that all this new Rome which we now see, large and beautiful as it is, adorned with palaces, churches, and other edifices, is all built with lime made from ancient marbles.

Some marbles, mercifully, escaped the lime kilns and were casually reused along the outer reaches of the road. There are bits and snatches up and down the route: a marble *cippus*, still gleaming white, as doorstep of a peasant house or sill of a barn; a beautifully worked column holding up one corner of an ancient church; an inscription set upside down in a wall, having been used as a simple building block. Stones of Roman moles are visible as fill in the retaining walls of modern seaside highways. Round, heavy millstones of ancient date are set into walls, or if they are broken, used as arches for the passage of people, beasts, water. Tumbled milestones, broken bridges . . . on the high ridge above the sea at Terracina, where the road went before Trajan made his cut, old stones straggle in the grass along a road reduced to a mule track, between dejected houses and ragged gardens.

Near the ruins of Minturnae, south of Terracina, is a bit of road, and a miraculously preserved bridge viaduct now known as the Ponte degli Aurunci. Once it connected the Appia with the Roman city of Sessa and the Via Latina. No signs direct the curious to this lovely remnant. It must be sought with the aid of Italian guidebooks and friendly peasants (see Appendix). There is no visible trace of it from the only modern road which passes nearby, but a five-minute walk in the right direction reveals it. Suddenly, between ancient rock cuttings in the enveloping cliffs made to extract the stones of the roadbed itself, it appears — neat, narrow, deeply set. The road goes on for almost a kilometer, arching upward in the telltale Roman fashion which modern Italians call *a schiena d'asino*, "the donkey's back," to cross a shallow valley on twenty-one arches. All twenty-one are still there, 450 feet of masonry construction, though the diminutive stream which flows today uses only the center and two smaller adjacent arches to dribble on its way. The stones of the road begin and end suddenly. All the miles of road on either side of the bridge-

viaduct were taken up by peasants centuries ago to use in their own buildings. All that remains is the difficult part, almost impossible to reach from ground level without complicated equipment. Only for this reason do they remain, now partly covered with weeds and closely bordered, on both sides, by the truck gardens and neat patches of small landowners. Once there was decoration and facing fixed to the structure, but all this has been removed.

An even less accessible Roman road monument, an Appian bridge which spanned a river near the present town of Buonalbergo, east of Benevento, was taken apart fairly recently by the same breed of energetic peasant. This bridge, now called the Ponte della Chianche, had six arches, each decorated with double rings of carefully set two-foot tiles. The entire inner ring of tiles in the highest, most-difficult-to-reach, central arch has disappeared: peasants discovered that the bridge tiles made perfect surfaces upon which to bake bread.

Of all the sagas of survival on the Via Appia, that of Cecilia Metella, Byron's "stern round tower," is the most astonishing. Having first been turned into a fortress in 1300, it was coveted again in 1589. By then it had passed to new owners of surrounding farmlands, and they wanted to pull down the tower to construct more useful buildings. They addressed themselves to Pope Sixtus V, who was on record as having said that he wished to "remove unsightly ruins in order to repair [buildings] that required it."

The archaeologist Rodolfo Lanciani unearthed the text of their request and published it in 1894 in an Italian archaeological bulletin. It needs no comment.

> Giovanni Battista Mottino, and Girolamo Leni and his brothers, are the owners of the farmlands of Capo di Bove, where there is a tomb, or tower, which it would be very advantageous to them to dismantle. They therefore humbly pray your Holiness that they may be granted permission in such way that the gentlemen of the city council [*signori conservatori*] cannot oppose it by saying it is an antiquity, which they ought not to say, as it is out of Rome and not in a public place, and others have been dismantled, one on the road to Tivoli, another of marble at Ponte dell'Arco, yet another at Casal Rotondo, and many others. If your Holiness will make this concession we think that the Roman people will do

*One of the most evocative traces of Roman road still existing. It was built to connect the Appia to the Via Latina and the town of Sessa.*

241

likewise to please him, and thus all we receive will be by special favor of our Master, and we will unceasingly pray God for his preservation, and that a long and happy life be granted. . . .

Sixtus V upon the evidence was nothing loath. The brothers had promised to pray for him, after all, and swore eternal gratitude, and anyway, he cared not a whit for antiquity. He granted the request, but he added a phrase which tripped him up and frustrated the brothers Mottino and Leni: "Our Sovereign Lord and Master grants the concession, provided that the Roman people are content."

At first the *popolo romano* hesitated and initial demolition work began. Then opposition began to grow. Three members of the city council, known as the Capitoline Assembly, objected. On a motion made by Paolo Lancellotti, and seconded by two colleagues, the council canceled the permission and the Tomb of Cecilia Metella was saved—for the moment.

Lanciani, whose retrospective rage at Sixtus V ranks with Livy's rage at Appius Claudius, even suggested in his article that "This incident, coupled with others of the same kind, may account for the change in public feeling toward Sixtus V." The very magistrates of Rome who on November 26, 1585, had voted to erect a monument to the Pope for having restored safety and plenty to the city, less than five years later announced his death as follows: "Today our most holy Lord, Pope Sixtus V, closed his life amidst general satisfaction and rejoicing."

Not even one century passed before the tomb was threatened again. This time it involved another pope, and the architect-sculptor Bernini, and of all things the Trevi Fountain, that baroque monument to dubious taste, beloved of sentimental tourists and small boys eager to filch tourists' votive coins from its depths.

It began with Pope Nicholas V, who in 1453 brought a new water supply to Rome from a spring in a village nine miles east of the city. The water, in the aqueduct called the Vergine Antica, was carried by gravity flow only, taking twenty-four hours to make the nine-mile trip from source to the Fontana di Trievi, as it was then called. Pope Nicholas' fountain was simple and dignified, its only decoration the crown and crossed keys of papal power and the letters S.P.Q.R.

By 1640, however, the pope was Urban VIII, who had torn the

remaining bronzes off the Pantheon. He commissioned Bernini to build a much grander fountain for the Vergine Antica. Bernini looked around and decided that the most convenient source of building material for a monumental fountain would be the Tomb of Cecilia Metella on the Appia. First he demolished the old fountain, then he shifted the outlet of the aqueduct to a new site. This move was a costly but graceful gesture, for by this time the popes had taken the habit of abandoning the Vatican during the worst of the summer heat and moving to a summer palace on the Quirinal Hill. Bernini did it so that the Pope would be able to see his new fountain from the vantage point of the Quirinal Hill (where stood the former papal summer residence, now the Quirinal Palace, official and ceremonial residence of the presidents of Italy).

After this, Bernini asked papal permission to pull down the sepulcher. Urban VIII granted it with no qualms, but again the people of Rome rose up and complained. Their outcry was so vociferous and so sustained that the Pope rescinded his demolition order and stopped the work on the new fountain. Cecilia Metella's tower was saved again, beside the basalt blocks of the road.

The Trevi Fountain was finally completed in May 1762, 122 years and fourteen popes after Pope Urban commissioned Bernini to do it. One of its many architects was Nicola Salvi, who couldn't finish because he died of a chill caught while he was inspecting the culverts which served the water source. There is a Roman tradition that before his untimely death, Salvi added a quite extraneous stone urn on the right side of the fountain to frustrate a garrulous barber who worked across the street and who between haircuts offered free advice to Salvi. Salvi designed and executed the urn just to block the barber's view. This strange, pitted stone addition to the fountain looks very like a design on Neapolitan playing cards, which are divided into suits called coins, swords, clubs and goblets. Salvi's urn looks like the ace of goblets and it is called that by Romans today. If that interfering barber who inspired it ever existed, his name has not survived. But there was, in the memory of residents of the quarter, an old barbershop at the correct site until just a few years ago.

Having been frustrated in one attempted rape of the Appia, Bernini was embroiled in another within a few years. This time it was

*All that remains of the once-great Roman amphitheater in Venosa, where Horace was born. It was demolished deliberately in the Middle Ages to build the Abbey of the Trinity across the street.*

for Pope Innocent X, whose family palace was on the Piazza Navona. He commissioned Bernini to do a fountain in the piazza, and decreed that an obelisk from the Appia should forthwith be brought to the piazza as part of the fountain design. The obelisk itself was an odd product of the pride of a first-century emperor, Domitian. He had ordered the stone quarried especially in Egypt, transported to Rome, and erected outside the Temple of Isis and Serapis in the Campus Martius. On its tapering sides he had himself portrayed as Pharaoh in the act of offering tribute to the Egyptian gods, and he had carved some accompanying hieroglyphs which scholars say mean nothing at all. They were fakes, designed to dazzle Domitian's public.

Somehow between the time of Domitian and the time of Innocent X the entire fifty-four-foot shaft of granite had been moved from the Campus Martius to the Via Appia. John Evelyn, Earl of Arundel, recorded in his diary that he had seen it there in 1645 lying in five pieces near the Tomb of Cecilia Metella. The Earl confessed that he coveted it and would have taken it back to England with him had it not been so confoundedly awkward to pick up and carry about.

Popes found transport simpler than did romantic, ruin-loving English travelers, so Innocent X got his way and the pieces of Domitian's obelisk were duly transported to the Piazza Navona and incorporated in Bernini's design for the central fountain of this lovely piazza. It is still there.

Even after the age of enlightenment and the dawn of archaeology, the pillage didn't stop. The excavation of the Appia which Pope Pius IX ordered in the middle of the nineteenth century gave him enormous pride and pleasure. Still visible on the left of the Appia going out of Rome, just opposite the church of St. Sebastian, are an open square and a column with an iron cross on top. Here are fixed three relatively modern inscriptions. The side facing the road has the coat of arms of Pius IX and a dedication to "Sebastian, unconquered martyr of Christ." Of the other two the first reads: "Pius XI *pontifex maximum,* in the year 1852, the seventh of his pontificate," and the second: "When the Appian Way was restored from here to Bovillae."

Pius traveled happily and proudly up and down his restored road, using it whenever he could. A local politician, one P. Trevisani, attached to a small house along the way a plaque written in ungrammatical Latin, on the occasion of the Pope's having gone south to witness some new "telegraphical experiments." Trevisani's plaque recorded that "Pius XI P.P.," while returning "by the Appian Way cleared of ruins, lent fame to this dwelling by the majesty of his presence."

Now the area is even more "cleared of ruins." Pius IX's motives were pure, his assistant Canina's efforts impeccable. Yet of all the once-lovely ten miles of road they restored, little remains. Exposure of buried remains subjected them to the ravages of rain and frost, the shelter fires of wandering shepherds and vagabonds, the depredations of art collectors and the mindless vandals who seem to exist in all eras.

Canina's walls have been ripped apart by thieves seeking statues and inscriptions. Much of the roadbed has been covered up again to prevent theft of its individual stones. Most of the marble which remained 120 years ago has been hacked away to leave crumbling brick cores. "All that lovely work, all that effort to preserve," says road scholar Sterpos, "has gone to rack and ruin."

Even nature complies in the destruction. Nature's plot is traceable, poignantly, over two millennia . . .

One of the tombs which Canina helped excavate and labored hard to identify was that which he finally judged to have been the mausoleum of Messala Corvinus, a victorious Roman general in 2 B.C. and a patron of the literary arts in the early first century A.D. Messala was a giant of his time, and his mausoleum a wonder of the age for its massive indestructibility. In the same century in which Messala died, the poet Martial referred to the tomb in his epigrams, comparing it, however, unfavorably with the immortality of the written word — especially Martial's written word. Martial was a Spaniard who had emigrated to Rome. Perhaps he resented the adulation of his new home for a dead general, or perhaps he was miffed that he hadn't arrived in time to receive some of Messala's largesse to struggling young poets. For whatever reason, he chose to use Messala's tomb as the symbol against which to hurl his words. In one epigram he wrote: "When the stones of Messala's sepulchre lie shattered on the ground, I shall still be read." In another he said: "The wild fig-tree splits the marbles of Messala's tomb; but writings are neither hurt by thieves, nor helped by time; they are the only monuments which know not death."

The second image seems an odd one, even a flight of fancy or poetic imagery on Martial's part. Yet time and nature have proved it literally true. In June 1973 several large chunks of mortar fell from the tall obelisk in the Piazza Santa Maria Maggiore in Rome, mercifully missing the few cars and pedestrians who were in the square at the time. Firemen, summoned to the scene with their ladders and crowd-containing cordons, identified the cause as a wild fig tree which had attached its roots high on the column and was busily dislodging both stone and mortar. This was the same culprit, said the firemen, which had caused the temporary closing of the remains of Trajan's market in Rome in 1971, and which was attacking the masonry of the Colosseum.

Just outside ancient Canusium near the Adriatic, a Roman gate stands still astride the remains of the Via Appia Traiana. It was built in the second century A.D. and long ago lost its marble facing, its frieze, its cornices. It looks sturdy from a distance, though the top has a strangely lacy profile. Upon closer examination the "lace" is revealed as a healthy crop of small but rapidly growing wild figs.

It is by miracle that the gate still stands, as well as the bridge at Sessa Aurunca, the Tomb of Cecilia Metella, the column by the sea at Brindisi, the scattered stones at Terracina and the battered amphitheaters, the little reach of ruined beautiful road near Rome.

# XIV
# HAS THE PAST
# A FUTURE?

Only a few years ago a cynical poster urged tourists to "See Italy
before the Italians ruin it."

For a decade there has been a rising chorus of wolf-wolf: Venice is
sinking into the lagoon; the Leaning Tower is going to fall over; a
maniac has hacked at the "Pietà" in the very nave of St. Peter's; the
Colosseum and the Forum are collapsing on tourists' heads; art
thieves are stealing everything that isn't under lock and key, and
quite a lot that is.

All these horrid things are true. And yet the "Pietà" was repaired,
Venice remains visible, the Forum and the Colosseum are reopened
as regularly as they are closed, after some plastic surgery and
emergency repairs, and until the Leaning Tower finally expires in a
heap of dust and shattered stone — which it surely will do, sooner or
later — all will remain the object of passionate pilgrimage and heroic,
inconclusive debate on how they are to be saved.

The sheer volume of wolf-crying, and the deafness it engenders,
mask a dreadful possibility. The lovely land of Italy could really suc-

cumb, finally and irrevocably, to the automobile, to speculative building, to human greed and indifference. If it happens, it will be the fault of the Italians, for the rest of the world demonstrates more respect for its beauty and its antiquity than do the natives.

Up and down the route of the Appia, where the miracle of survival has left anything at all, the remains are in mortal danger. A few kilometers southeast of Benevento, on route 90, only 200 yards off the main road, are the ruins of Roman Aeclanum, excavated in 1954. There is no signpost on the road to signal their presence, though there is a little guard shack all but invisible in weeds. The guards, delighted to have company, eagerly trace the route of the Appia with extended fingers, show the remains of sprawling public baths, a circular market, villas, mosaic floors, a road of massive stone which connected Aeclanum with the Appia as it snaked here across the hills.

As recently as ten years ago there were still square columns of thin Roman brick in Aeclanum, and great terra-cotta jugs set into the earth in a storehouse for wine and oil, or perhaps the reserve supplies of one of those inns of ill repute. Vandals have knocked down the columns and broken the vases, and weeds grow so high in summer that even the guards can hardly make their way through. How does anyone ever find the place, to come and look? "Only foreigners come," the guards say. "They inform themselves well, from books, and then they find it."

More on the beaten path are the monumental walls, gates, floors and paving of Minturnae, just off the modern Via Appia on the coast below Terracina. This excavated city at least has a small yellow sign indicating an archaeological site. It also has an overgrown parking lot and a small museum, from which lethargic, unshaven functionaries emerge to demand that the occasional visitor walk over and sign the guest register. They never leave their ritual guest book in order to lead visitors to the excavation, and they have neither guidebooks nor information to offer. At the risk of sprained ankles or sudden encounters with snakes, brave tourists may see a handsome amphitheater, a lovely small stretch of paved Appia, some slim delicate arches and mosaic floors, a row of ceremonial inscriptions. It is a beautiful site, expertly excavated. It will not last another decade, exposed to weather and weeds and the unsupervised visits of the unscrupulous. Perhaps the guest book can be preserved in plastic to prove that once there was an archaeological curiosity here.

Just past the modern bridge beyond Minturnae, at the right, is a small *trattoria* beside a stream. The proprietor helped excavate Minturnae, and he both knows and cares far more than do the state employees at the scene. For anyone who can speak Italian, or a little German or Swedish, he will leave his pasta and go for a walk, explaining as he goes along.

In Benevento neither of the Roman bridges is marked. A tourist wishing to see them—either the big one by which the old Appia entered the city, or the small one by which the Via Appia Traiana left it—must read some very detailed guidebook and then either buy and decipher a city map or master enough Italian to ask directions. Beside the little *Ponticello* which took the Traiana out of town toward the east is the shop of a young man who sells cooking gas. He loves the old bridge and he tries to keep it clean, but every night people come along and toss plastic bags of garbage over its side, or broken chairs, or children's potties. The last time the authors saw it, it had become the repository for a half-burned mattress and two broken suitcases.

In Teano the Roman theater has been excavated and abandoned, surrounded by a high fence which keeps out the eager searcher for antiquity but does not prevent the neighbors from tossing refuse over the top. In Lecce a magnificent amphitheater has been preserved, less than half excavated, in the town's main square, and it is flanked, effectively, by that second column from Brindisi, soaring grandly over the scene. Less than five blocks away a charming smaller theater has been dug out and then abandoned. It is filling, inevitably, with potties and plastic bags.

At Venosa there are two signs to a dilapidated building which purports, unconvincingly, to be Horace's house, but the renowned Jewish catacombs on the edge of the city, the object of scholarly study for years, have been closed for lack of funds to maintain a minimum of safety inside. Even the sign which once marked the site has been demolished, by hunters and small boys with rocks. No anti-Semitism is involved; just neglect, and lack of funds.

The list is dreary and disheartening, and it could be extended to several thousand words and examples. It is not true that every garbage dump in Italy is an ancient site, but it is nearly universally true that every ancient site has become a garbage dump.

There has been no outcry about the casual erosion of the vestiges

of the Appia in outlying districts, but for a decade there has been a bitter battle to save what is left on the outskirts of Rome.

More than a hundred years ago, in the great surge of patriotism and optimism which followed the unification of Italy, Guido Bacelli as minister of education proposed that the state create a *passeggiata archeologica,* an archeological walk, with parks and trees and pathways, between the excavations in the Roman Forum, the Palatine Hill, the first reaches of the Via Appia, and the old Porta Appia itself.

At about the same time a Milan journalist and antiquities lover named Ruggero Bonghi proposed almost the same thing. He wrote passionately of the need to create what he called "the third Rome." There had already been, he said, two Romes: the first one created by the Roman legions, using all the treasure they could capture from the world around them; the second built with indulgences offered for sale to the world by the popes.

"Now we must make the third Rome, with our own money," Bonghi wrote. Using one's own money for public amenities has seldom been a popular idea, in Rome or anywhere else, and neither Bacelli nor Bonghi received much more than enthusiastic praise for their ideas.

Both considered themselves pioneers, but they were in fact rather late into the great "save Rome" caper. One of the first to launch himself at this problem was a strange man called Cola di Rienzo, the son of a tavern keeper who in 1344 tried to rally the dispirited citizens of Rome around his own person as a latter-day Augustus. His stated aims were to restore the city's ancient monuments, reopen the Appia, revive the manners and morals of more than a millennium earlier. With the blessing and support of the exiled Pope Clement VI in Avignon, Cola di Rienzo got dressed up in armor, declared himself tribune, and exhorted the Romans to follow him faithfully and restore the city to its divine position of *caput mundi,* "head of the world."

Cola lost. Alliances were fragile in the fourteenth century and the powerful noble families combined against him and forced him to flee the city. In 1354 he tried again. The populace received him with enthusiasm, but while he was making a public address the building was set afire and Cola was caught and murdered while trying to escape.

Two centuries later Pope Paul III commissioned a man named La-

*The core of a Roman funeral monument near the arch at Venosa, in a field.*

253

tino Giovenale to create a master plan for Rome and its development and to include in it the routes and remains of the roads which made the city great. Giovenale was nicknamed "master of the roads," and he managed to open a monumental street which began at the Porta Appia and entered the city in a Y-shape to afford views of the Baths of Caracalla, the Colosseum, and pass under the arches of Constantine, Titus and Septimius Severus. Both Giovenale and Pope Paul III had hoped for more. Their vision was as vast as the plan which Baron Haussmann made — and completed — for Paris in the nineteenth century, but in sixteenth-century Italy it never came true.

Napoleon, too, had his visions for Rome and the road. He signed a decree at Saint-Cloud on June 27, 1811, which delegated to Count Camille de Tournon the supervision of a special fund to "get Rome together," and to restore and protect its antiquities. Count Tournon devised a handsome project which included the heart of the city from the Colosseum to the Porta Capena, where the Appia began, including the Forum and the three big commemorative arches. By 1811, however, Rome had been reduced to 117,000 inhabitants and Tournon's "park" reached to the farthest inhabited limits of the city. When Napoleon fell, Tournon's plan fell with him.

It was into this pattern, both of thought and of geography, that Bacelli and Bonghi emerged a century ago. They wanted almost a mile of greenery, beginning at the Forum and going south past the Porta Capena, the Baths of Caracalla, the lower reaches of the Palatine and Aventine hills, to the old Appian gate in the Aurelian Wall. Both men were visionaries, lovers of history, impelled by education and good will to create something for the nation. They also fought like devils with each other in print. Each claimed the idea for an archeological walk as his own. Each had a degree of corroborating evidence.

Their exchanges make charming, if rather wistful, reading today. They never argued about the need for such a park, or about the credit it would bring to Rome and the nation. Each described with fervor the pleasure it would afford to "those in carriages, or on horseback," to proceed on shady pathways through the remains of ancient glory, with the song of birds in the air and the blazing Italian sun filtered through the leaves of graceful trees.

Unfortunately, it took seventy-five years for their dream to come

*Roman remains where the old "high Appia" passed in Terracina, incorporated into one of the main squares of the present city, the Piazza Municipio.*

true. Law after law, plan after plan were proffered, approved, ignored. By the time the *passeggiata archeologica* became a reduced, compromised entity, the combustion engine had banished forever the song of birds and the peaceful passage under the trees. What were to have been carriageways became roads, to accommodate private cars and the two thousand trucks a day which even in the early 1930s carried loads of garden produce, pozzolana, blocks of building stone, on the old Appia from the Alban Hills through the gate in the Aurelian Wall and into the city.

Mussolini aided final stages of the archaeological park by razing slums and latter-day accretions all the way from the Capitoline Hill to the Colosseum and beyond, to highlight the grandeur that had been Rome. His workmen, in passing, demolished a Roman fountain called the Meta Sudante which had stood for centuries near the Colosseum. More to his credit, he finished demolition of a gas company's sprawling works which had for years, to the fury of archaeologists, occupied the Circus Maximus.

In vain, in 1932, the Duce pleaded that the first few kilometers of the Appia should be turned into a "great green park for the pleasure of the people." He was defeated by the same people who had brought down Cola di Rienzo seven hundred years before—the powerful old landowning families, unwilling to cede their property to the public even for money.

The *passeggiata archeologica* exists, pallidly, in a green incline around the Porta Capena and the Baths of Caracalla, and in tree-lined boulevards which separate them, but the pedestrian who attempts to enjoy it must be quick. The traffic is horrendous and implacable, the space carved out for parking or driving ever wider.

Now the debate, the battle, has shifted a mile farther south to the very gate of the outer wall, the beginning of the Appia where it is still visible. The proposal is to create an Appian park from the Porta San Sebastiano and out for 12 kilometers until the old stones vanish into grass and garbage.

In 1962 the city of Rome, in the person of its planning committee, passed a local law which forbade building on either side of the road from kilometer 1 to 12. In 1965 the minister of public works pushed through a zoning plan which set aside more than 6,000 acres for parkland near the road. It was a modest enough proposal, calling for a park only 150 feet wide outside the Porta San Sebastiano, where the area is most heavily built up. From there it would grow, on alternate sides of the road, to almost one mile wide where it reaches the 12th kilometer. Most of the world's parks are meant to preserve bits of nature for the edification of men who have almost destroyed it. This one would save an entirely different segment of the human experience: the monuments made by man, triumphs from an era when nature itself was dominant. The Appia park would also, almost as an afterthought, present to Romans a tiny strip of grass and trees. Of all the major cities of the world, Rome offers the least greenery—less than one meter and a half of green space for each citizen. By comparison, Munich has 30 meters, Leningrad 25, Amsterdam 20.

In 1969, modern equivalents of the triumvirs of old—three politicians of the Socialist, Republican and Social Democratic parties—presented a bill for the immediate expropriation of the necessary land and asked the federal government to provide $50 million, the city of Rome $3 million.

One of the sponsors was Socialist Antonio Giolitti, whose grandfather had almost single-handedly forced expropriation of the Villa Borghese in 1901 to make it a park. Giolitti's father was a prime mover in the acquisition of the Villa Pamphili in Rome for the same purpose. The Villa Borghese has been a success, but the Villa Pamphili was promptly stripped of most of its ornamental urns and statuary within weeks of its opening to the public. Perhaps Antonio Giolitti should have been cynical, but he was not. In 1970 he proclaimed: "The constructors and the landowners [on the Appia] don't have a chance any more to stop the park project. It has been promised to the people of Rome, and it will be built. Work on it will commence this year."

Work has never commenced. Cola di Rienzo, Giovenale, Napoleon, Bacelli and Bonghi, even Mussolini may be thrashing wildly in their graves.

After the 1965 law, Rome issued no building licenses along the Appia, and the government even expropriated about 200 acres in a valley which separates the old Appia from the modern one. Park planners could offer landowners along the way only 1,000 lire per square meter, about $1.60 at 1965 prices. Far less desirable, less beautiful, less historic land was even then going for triple that price, and building speculators were offering a hundred times the price with the hope of putting up expensive high-rise apartments. Despite the ban on building, at least a hundred illegal structures have gone up within sight of the Appia, and the expropriated valley has been altered forever by detritus carried from nearby subway construction and dumped into the hollow. Dozens of supposedly "frozen" peasant houses and ancient villas have quietly sprouted "repairs," which turn out to be entire extra wings or stories, guesthouses, swimming pools. These rise behind screens of newly planted trees or temporary matting which Italians customarily use on construction projects.

In mid-1973 a photographer, chronicling frantic Sunday work on an illegal housing complex within sight of the Appia, was almost run down by the driver of a cement truck and was fortunate to survive to publish his damning photographs. At the end of 1973 police who were sent to halt illegal construction not far from here were frustrated by women and children who climbed to the roof of the structure and refused to come down so it could be demolished. After an exchange of rock volleys, insults, and one pistol shot into the air, both sides retired.

At the heart of the problem is money. The brave Bonghi, addressing the British Archaeological Society in 1889 about his proposed *passeggiata archeologica*, remarked ruefully: "We Italians are very strong legislators, stronger perhaps than you would even tolerate. We make dozens of laws in principle, and then we always put off the financial laws needed to translate the principle into reality."

Right on, Mr. Bonghi. Neither the city of Rome nor the federal government has provided realistic financial support for the park of the Appia. Chronically unable to collect its taxes, hampered by an almost total lack of natural resources, conditioned to chicanery by centuries of practice, Italy has a deficit economy. The much-touted economic miracle, achieved within the Common Market when both Italian labor and the national genius for invention were in demand, has run out of steam. Rome has an operating deficit, and a civic debt which would have sent even Franklin Roosevelt straight off the top of the Empire State Building, cigarette holder and all.

As a result, Italy's total budget for the maintenance of its ancient ruins, their continuing excavation and preservation, supervision of monuments and museums, is less than the annual budget of one single U.S. institution, the Smithsonian. It has in 1973 no more archaeological technicians and supervisors than it had in 1909.

There are voices in the wilderness. Many an underpaid Superintendent of Antiquities tries his best. Many an inspired amateur trudges out, staff in hand and pack on back, to discover again the traces of the road and its artifacts. A national volunteer organization called Italia Nostra watchdogs both antiquities and pollution and mounts noisy, if often ineffective, campaigns against violations. A newer organization, Gruppi Archeologici d'Italia, accepts dues-paying volunteers, who last year cleaned up and reopened the ruins of Largo Argentina, a group of four Republican temples, to the Roman public and foreign tourists. These groups swim mostly upstream. Italy has neither a tradition of public concern nor concerted citizen activism like that inherited by Americans from their pioneer ancestors. Italians, while complaining loudly that the mayor is a crook and the premier an opportunist, happily throw their garbage out of car windows and vote against any measure which would require them to contribute fifty cents to save the Appia park, or any other bit of antiquity.

They do understand the system of patronage and patrons, the tradition of popes and noblemen like the Medici who supported the geniuses of bygone centuries. There was a howl of outrage just a few years ago when an American millionaire offered specifically to buy the Colosseum and restore it, but the nation has, and will, accept financial aid offered less crassly. Florence welcomed and then made scrupulously honest and brilliantly innovative use of international money which poured in to help after the disastrous flood of 1966. Venice, locked for months in intramural political argument over how to spend United Nations funds appropriated for its salvation, is moving toward sensible agreement.

Rome, stumbling along without the glamour of the gondolas or the drama of a flood, has had no substantive help. An international fund to buy the land and administer an Appian park would no doubt be welcomed, after some chauvinistic maneuvering about responsibility and the legal intricacies of land acquisition. Once this was done, there would be allies a-plenty. Traffic barriers could close the road from the Porta San Sebastiano for 12 kilometers, and funds for upkeep could be extracted from visitors and private citizens whose property

is reachable only from the road. In a second phase, new access roads should be opened to keep all private traffic away.

Fifty cents would be a small price to pay for the privilege of walking undisturbed across the old stones and the remains of sidewalks, for being able to sit quietly in the shade and study the tombs, decipher the remaining inscriptions. Access would at last be granted to ruins of the Quintilian villa, now closed, and to a view of the ruined arches of the nearest aqueduct to Rome as they vault still across the plain.

Some decision must be made very soon, because as one of the most recent of the Via Appia's devoted prose-poets, Rodolfo de Mattei, wrote in 1968:

> The Appia is a stopped clock. It sounded all its hours 2,000 years ago . . . but these ruins scrutinize you, judge you. They grant you (maybe, they ask of you) a part, a role, in their final destiny.

*A stretch of the Appia at Minturnae.*

# *Appendix*

## A Guide to Some Sites,
### for Amateur Road-Trace Hunters

On a blustery day in March 1973, the authors were driving from Rome to Benevento on the modern Via Appia, SS 7, looking for remnants of the old road. Between Santa Maria Capua Vetere and Benevento the drive is beautiful, plunging through a narrow valley which probably was the site of the battle of the Caudine Forks. No ruins are marked on the maps, but one guidebook indicated that recent excavation had turned up the remains of Republican villas very near the road. The *scavi*, said the book, were in a hamlet called Costa, a *frazione*, or outlying dependency, of the town of Arienzo. Finding Arienzo was easy, but there no one knew of any *scavi* and people were vague about the location of Costa. Attempts to find it landed us in three wrong villages, all full of ancient-looking arches, stone doorsills which could have been antique, and friendly natives who were bored by discussion of *antichità*.

In final desperation we followed an unmarked track into an unnamed clutch of houses straggling dispiritedly beside a narrow asphalt road. This road, and our journey, ended abruptly when we fetched up between somebody's front door and a row of potted geraniums which marked the edge of a precipice about twelve feet from the door. There being nothing to do but stop, we stopped.

Regarding us with singular lack of enthusiasm was a young man wearing a black mourning button in his jacket lapel. Because we seemed to be, car and all, on what served as his front porch, we felt the burden of conversation was on us.

"Please forgive the intrusion," we said. "Are there by chance any *scavi* in this vicinity?"

Silence for a moment, then a jerk of the head. "*Si,* right up that path, about fifty meters."

Having received permission to leave the car where it was, we set forth with light cameras and heavy doubts, slipping and sliding through a grove of olive trees sprouting gray-green among the gray rocks. Before long the young man had joined us, looking far less surly.

"Here," he kept shouting, "here!" There among the trees, invisible from a distance of more than thirty feet, were the tumbled, earth-colored remains of two villas of the second or first century B.C. Partly excavated in 1965 and 1966, they have been abandoned for lack of funds. Weeds grow over lovely mosaic floors with patterns of running deer and black-and-white vases. Across the disintegrating plaster walls are bits of red and gold fresco, and a graffito of hunters pursuing wild boar.

An enormous underground cavern which once was the double-floored structure of a centrally heated Roman bath has silted almost full from winter rains. Our flashlight revealed a dozen stubby stone columns; the young man said he had counted sixty-seven of them during the excavation.

From within these ruins, so still and so beautiful, we could hear, dimly, the traffic on the Appia. Across the valley towered Monte Castello, 2,000 feet high, named for a medieval castle which once stood there. And here, right where we stood, some peasant in 321 B.C. must have heard the Roman army marching toward its rendezvous with disaster at the Forks. Perhaps he too raised olives on this hillside. Perhaps his descendants served the grand owners of the villas built along the Appia a couple of centuries later. Certainly here in the days when Augustus ruled the Empire and Agrippa was making his map, well-connected travelers must have stopped often to stay with friends in these lovely, sprawling villas.

Our accomplishment in finding the site was so negligible as to be unworthy of mention, except for the fact that we were exhilarated for twenty-four hours afterward. Reason and logic fled completely, vanquished by excitement. For ruin lovers, road lovers, mild-adventure lovers, nothing compares with the joy of locating, preferably with a little bit of difficulty, an ancient trace. For a few minutes anyone can believe that he found, excavated, owns forever, this piece of the past. The glow truly lasts for hours.

In the course of research for this book, the authors drove 6,000 kilometers in intermittent forays which spanned two years and which almost demolished a spectacularly courageous Fiat 850 automobile. After four new tires, one new muffler, a valve job and a clutch assembly, we can present a collation of achievable sights for anyone who may become as fascinated as we did. We offer it because the best guides to sites off the beaten track, provided by the Touring Club Italiano, are published in elegant red-bound volumes only in Italian and sold only to its members.

Even the TCI guides haven't always enough space to be detailed, so recourse must be made to the natives who live nearby. These friendly folk seldom speak anything but Italian. But because they regard ruin-hunting as a harmless aberration of foreigners and professors, most can guess what the tourist is looking for even before he opens his mouth. As a general rule, it would be wise to memorize the Italian words for bridge (*ponte*), gate (*porta*), ancient road (*strada antica*), amphitheater (*amfiteatro*) and ruins (*rovine*), and to keep in mind the generic term for any dug-up ancient site—*scavi*. Other general rules: keep smiling, particularly when words fail; carry candy for small children, who are eager showers-of-the-way and couldn't care less what sweets will do to their teeth; try not to trample the farmer's crops while intent upon the remains in his fields.

The Via Appia sites to follow are arranged in geographical order proceeding south and east from Rome on the original route of the road, through Capua to Benevento and Taranto and Brindisi. Sites on the Via Appia Traiana are listed from Brindisi north and then west to Benevento.

Because of the rapid deterioration of some sites, you may find this Appendix out of date by the time you get to Italy. Some greatly imperiled sites will be indicated below as warning. On the other hand, new sites are constantly being found and excavated. Normally for the first few years after discovery and excavation the work is well marked with yellow highway signs, and well guarded and maintained, so you will have no difficulty finding them.

Three stars mean "don't miss it" even if you miss lunch and must hike for half an hour. Two stars mean "well worth some effort." One-star sites are for the hopelessly hooked, or for everybody's list of things to do next time, when-we-aren't-in-such-a-hurry.

\*\*\* **Rome to the Via di Fioranello,** on the road marked Via Appia Antica, 12 kilometers south from the Porta San Sebastiano. Sights described in Chapter III. Sightseeing tours are available in Rome, but a standard guidebook and your own feet, or car, are far more satisfactory.

\* **Via di Fioranello,** south to the town of Santa Maria del Mole, where the Appia Nuova, SS 7, merges with this track of the earlier road. This must be done on foot. Leave the car at the crossroads of the Appia Antica and the Via Fioranello. The walk takes an hour, round trip, but it is beautiful. Remains of the paving, of monuments, tumuli. Rubber boots required after winter rains or sudden summer storms.

\*\* **Albano,** a town in the Alban Hills, directly on the route of SS 7, 25 kilometers from Rome. The main street, Corso Matteotti, lies on top of the ancient Via Appia. No traces remain. In the town, however, there are ruins of a **Roman amphitheater,** the **villa and tomb of Pompey,** and a **Porta Praetoria** which once served the Appia. All are marked.

Proceeding straight through the town, the Corso Matteotti turns into the Borgo Garibaldi and rises slightly. Watch the right-hand side of the road and you will see yellow signs indicating the **Chiesa Santa Maria della Stella** and the **Tombs of the Horatii and Curiatii.** Turn right where the signs indicate and only a few meters beyond is a large monument, on the left. This is probably Republican, much too late to have been the Horatii and Curiatii, but it is impressively large and rather Etruscan in style. Parking in the forecourt of the church across the street. From here the road proceeds to . . .

\* **Ariccia,** on or near the site of Roman Aricia. Here the road is marked "Via Appia Antica" for about one kilometer. In winter one can see the great Roman viaduct to the left; at other times of year it is hidden by foliage. The roadbed here is evocative, and remains of brick gates and outbuildings are visible among the vineyards and weeds at the left of the road.

\* **Cisterna di Latina** on SS 7, 52 kilometers south of Rome. Here the road begins to cross the Pontine Marshes, on top of foundations of the ancient road. There are no visible remains but the road is narrow, lovely, bordered with trees. A drainage canal on the right, taking swamp water to the sea, probably is in or near the channel on which Horace traveled so uncomfortably by night boat in 38 B.C.

\*\* **Mesa di Pontinia,** at 87 kilometers south of Rome, is on or near the site of Roman Ad Medias. The structure now standing here began life as a papal post station in the eighteenth century, and has two well-preserved Appian milestones set into the main entrance. A dangerous turn across the highway provides parking space for a close inspection of the milestones.

\*\*\* **Terracina,** 103 kilometers south of Rome on SS 7. (If you wish to skip the sights between Rome and Terracina, there is no need to take SS 7; other roads also reach it.) The most dramatic Appian sights here are the **Temple of Jove Anxur** high on the rocky cliff, visible from far away (Chapter VI) and the great cut down by the sea, made by Trajan. Traffic on the modern road goes directly past Trajan's cut, shortly after SS 7 reaches the sea and turns left. There is no sign, but the cut is obvious. There is also no parking to the left, but to the right of the highway are filling stations and a restaurant where the curious may pull in and stop.

The old town, Roman Tarracina, lies partway up the bluff, halfway between the modern seaside buildings and the Temple of Jove. Access to it is easy: signs point to the Duomo and the Piazza Municipio from within the modern town. In the piazza between the church and the city hall are stones of Appia pavement; nearby is a little arch which was exposed by 1943 bombing. There are in the vicinity — just get out and wander around a bit — some remains of city wall, an old gate and columns of a temple.

As well marked as the Duomo itself is the road to the **Temple of Jove Anxur.** Not for those who suffer from vertigo, but otherwise a magnificent site and breath-taking view up and down the coast. On the road to the temple you will encounter a Y-fork at one point. The right fork goes to the temple; the other, to the left, is marked to the *"cimitero."* Take this cemetery fork. Within a few meters another turn, to the right, is marked "Piazza Palatina." The road looks impassable, but a small Italian car will make it. The route bumps up and down, meanders generally left, goes past a row of sagging houses and abandoned automobile carcasses and arrives at last at a great green flat place which was once the great "resting piazza" on the "high Appia" through Tarracina and Anxur (Chapter VI). This is seen much more satisfactorily if you leave the car after only a few hundred yards and walk. The track between the houses is littered with ancient paving stones, funerary inscriptions, and bits and pieces. There is curbing all-but-hidden in the bushes, and near the piazza itself, clear buttress walls which once supported the high road and the piazza. An easy half-hour walk, though we spent an hour examining priceless finds along the way.

\*\*\* **Fondi-Itri.** Farther south on SS 7, the first town after Terracina is Fondi, Roman Fundi. There are stubby cones of funerary monuments at the left of the road as it enters the town, but the most interesting part comes at Kilometer 126.5. Here the modern road proceeds to the left of a valley, but the old Appia route is clearly visible on the right. To help locate it, look for tall, ugly concrete telephone poles. Some idiotic bureaucrat has chosen to place them smack in the middle of the old road. At about Kilometer 129 there is a widening of the modern road to the right, and a place to drive off and park. It is exciting to walk back down the valley on the track of the Appia. There is paving, sidewalk, retaining wall, and the remains of a fortress where neighboring villages today dump and burn their garbage. You may have to hold your nose, but it is otherwise beautiful.

\*\*\* **Itri.** As SS 7 enters the city, the eye is caught instantly by a dramatic castle straight ahead. On the left of the road, however, is an older monument—a long stretch of Appia pavement, very well preserved. Inside the town is a fine bit of viaduct which probably is the oldest such structure on the entire route of the road. Scholars date it to Appius Claudius' time, while the one at Ariccia was a bit later. The Itri viaduct is visible in small segments between later buildings, but it is worth asking for the *viadotto antico*.

** Between **Itri** and **Formia,** at Kilometer 136, there is a delicious small surprise to the left of the road: a milestone and a bit of pavement dug up and nicely resited in a little planting of trees and shrubs. The milestone is number LXXXV from the original Appia.

** **Formia.** At 137.3 kilometers south of Rome, on the right, is an impressive circular tower in a pleasant garden setting. A marble plaque, too high to read, says enigmatically that this is a "Roman edifice, commonly called the Tomb of Cicero." Probably it isn't, but it is ancient and handsome, and caretakers on the site will unlock an iron gate to reveal a small museum inside.

In the town of Formia itself is Villa Rubino, in private hands, which very likely includes the ruins of Cicero's villa by the sea. Don't bother, though; it is unkempt and dirty. In the center of town, on the sea front and visible in the shallow water, are the mossy masonry remains of a Roman fish hatchery, and right beside the main highway a tall, ruined medieval **Torre di Mola.** The road passed this town in the Middle Ages, and Torquato Tasso was almost captured by highwaymen right here (Chapter XI).

*** **Minturnae.** Start watching at Kilometer 154 on SS 7 going south. At 155 the modern road passes through remains of a low, fine aqueduct. It is almost hidden by vegetation except as it reaches the road, but it extends for a hundred yards on either side. There is a lane to the right, immediately under the aqueduct, which provides temporary parking space for a better, closer look.

About one kilometer beyond, at 156, is a yellow sign indicating ruins. Entrance to a parking lot on the right. The **amphitheater** is visible from the road, but behind it are far more wondrous sights: four or five acres of graceful little arches, mosaic floors, block-long sections of Appian pavement, commemorative inscriptions, the exposed lower level of a double-floored Roman bath with neat little brick pillars still in place (Chapter XIV).

\*\*\* **Sessa Aurunca** and the bridge-viaduct. If we had a four-star category, this would be it. Here is a twenty-one-arched bridge-viaduct almost intact for 300 yards. It was not on the direct route of the Via Appia, but it is contemporary with it and once connected the Appia to an ancient city of the Aurunci tribe and to the Via Latina.

To find it, take SS 7 immediately after the ruins of Minturnae. Avoid the right fork, which runs nearer to the sea and is marked "SS 7 Quater." The "Quater" is written in black under the road name. Stay on SS 7 until the mileage markers indicate 4 kilometers to Sessa Aurunca. At this point there is on the right a blue highway sign which says "Mondragone 17 km." Stop here and park. There is no parking lot, but you can edge off the road a bit somewhere. Directly opposite the blue Mondragone sign are two mule paths leading downward into fields. Take the one on the right. It descends fairly steeply, and within a few yards you will see on the left a masonry wall which may once have retained the roadbed. On the right are rocky hills with vertical cuts, made by the Roman roadbuilders to get stone for their highway. Even a slow walker will arrive in ten minutes at the stark, gray-white, narrow, beautiful reach of road. It begins suddenly, arches over a little valley and a stream, and ends suddenly on the other side. The name of the bridge in modern Italian is **Ponte degli Arunci.**

\* **Mondragone.** Ruins exist on the road marked SS 7 Quater, by the sea, at a point 4 kilometers north of the town of Mondragone. This was Roman Sinuessa, famed for its sulfur baths. It still smells to high heaven. No archaeological notice marks the site, but a small sign at the right of the road indicates (or did, in 1973) "Lido di Sinuessa." Some of the remains of Roman masonry are underwater near the beach, other bits remain in the sand defaced by large "land for sale" signs erected by speculators. There may be nothing left at all here in another year or two.

Proceeding south, you will see on the left of the road, up rather high, a large hotel complex with a ruined hilltop fortress behind it. You can leave your car at the Hotel Sinuessa and walk in ten minutes to the fortress, which commands a wonderful view up and down the coast. The track of the Appia is clearly visible from here.

**\* Capua.** This was the Casilinum of the Romans, a fortress town guarding the crossing of the Volturno River. Their bridge was rebuilt dozens of times and finally done in by World War II. Parts of the round towers and the retaining walls are all that remain. The main street of town, now the Corso Appio, lies on Appius Claudius' road. There is an excellent museum here, housed in a handsome old *palazzo*, well worth a stop.

**\*\*\* Santa Maria Capua Vetere.** This was Roman Capua originally, until all the name changing started (Chapter XI). As SS 7 enters the town along a spectacularly ugly road lined with dingy small businesses and stores, it passes through remains of a **Roman arch** sometimes ascribed to Hadrian. A rather tatty arch it is, too, though once it must have been grand. Affixed to the middle of it now is a marble plaque commemorating Garibaldi's triumphant passage a hundred years ago.

Farther on, in the center of the city, is the **Roman amphitheater,** well worth a daytime visit and well worth seeing at night when it is dramatically lighted.

**\*\* Costa,** site of the Republican villas mentioned at the beginning of the Appendix. This is difficult to find, but possible. Stay on SS 7 through Caserta and Maddaloni, past signs to the towns of Montedecoro and Santa Maria a Vico, until you come to a sign marking a right-hand turn off No. 7 to Arienzo. Don't take this, but very near it you will see on the opposite side of the road a restaurant near the highway, and an unmarked macadam road leading inland. Take that little road, and with any luck you'll wind up on the same young man's front porch. He helped excavate the site, and he loves to show it. Don't tip him; take his picture and then remember to send him a print.

**\* Montesarchio.** This probably was Roman Caudium. No Roman remains, but a dramatic hilltop site with a medieval castle and a fort, a fine view back down toward the Caudine Forks and the wild river valleys.

**\*\*\* Benevento** (Chapter VIII). Locals dote on the fine **Arch of**

**Trajan,** near the center of town at the foot of the Via Traiana. The arch has been half covered with scaffolding for three years, but some day they'll have to take it down.

The two bridges, both worth a walk. From the Arch of Trajan the Via San Pasquale leads away from town and arrives within minutes at the **Ponticello,** the small bridge which took the Appia Traiana out of town. It has been much rebuilt, but if you squat down and study it from below and up close, the Roman structure is visible in the center.

Much more impressive is the other bridge, now called **Ponte Leproso,** which brought the original Appia into Benevento over the river Sabato. It is an easy walk from the vast, well-preserved remains of a **Roman theater** which houses summer opera in July and university art classes the year round. En route to it — on foot is far best — is the **Porta d'Arsa,** which has Roman columns set into later, Longobard, walls.

Benevento has two museums very near each other. The principal one, in the ancient **Abbey of Santa Sophia,** is excellent in every way. The so-called historical one, in the **Rocca dei Rettori,** is chiefly interesting outside. Near its main gate is a bad statue of Trajan and a much-eroded milestone, and in the entrance is a bit of Roman pavement, probably the Appia and a statue of Diomedes. Around the side of the building, which still looks like the castle it once was, are five milestones and some Roman inscriptions nicely arranged in a tiny park. The milestones come from the original Appia between Beneventum and Aeclanum and date from Hadrian's time, A.D. 123.

*** **Passo di Mirabella.** Beyond Benevento on SS 7, still going southeast, at a small place called Passo di Mirabella, are the ruins of **Roman Aeclanum.** At about 24.6 kilometers out of Benevento, SS 7 wanders off to the south and the main road becomes No. 90. Take it, almost straight east. Do *not* turn off at a sign toward Mirabella Eclano to the right. Stay on 90. As you enter the hamlet marked "Passo di Mirabella" you will see on the right a large building painted dark red and marked "Casa Cantoniera," a highway headquarters. Immediately past it, a small unmarked track goes off at 90 degrees to the right. Take this. After about 200 yards there is a shack at the right for the excavation guards. If they are there, they will take you around. If they are not, you may leave the car by their shack and explore ruins to both left and right.

** **Route of the Appia across the mountains.** No modern road completely matches the Appia route here, though No. 303 passes some sites which must have lain on or near the old road: Bisaccia, Lacedonia (Roman Aquilonia), Melfi. The scenery is spectacular with the great Ofanto River valley and its tributaries far below. One can appreciate the feat of Roman road building by driving on route 303.

*** **Venosa.** Ancient Venusium, Horace's hometown. To reach it, leave Melfi on 303. After 5 or 6 kilometers it becomes No. 93. After about 8 kilometers on 93, turn right on No. 168. This road enters Venosa from the northwest. There are no signposts to its antiquities. The main route into town goes past a fifteenth-century castle, with turrets, a rather nice one. Traffic proceeds down the town's main street, the Via Vittorio Emmanuele, and is (or was) marked to the "Abbazia SS Trinità." Midway inside the town is a small piazza on the left with a statue of Horace on a pedestal, and beyond it to the right, yellow signs indicate his house. Not at all convincing; don't bother unless you like ruined old stone houses with musty smells.

Eventually the road leads out of town to the Abbey of the Trinity. This is worth attention: incorporated in its walls are fragments from the Roman amphitheater just across the road, from the Jewish catacombs nearby, and from the ancient city of Venusium. Everything within reach was plundered centuries ago to build this enormous, unfinished abbey.

Parts of ancient Venusium, and the Via Appia, have been excavated recently. To see them, face the abbey and then walk from the front to the back and turn right on a footpath. The excavation site is fenced and locked, but the remains are clearly visible at eye level through the fence.

** **Route of the Appia** between Venosa and Gravina di Puglia (Chapter XII). No present road exactly duplicates the track of the Appia. The nearest road is No. 168 out of Venosa to the east, but only so far as Spinazzola. From there it is most convenient to take No. 97, which runs north of the old route, to Gravina. It is worth the trip just for the scenery across the high plateau. In late May and early June the hills are a wonderland of purple thistle, red poppy, early spring wheat and sweeping vistas.

* **Gravina** has no comprehensible Roman remains, though the Appia surely passed very near here. The local museum, called Pomarici-Santomasi, displays some pottery and artifacts dug up by the British in their search for Silvium and for the road itself. It also has a magnificent set of Byzantine frescoes excavated in the vicinity and reconstructed in an underground crypt. These alone are worth a stop in Gravina, though they having nothing to do with the Appia.

* **Route of the Appia** between Gravina and Taranto. One highly evocative stretch of road, marked "Via Appia Antica," exists northeast of the city of Matera. Go out of Matera to the northeast on road No. 271. After about 11 kilometers there is a narrow road to the right, pitted and pockmarked, which runs dead straight for 6 kilometers and which surely lies on the bed of the Appia. Matera also has an excellent archaeological museum.

* **Matera to Taranto.** Taking SS 7 from Matera to Taranto, you go through Castellaneta, which turns out to be Rudolph Valentino's hometown. Right on the road, at the edge of town, is so gaudy a ceramic monument to the Latin lover that it demands a color photograph. After Castellaneta, SS 7 turns south and then east again before the village of Palagiano. Here the kilometer markings are suddenly in the 600s, but no matter.

Proceeding toward Massafra on SS 7 at about Kilometer 622.8, you find a narrow dirt road to the left. If you take it for .5 kilometer, it intersects with a new gravel road. Turn right on the gravel, go .8 kilometer, and on the right are the enormous remains of a reticulated Roman wall, at least 240 by 120 feet. No one seems to know what it was and perhaps you have to be a little bit crazy to want to see it, but finding it is fun. As a bonus there are quite beautiful olive groves on both sides of the road, some of the trees so old and gnarled that their main branches are supported by little columns of native stone.

\* **Taranto.** The Appia came here, but nothing remains. The archaeological museum is good, the port interesting, the city surprisingly
handsome.

\*\*\* **Lecce** has a spectacular main city square, the Piazza
Sant'Oronzo, in which lies a partially excavated **Roman amphitheater**
in fine repair. Beside it towers that second column which had
marked the end of the Appia at Brindisi. On top of it now is a statue
of St. Oronzo, for whom the square is named. At the rear of the
piazza is a bank called the Piccolo Credito Salentino in which works
an English-speaking Americanophile named Giuseppe Giurgola. If he
is not too busy, he loves to take Americans down into the bank's
vaults and safe-deposit boxes, which are set between the great arches
of still more of the buried Roman amphitheater, under the bank.

On the Adriatic coast outside Lecce, 12.5 kilometers east and well
marked to "San Castaldo," are remains of a mole built by Hadrian.
The main road delivers you to the beach near a small refreshment
stand, and then turns right. Stop near the stand and walk toward the
sea. The ruins are difficult to detect at first, but if you examine what
appear to be natural rock outcrops, you can see the lines of the huge
fitted stones. Most of Hadrian's mole was demolished, unfortunately,
to build the present sea wall.

\*\* **Baletium or Valesium** was an ancient Roman city, mentioned in
many of the itineraries, which lay almost midway between Lupiae
and Brundisium. A new *superstrada* (not an *autostrada,* there is a
slight difference) now connects the two cities, Lecce and Brindisi,
and at about Kilometer 24 north from Lecce there should appear the
remains of what the Italians now call **Valesio.** Many detailed road
maps show the three little dots which mean "antiquities," and the
new *superstrada* itself shows a slight bend at the spot where the road
was detoured to avoid the ruins. Despite all this the authors, in a full
day of trying, never managed to find the remains. They are alleged to
lie east of a village called San Pietro Vernotico, north of a hamlet
called Torchiarolo. We found no natives who knew what or where
the ruins were, however, and we subjected the car to its worst torture
pursuing cart paths in all the right directions, with no luck. We

would be most grateful to receive instructions on precisely how to get there, if anyone manages to find these ruins.

*** **Brindisi.** Brindisi can be reached from Lecce, but the usual route is to proceed on SS 7 directly from Taranto to Brindisi, as the old Appia did. Most of this route lies on top of the old road, though it is not noticeable until after the town of Mesagne, from which the road drives straight east for 16 kilometers toward the sea. This stretch is marked "Appia Antica" on many modern road maps. Nothing remains of the monuments which once stood here. Recent road building has altered the entrance to Brindisi, but most traffic is still directed toward the port down the central Via Roma, which turns into the Corso Garibaldi and then reaches the sea. From any point along the sea front the tall **Appia column** is visible and unmistakable.

Remains of a **Roman gate and wall** lie on the outside of the **Porta Mesagne,** once main entrance to the city, and inside the Porta Mesagne on the Via Cristofor Colombo in the garden of an open-air *trattoria* are remains of a **Roman water reservoir** (Chapter XIII) with brick columns which once held up its roof, a narrow brick wall, and ducts carved into the floor. Sightseers are welcome even if they don't want a meal.

Just off the Piazza Vittoria in the center of town, where the Via Roma turns into the Corso Garibaldi, is the little **fountain made of Roman stones** and dedicated to the Spanish governor. Going up the little incline from this site, through the tiny Piazza Sedile and Piazza G. Matteotti, a five-minute walk brings you to the Vico Romano, which turns to the right into the Via G. C. Casimiro. Here are the remains of a **"Roman edifice"** under an apartment-house entrance walk.

** **Route of the Appia Traiana** from Brindisi to the north. The modern route which most closely approximates the Appia is No. 379, which hugs the Adriatic coast and passes a series of medieval defense towers. **Torre San Sabina,** about 28 kilometers north of Brindisi, is probably the site of Roman Speluncae. No remains, but an evocative site and the tower is nice. About 10 kilometers farther north, at Castello Villanova, a road turns left, inland, toward Ostuni. Just past one kilometer inland on this road, you will note rather small, rough-looking tracks branching from it on either side. This is the track of the old Traiana, and you can follow it a short distance either to the left or to the right, or both. No monuments, but the road is recognizable; worth a half hour's fun.

*** **Torre Egnazia.** Halfway between Brindisi and Bari, on No. 379, are excavations of a town the Greeks called Gnathia and the Romans Egnatia. A yellow *scavi* sign on the highway indicates the locale, and the ruins are visible just to the left of the road. You can pull off and park here, and if you have time, walk also to the right, to the sea, where in the weathered rocks there are clear remains of a Roman fish hatchery, some mysterious rounded hollows and rectangular remains. Geology lovers will note some excellent potholes along the shore.

The ruins of Egnatia were being restored in 1973 and may soon be open and labeled for the public. Even if they are not, the place is worth an hour or so, and is a fine place for a picnic by the sea.

** **Bari.** This was Roman Barium, a handsome town. The archaeological museum near the university in the center of town is worth a visit. Even better is the **Lungomare Imperatore Augusto,** along which are installed a row of Roman columns and one impressive milestone. This very old city also has the bones of Santa Claus — so they say — in the **Chiesa di San Nicola.** Well worth a walk, but watch your purses: local hoodlums haunt the Lungomare, the delightful walk beside the Roman columns and the sea.

*** **Trani.** Straight up the coast from Bari, on No. 16, is the little town of Trani. It was not on the Appia Traiana, but in a charming small park by the sea are eight **Roman milestones** set in a semicircle, very nicely displayed.

* **Route from Bari to Canosa.** The Appia Traiana went from Barium to Butuntum to Rubi (a fine private museum of ancient pottery at **Ruvo di Puglia**) and then to Canusium. This is a nice drive, beginning as No. 96 going out of Bari, then becoming No. 98 into Canosa.

*** **Canosa.** This can be a very frustrating city, as the remains are so badly marked. If the good local museum is open when you arrive (it is called the Museo Civico), it can provide a map of the principal sites, which is a great help. There are signs indicating the direction of **San Leuceo,** an impressive excavation just outside Canosa. Well worth a visit, though the authors went three times and never found anyone on the premises to let us inside the fence for a better look. The caretaker must be there occasionally, even if by accident, but the ruins may be seen fairly well from outside the fence. Handsome columns, beautiful mosaic floors, a nicely landscaped excavation.

There is also a Greek acropolis high above the old city, much altered by the Romans and by medieval wall builders. Signs inside Canosa direct you to it. Not much to see except three much-ruined towers and a fine view across the plain.

Relatively easy to find are three Roman remains in a row: take highway 98 out of Canosa in the direction of Cerignola. Just outside of town, on the left of the road, is a **monumental arch** from Trajan's time, now in a field. Beyond it, still on the left, the brick core of what was once a huge **tomb,** and about 3.3 kilometers out of town a **Roman bridge,** much restored. You must leave No. 98 to see the old bridge up close, but should you not be that curious, there is a good view of it from the present bridge on No. 98.

** **Battle of Cannae.** Northeast of Canosa and indicated on numerous highway signs is the site of **Canne della Battaglia,** where the Romans were routed by Carthaginians under Hannibal. There is a small museum on the site which explains the battle. Behind the museum and above it, a good pathway leads through the ruins of the city, or more accurately, the series of cities which stood here. All are now in ruins, but their walls and gates, rooms and some roads may be seen. It's a jumble but a fascinating one, about half an hour's walk with funerary monuments, inscriptions, milestones piled and turned every which way and, at path's end, a magnificent view of the Ofanto River valley. On a clear day you can see all the way to Canosa, Roman Canusium.

* **Cerignola** was on the Appia Traiana but there is little to see. There is a milestone set up along the main street, and two more are inserted into an arcade at the entrance of the Palazzo Municipio, the city hall.

** **Ordona.** Ancient **Herdoniae** lies west and slightly north of Cerignola. Route 16 northwest out of Cerignola turns into No. 161 and passes the site. In 1973 a temporary sign on the edge of Ordona indicated Belgian excavations. It also said "No entry," but we entered. The excavation is extensive and impressive with remains of houses, a section of what must have been a vast forum with massive columns and scattered capitals. There is a dig headquarters house with space to leave a car, from there a clear though unmarked path leads toward the excavation, a five-minute walk.

** **Ordona to Benevento.** Highway 161 west from Ordona turns into 90, then into 90 Bis, roughly on the track of the Appia Traiana. Little to see, but a beautiful drive through mountain scenery never steep enough to be scary.

* **Troia.** Tracers of the fine lines of the route may want to leave the highway to visit Troia, ancient Aecae, a pleasant town strung across a very high ridge, a magnificent location. Its main street, according to Dr. Giovanna Alvisi (Chapter XII), is built over the Appia Traiana.

* Between **Troia** and **Buonalbergo,** a country road leads from 90 *bis* off to the right and meanders toward Castelfranco in Mescano, through the mysterious plain of San Eleuterio. No remains above ground, yet somewhere in this beautiful setting, still unspoiled by real estate developers and traffic snarls, is the site of the ancient city of **Equum Tuticum,** where in the late empire the Via Herculia was connected to the Appia Traiana. (See R. J. Buck, "The Via Herculia," in Reading List.)

** **Buonalbergo** along this route probably is the site of **Forum Novum** of the Romans. It is situated dramatically on a peak, visible for miles. Its most prominent monument is a seventh-century Longobard castle, but south of the city is the ruin, well preserved, of a handsome Roman bridge on the Appia Traiana. It is now called the Ponte della Chianche.

# Source Notes

I: THE APPIAN WAY, QUEEN OF ROADS

PAGE

3   Epigraph. Edith Hamilton, *The Roman Way*. New York: Norton, 1932. (This quote is taken from the New American Library 1963 Mentor edition, p. 116.)

3   Epigraph. From Albert C. Rose, p. 347. See Reading List.

3   "queen of long distance roads"   Statius, *Silvae*. II.ii.14.

5   "The Great Sacred Antonine Travelling Company . . ."   From Ludwig Friedlander, Vol. I, p. 319. See Reading List.

9   "the stern round tower . . ."   Lord George Gordon Byron, *Childe Harold's Pilgrimage*. Canto IV.xciv.

10   "The Appian Way . . . leads you . . ."   Henry Wadsworth Longfellow, *Outre-mer, a Pilgrimage Beyond the Sea*. Cambridge: Riverside Press, 1886.

10   "a little one-horse carriage . . ."   Nathaniel Hawthorne, *Passages from the French and Italian Notebooks*. London: Strahan, 1871.

10   "After they had exhausted their enthusiasm . . ."   Mark Twain, *The Innocents Abroad*. New York: Harper, 1911. (We used the New American Library 1966 Signet edition, from which this and a later excerpts are taken. This is p. 212.)

11   ". . . a very wonderful arrangement of Providence . . ."   Hawthorne, *op. cit.*

## II: Appius Claudius, His Water and His Road

13 Epigraph. Robert Graves, *I, Claudius.* New York: Smith & Haas, 1932. (This quote is from Vintage Books, 1961, p. 14)

13 Epigraph. Livy. IX.xxix. Loeb Classical Library.

15 "under the ridge of Alba Longa . . . now the Appian Way." *Ibid.,* VII.xxxix.

15 "southern lobby" E. T. Salmon, *Samnium and the Samnites.* Cambridge University Press, 1967.

16 "the descendant of that Appius . . ." Livy, *op. cit.,* IX.xxxiv.

17 " 'Will this be your contention . . .?' " *Ibid.*

20 "twelve families of the Potitii . . ." *Ibid.,* IX.xxix.

20 "greatly to the indignation of all classes." *Ibid.,* IX.xxxiv.

22 " 'Up to this time, O Romans . . .' " Plutarch, *The Lives.* "Pyrrhus," xix. Loeb Classical Library.

23 "did not languidly succumb . . ." Cicero, *De Senectute.* XI. Loeb Classical Library.

24 ". . . then let them drink." Robert Graves, *op. cit.,* p. 14.

25 "most happily in the founding of cities . . ." Strabo, *The Geography.* V.3.8. Loeb Classical Library.

25 "the whole globe . . ." Pliny, *Natural History.* XXXVI.24.123. London, 1855. Quoted in Will Durant, *Caesar and Christ,* Vol. III in The Story of Civilization. New York: Simon & Schuster, 1944. Chapter XV, p. 327.

25 "Who will venture to compare . . ." Frontinus, *The Aqueducts of Rome.* I.16. Loeb Classical Library.

26 "Wash away the perjuries of past time . . ." Ovid, *Fasti.* V.665. Loeb Classical Library.


## III: Skeletons in the Outskirts

31 Epigraph. Leandro Alberti, *Descrizione dell'Italia.* Bologna, 1550.

31 Epigraph. From Umberto Leoni and Giovanni Staderini, pp. 158–59. See Reading List.

38 "To love a wife while she lives . . ." Statius, *Silvae.* V. Quoted *ibid.,* pp. 88–89.

38 ". . . discovered whose footprints they were . . ." Mark Twain, *The Innocents Abroad*, p. 198.

41 "Pliny tells of a raven . . ." Pliny, *Natural History*. X.lx. Loeb Classical Library.

42 "Stranger, I thank you . . ." From Leoni and Staderini, p. 172. See Reading List.

42 "Stop, stranger . . ." *Ibid.,* p. 206.

50 "set to bury their dead . . ." Livy. I.xxii–xxvi. Loeb Classical Library.

## IV: Hospices and Hazards

55 Epigraph. Horace, "From Rome to Brindisi, with Stops," *Satire I.5,* pp. 58–62. See Bovie translation in Reading List.

55 Epigraph. Jerome Turler, *The Traveiler*. Gainesville, Fla.: Scholars' Facsimiles and Reprints, 1951. P. 65.

57 "blind flatterer . . ." Juvenal, *Satire IV*. Loeb Classical Library.

60 "But surely, friend, the man who gains an inn . . ." *The Works of Horace*. Translated into English Verse by Sir Theodore Martin. New edition. Edinburgh and London: Blackwood & Sons, 1888. (Epistle I.ii.)

60 ". . . skinny little thrushes . . ." Horace, "From Rome . . . ," *Satire I.5*. See Bovie translation in Reading List.

61 "I made war on my stomach . . ." *Ibid.*

61 "The rains this year . . ." Martial, *Epigram*. From Lionel Casson, "In 2,000 Years, Traveling Has Changed but Not the Tourist." In *Smithsonian*, Vol. 2, No. 6 (September 1971), p. 56.

62 Alessandro Donati, *Iter Neapolitanum*. Rome: The Vatican, 1625. Pp. 363 ff. From Daniele Sterpos, *Roma-Capua*, pp. 156–61. See Reading List. Excerpt translated by Dora Jane Hamblin.

63 "How glad we are at the sight of shelter . . ." Seneca, *De Beneficiis*. VI.15.7. Quoted in Friedlander, Vol. I, p. 291. See Reading List.

64 Epistle of Paul the Apostle to the Romans 12:13.

64 First Epistle of Paul the Apostle to Timothy 3:2.

64 First Epistle General of Peter 4:9.

64 Epistle of Paul the Apostle to the Hebrews 13:2.
    (All Bible quotations are from the King James Version.)

PAGE

65 "I was shipwrecked . . ." Seneca, *Epistle 87.* Loeb Classical Library.

66 ". . . there would be no robbers" . . . "Why are you a prefect?" . . . "robber of the better sort." From Friedlander, Vol. I, p. 297. See Reading List.

67 "Thedesco Italianato . . ." Turler, *op. cit.,* pp. 65–66.

67 ". . . let him bolt or locke the doors . . ." Fynes Moryson (Gent.), *An Itinerary* containing his ten yeeres travell through the twelve dominions . . . London: John Beale, 1617. Reprinted in Glasgow: MacLehose and Sons, Publishers to the University, 1907. Part III, Booke I, p. 19 (original page numbers).

67 "The Italian Hosts . . ." *Ibid.,* III.ii.116.

68 "treat not of . . . Religion . . ." *Ibid.,* III.i.19.

68 ". . . I avoyded the Priests . . ." *Ibid.,* III.i.31.

68 "some five thousand pound, to be paid me . . ." Ben Jonson, *Every Man Out of His Humour.* Quoted in Clare Howard, *English Travellers of the Renaissance.* London: John Lane, 1914.

68 "Our manner of travelling . . ." Sterpos, *Roma-Capua,* p. 277. See Reading List. Sterpos' source: Valery: *Voyages Historiques et Littéraires en Italie* . . . Bruxelles, 1835. (Lady Morgan, p. 378.) Excerpt translated by Dora Jane Hamblin.

69 "Yesterday [Marco] killed many men . . ." *Ibid.,* pp. 138–40. Sterpos' source: *Letters of Tasso.* Edited by Cesare Guasti. Florence, 1855. Vol. V, pp. 99 ff. Excerpt translated by Dora Jane Hamblin.

71 ". . . we seek omens by the inspection of entrails . . ." Cicero, *On Divination.* I.15.16. Translated by Hubert M. Poteat. Chicago: University of Chicago Press, 1950.

72 "We shall begin at the head . . ." *Medicina Plinii.* Edited, with an introduction, by Valentin Rose. Leipzig: Teubneri, 1875. Excerpts translated by Dorothy R. Patton.

73 "resonant swamp frogs" . . . "black salve" Horace, "From Rome . . . ," *Satire I.5.* See Bovie translation in Reading List.

73 ". . . if hee come from suspected places . . ." Moryson, *op. cit.* II.i.

V: Milestones, Maps and Guidebooks

75 Epigraph. Quintilian, *Institutio Oratoria.* IV.5.22. Quoted in G. H. Stevenson, p. 157. See Reading List.

75    Epigraph. Frank N. Jones, ed., *Roads through History: Road Maps from Rome to Today.* (An annotated checklist of an exhibition.) Baltimore: Peabody Institute Library, 1966.

75    Acts 28:14–15.

77    "caused the roads to be all divided into miles . . ." Plutarch, *The Lives.* Translated by John Dryden and revised by Arthur Hugh Clough. New York: The Modern Library. "Caius Gracchus," pp. 1011–12.

78    "The Emperor . . ." From Daniele Sterpos, *The Roman Road in Italy,* p. 107. See Reading List.

82    "the head of the world . . ." *Mirabilia Romae.* Quoted in Georgina Masson, p. 21. See Reading List.

85    "bits of columns . . . medals, inscriptions . . ." From Sterpos, *Roma-Capua,* p. 218. See Reading List. Excerpt translated by Dora Jane Hamblin.

90    "a brazen tablet . . ." Herodotus. V. 49. The Bohn Classical Library.

93    "for teaching of geography" . . . "a map of the eastern front" From Stevenson, p. 158. See Reading List.

95    Mr. Schott of Antwerp; Pighius; and the *Itinerarium Italiae.* From Sterpos, *Roma-Capua,* Chapter IV, pp. 129 ff. See Reading List. Excerpts translated by Dora Jane Hamblin.

97    ". . . a useful invention . . ." Vitruvius, *The Ten Books on Architecture.* Translated by Morris Hickey Morgan. New York: Dover, 1960. Chapter IX, p. 301 ff. (This is a reissue of the first edition, originally published by the Harvard University Press in 1914.)

98    "We next rolled downhill . . ." Horace, "From Rome . . . ," *Satire I.5.* See Bovie translation in Reading List.

98    "No matter how one tries to mark the distance . . ." Guiseppe Lugli, "Osservazioni sulle stazioni della via Appia antica de Roma ad Otranto." In *Festschrift für Rudolf Egger, Beiträge zur Alteren Europäischen Kultur Geschichte.* Klagenfurt, 1952. Vol. I, pp. 276 ff. Excerpt translated by Dora Jane Hamblin.

VI: HURRY, HURRY, HURRY

101    Epigraph. Durant, *Caesar and Christ.* Chapter XV, p. 323.

101    Epigraph. Horace, "From Rome . . . ," *Satire I.5.* See Bovie translation in Reading List.

PAGE

103 "We wormed our way . . ." *Ibid.*

108 "The Appian Way is less rough . . ." *Ibid.*

108 "Neither snow, nor rain . . ." Inscription on the Main Post Office, New York City. From Herodotus, VIII.98.

109 "When I arrive in Rome . . ." Cicero, *Ad Quintum Fratrem.* II.14. Loeb Classical Library.

109 ". . . waiting at the gate." Cicero, *Ad Familiares.* XV.17.1. Loeb Classical Library.

109 "I received your letter . . ." Seneca, *Epistle 50.* Quoted in Leoni and Staderini, p. 73. See Reading List.

110 "the flower of Roman knighthood . . ." Cicero, *Pro Plancio,* IX. Loeb Classical Library.

110 Luke 18:10.

110 ". . . he kept in close touch . . ." Suetonius, *The Twelve Caesars.* "Augustus," 49. Translated by Robert Graves. Penguin Books, 1957.

111 "To all our officials . . ." W. C. Firebaugh, *The Inns of Greece and Rome.* Chicago: Frank M. Morris, 1923.

112 "Thou didst well . . ." Pliny the Younger. Letter X.cxxi. Loeb Classical Library.

113 "Wearied with the discomfort . . ." Seneca, *Epistle 123.* Loeb Classical Library.

114 "As the multitude flock . . ." Dante, "Purgatory," II.v.71–72. Quoted in Leoni and Staderini, p. 70. See Reading List.

VII: THE MANY MEANS AND MISSIONS OF THE ROAD

115 Epigraph. Epictetus, *Discourses.* III.xxiv.36. Quoted in Friedlander, Vol. I., p. 299. See Reading List.

115 Epigraph. Seneca, *Epistle 104.* Loeb Classical Library.

115 "Everyone now travels . . ." *Ibid.*

118 "a three-legged truckle bed . . ." Martial, *Epigrams.* XII.xxxii. Loeb Classical Library.

120 Hilaire Belloc on *gauge:* See Reading List.

124 "with five slaves . . ." Horace, "I Am Only a Freedman's Son," *Satire I.6.* See Bovie translation in Reading List.

PAGE

124    "Persons who had occasion . . ." Apuleius, *The Florida*. 4.21. Quoted in William West Mooney, p. 63. See Reading List.

124    "Only by walking . . ." Seneca, *Epistle 87*. Loeb Classical Library.

129    "swarms of artists . . ." From Friedlander, Vol. I, p. 319. See Reading List.

129    "which made so much work . . ." Horace, *Epistle I.7.5*. Quoted in Gaston Boissier, *The Country of Horace and Virgil*. Translated by D. Havelock Fisher. London: Unwin, 1896.

129    "He rushes headlong . . ." Lucretius, *De Rerum Naturalis*, III. Quoted in Leoni and Staderini, p. 53. See Reading List.

130    "Thou who dost wish . . ." Martial, *Epigrams*. XIV.188. Quoted *ibid.*, p. 55.

130    "We avoid it . . ." From Sterpos, *Roma-Capua*, p. 174. See Reading List. Excerpt translated by Dora Jane Hamblin.

131    "The plough is not more worn . . ." Ovid, *Epistles from Pontus*. II.7.v. Quoted in Leoni and Staderini, p. 52. See Reading List.


VIII: THE NETWORK

133    Epigraph. Guiseppe Lugli, "Il Sistema Stradale di Roma Antica," in *Etudes Etrusco-Italiques*. Louvain, 1963. Excerpt translated by Dora Jane Hamblin.

133    Epigraph. Aristides, *The Orations*. Quoted in Friedlander, Vol. I, p. 13. See Reading List.

137    ". . . an ill wind . . ." Procopius, *History of the Wars*. V.15. Loeb Classical Library.

144    "Christianity spread first . . ." W. M. Ramsay, "Roads and Travel in the New Testament," in James Hastings, ed., *A Dictionary of the Bible*. New York: Scribner's, 1904. Extra Volume (5).

144    "All is common . . ." Quoted in Stevenson, pp. 142–43. See Reading List.

144    "Could not every man go whither he would . . ." Aristides of Smyrna. Speech quoted in Friedlander, Vol. I, p. 269. See Reading List.

145    "globe-trotters" Plutarch, *Moralia*, "On Exile" 604-A. From Durant, *Caesar and Christ*, p. 324.

145    ". . . some remote site . . ." Seneca, *Ad Helviam*, vi. Quoted *ibid.*

145 "Abolish fabulous tales . . ." Lucian, quoted by Casson, *op. cit.*, in *Smithsonian* (September 1971), p. 56.

146 " 'The guides went through . . .' " Plutarch, quoted *loc. cit.*

146 "bread and circuses" Juvenal, X.81. Loeb Classical Library.

146 "Orontes . . . emptied . . ." *Ibid.*, III.62.

146 ". . . cesspool . . ." Tacitus, quoted in Stevenson, p. 143. See Reading List.

147 Pliny reported devaluation: *Natural History.* Xxxiii.13.

148 "You can persuade me . . ." Seneca, *Epistle 53.* Loeb Classical Library.

148 "Never take a night boat, reader . . ." Horace, "From Rome . . .," *Satire I.5.* See Bovie translation in Reading List.

### IX: Of the *Groma, Agrimensores* and Construction

151 Epigraph. Hamilton, *The Roman Way.* (Quote is from New American Library Mentor edition, 1963, p. 116.)

151 Epigraph. Procopius, *History of the Wars.* V.xiv.6–11.

156 "the changes which the passage of time bring . . ." Maximillian Misson, *Nouveau Voyage d'Italie.* 5th ed. Utrecht, 1922. Quoted in Sterpos, *Roma-Capua,* p. 174. See Reading List. Excerpt translated by Dora Jane Hamblin.

157 "Oh! how many gangs . . ." Statius, *Silvae.* IV.iii. Loeb Classical Library.

160 "The fact remains . . ." R. J. Forbes, p. 164. See Reading List.

160 ". . . did not even walk like other men . . ." E. M. Winslow, p. 13. See Reading List.

167 "Two slopes lead up . . ." Procopius, *op. cit.,* I.17. Quoted in Sterpos, *The Roman Road,* p. 48. See Reading List.

168 "In my 7th consulship . . ." Quoted *ibid.,* p. 42 (from *Res gestae,* "Monumentum Ancyranum," Malcovati 20, 22–24).

168 ". . . little brother of the road . . ." From Victor W. Von Hagen, p. 45. See Reading List.

### X: Rules of the Road

169 Epigraph. *The Corpus of Roman Law,* Vol. II, *Ancient Roman Statutes.*

PAGE

Translated by A. C. Johnson, P. R. Coleman-Norton and F. C. Bourne. Austin: University of Texas Press, 1961. Document 113.14–15, pp. 94–95.

169 Epigraph. *Ibid.* Document 244. 237b, p. 192.

170 ". . . no one shall drive a wagon . . ." *Ibid.* Document 113.16, p. 95.

170 "where is sleep possible?" Juvenal. iii.234.

174 "Considering . . . cudgels . . ." *Codex Theodosianus.* VIII. tit. V.2. Quoted from Leoni and Staderini, p. 69. See Reading List.

175 "No sort of man, of any dignity . . ." Quoted from Von Hagen, p. 71. See Reading List.

176 "brought a number of usurers to trial . . ." Livy. X.xxiii.12–13.

176 "the aediles procured . . ." *Ibid.* X.xlvii.4.

178 "His . . . exertions were given . . ." Plutarch, *Lives.* Dryden translation. "Caius Gracchus," p. 1011.

180 "work brought him censure . . ." Livy. XL.li.

181 Senator Corbulo and the condition of the roads: Tacitus, *The Annals,* III.31, and Dio Cassius, LIX.15.3. Reported in Forbes, pp. 156–57. See Reading List.

182 "He caused the pipes . . ." Plutarch, *op. cit.,* Dryden translation. "Cato," p. 425.

184 "Send . . . a bathing costume . . ." Casson, *op. cit.,* in *Smithsonian* (September 1971), p. 59.

184 "We object to customs officials . . ." From Friedlander, pp. 293–94. See Reading List. (And his sources: Quintilian, *De Curiositate,* c.7, and *Declamations,* 349, 359.)

184 "Our dames . . ." *Ibid.*

184 "the official is entitled . . ." *Ibid.*

XI: The Bloody Road

187 Epigraph. H. G. Wells, *Outline of History.* New York: Macmillan, 1921. Pp. 435–36.

187 Epigraph. Cicero, *Pro Milone.* Quoted in Sterpos, *Roma-Capua,* p. 34. See Reading List. Excerpt translated by Dora Jane Hamblin.

190 ". . . If you had only spoken . . ." Dio Cassius, xl.57. Quoted in Durant, *Caesar and Christ,* p. 180.

PAGE

191 "When this same Clodius . . ." Cicero, *op. cit.* In Sterpos, *Roma-Capua, loc. cit.* See Reading List.

195 "Have I played my part . . ." Suetonius, *The Twelve Caesars.* "Augustus," 99.

195 Tiberius' pet snake: *Ibid.,* "Tiberius," 72.

197 "a man not only of high spirit . . ." Plutarch, *The Lives.* Dryden translation. "Crassus," p. 655.

198 The Twelve Martyrs of Hadrumentum: See R. J. Buck, pp. 69–71, in Reading List.

201 ". . . a band of philosophers . . ." Quoted in Pierre Grimal, *The Civilization of Rome.* Translated by W. S. Maguinness. New York: Simon & Schuster, 1963. P. 311.

201 "Belisarius commanded all the Romans . . ." Procopius, *History of the Wars.* V.xxv.

202 "On the grand Roma-Capua of antiquity . . ." From Sterpos, *Roma-Capua,* p. 89. See Reading List.

202 "at the site of Roman Casilinum . . ." *Ibid.*

203 "slippery and slimy" Lucilius. III.98. In *Remains of Old Latin.* Loeb Classical Library.

203 "the marvelous work of a road . . ." From Sterpos, *Roma-Capua,* p. 99. See Reading List. Excerpt translated by Dora Jane Hamblin.

203 "bandits brought to justice" *Ibid.,* p. 172.

204 Consalvi's *Memoirs: ibid.,* pp. 251 ff.

206 ". . . a peculiar old drain . . ." Tenney Frank, *Roman Buildings of the Republic.* Rome: American Acadamy, 1924. Pp. 51 ff.

206 "When she recognized . . . the military cloak . . ." Livy. I.xxii-xxvi.

XII: ARCHAEOLOGY AND THE ROAD

209 Epigraph. Paul McKendrick, *The Mute Stones Speak.* New York: St. Martin's Press, 1960. P. 2.

217 "The tales they tell . . ." J. B. Ward-Perkins in Introduction to Thomas Ashby, p. viii. See Reading List.

## XIII: The Miracle of Survival

PAGE

231 Epigraph. *Memoirs of a Renaissance Pope: The Commentaries of Pius II.* Translated by F. A. Gragg; edited by L. C. Gabel. New York: Putnam's; Capricorn edition, 1962. P. 319.

231 Epigraph. Ferdinando Castagnoli in Introduction to Sterpos, *The Roman Road,* p. 5. See Reading List.

235 "their part in the destruction . . ." Rodolfo Lanciani, *The Destruction of Ancient Rome.* New York: Macmillan, 1903. P. 9.

236 "the breadth of this road . . ." Procopius, *History of the Wars.* V.xiv.

237 ". . . after celebrating . . . the feast . . ." Pius II, *op. cit.,* p. 314.

238 "He went by the Appian Way . . ." *Ibid.,* pp. 317, 319.

238 "It delights me . . ." Quoted in Leoni and Staderini, p. 23. See Reading List. From Aeneas Silvius Piccolomini, Pope Pius II, *Inedited Works,* in "Atti della R. Accademia dei Lincei," 1883. Vol. VIII, p. 674.

239 "I should even go so far to say . . ." Leoni and Staderini, *loc. cit.*

241– "remove unsightly ruins . . ."; ". . . owners of farmland . . ."; "This
242 incident . . ." Lanciani, *op. cit.,* pp. 235 ff.

246 "When the stones . . . lie shattered . . ." Martial, *Epigrams.* VIII.3. Quoted in Leoni and Staderini, p. 196. See Reading List.

246 "The wild fig-tree . . ." *Ibid.* Epigram X.2.

## XIV: Has the Past a Future?

249 Epigraph. Leoni and Staderini, p. 25. See Reading List.

253 ". . . the third Rome . . ." Ruggero Bonghi, in *Capitolium* (official publication of the *Comune di Roma*), Vol. XLIII (July-August, 1968), p. 262. Excerpt translated by Dora Jane Hamblin.

257 "The constructors . . ." Antonio Giolotti. From newspaper reports at the time.

258 "We Italians . . ." Bonghi, *op. cit.*

261 "The Appia is a stopped clock . . ." Rodolfo de Mattei, "Introduzione all'Appia," in *Capitolium (op. cit.),* pp. 251–54. Excerpt translated by Dora Jane Hamblin.

# Reading List

Ashby, Thomas, *The Roman Campagna in Classical Times*. New ed., with an introduction by J. B. Ward-Perkins. London: Ernest Benn, 1970.

Ashby, Thomas, and Gardner, Robert, "The Via Traiana." Papers of the British School at Rome, Vol. 8. 1916.

Belloc, Hilaire, *The Highway and Its Vehicles*. Edited by Geoffrey Holme. London: The Studio, 1936.

Bergier, Nicolas, *Histoire des Grands Chemins de l'Empire Romain* (Paris, 1622). Brussels: Leonard, 1736.

Buck, R. J., "The Via Herculia." Papers of the British School at Rome, Vol. 39. 1971.

Canina, Luigi, *La Prima Parte della Via Appia della Porte Capena e Bovillae*. 2 vols. Rome: Bertinelli, 1853.

Forbes, R. J., *Notes on the History of Ancient Roads and Their Construction*. Amsterdam: Adolf M. Hakkert, 1934. Second unrevised edition, 1964.

Friedlander, Ludwig, *Roman Life and Manners under the Early Empire*, 4 vols. Authorized translation of the 7th enlarged and rev. ed. by L. A. Magnus, et al. London: George Routledge & Sons (n.d.) and New York: Barnes & Noble, 1965.

Hoare, Sir Richard Colt, *Recollections Abroad: A Classical Tour*, London: J. Mawman, 1819.

Horace, "From Rome to Brundisi, with Stops." *The Satires and Epistles of Horace: A Modern English Verse Translation,* by Smith Palmer Bovie. Chicago: University of Chicago Press, Phoenix Books, 1959.

Jones, H. Stuart, *Companion to Roman History.* Oxford: Clarendon Press, 1912.

Labruzzi, Carlo, *La Via Appia: 24 Aquarelli.* Text by Giuseppe Lugli, English translation by Denys and Sybille Haynes. Rome: Ed. Dell'Elefante, 1967.

————, *Via Appia Illustrata Ad Urbe Roma Ad Capua.* London: 1794.

Leoni, Umberto, and Staderini, Giovanni, *On the Appian Way: A Walk from Rome to Albano.* Translated from the Italian by E. Fitzmaurice. Rome: R. Remporad & F., 1907.

Masson, Georgina, *The Companion Guide to Rome.* Rev. ed. London: Collins, 1972.

Mooney, William West, *Travel among the Ancient Romans.* Boston: Richard G. Badger, The Gorham Press, 1920.

Morton, H. V., *The Fountains of Rome.* London: The Connoisseur and Michael Joseph, 1970.

Paget, R. F., *Central Italy: An Archaeological Guide.* London: Faber & Faber, 1973.

Pratilli, Francesco Maria, *Della Via Appia Riconoscuita e Descritta da Roma a Brindisi.* Naples: 1745.

Rose, Albert C., *Via Appia in the Days When All Roads Led to Rome.* Washington, D.C.: Smithsonian Institution, Annual Report, 1934.

Sterpos, Daniele, *The Roman Road in Italy.* Introduction by Ferdinando Castagnoli. Translated by Frank B. Sear. Rome: Quaderini di "Autostrade"-17., 1970.

————, *Roma–Capua,* in the series Comunicazioni Stradali Attraverso i Tempi. Rome: Autostrade S.p.A., 1966.

Stevenson, G. H., "Communications and Commerce," in Cyril Bailey, ed., *The Legacy of Rome.* Oxford: Clarendon Press, 1924.

Touring Club Italiano, *Guida d'Italia.* Milano. Roma c Dintorni, 1965, Lazio, 1964; Campania, 1963; Basilicata e Calabria, 1965; Puglia, 1962.

Tozer, H. F., *A History of Ancient Geography.* 2nd ed., with additional notes by M. Cary. Cambridge: Cambridge University Press, 1935.

Vinson, S. P., A forthcoming article on the Via Appia between Venosa and Gravina di Puglia, in Papers of the British School at Rome, Vol. 40. 1972.

Von Hagen, Victor W., *The Roads That Led to Rome.* Cleveland and New York: World Publishing, 1967.

Winslow, E. M., *A Libation to the Gods.* London: Hodder & Stoughton, 1963.

ABOUT THE AUTHORS

DORA JANE HAMBLIN was born in Iowa and was for more than twenty years on the staff of *Life* magazine as correspondent and writer. She headed *Life's* Rome office for several years and became so fond of Italy and its many-layered history that in 1970 she went back to establish permanent residence near Rome. She is the author of books and magazine articles on archaeology and of two volumes in the Time-Life Books series The Emergence of Man.

MARY JANE LOEB GRUNSFELD was born in Chicago and still makes her home there, although she spends several months in Italy each year. She is a research specialist with a background in market research for advertising agencies in Chicago, and in-depth studies in areas of social problems and race relations.

Though the Appian Way was only 360 miles long, the authors hiked and drove more than 3,500 miles over a period of two years to find every trace which still remains of it, and to interview experts in the history and legends of the most famous road in the world.

*Index*

# Index